40 Classic Trades in the Environmental Markets

The environmental markets have never been more important or more widely discussed. But who exactly are the individuals that trade in the carbon markets, or who trade biofuels, biomass and water? Few non-specialists appreciate how traders approach the environmental markets, what their strategies are, and how they make money.

The trading world is not usually open to outsiders, but this book brings the environmental markets to vivid life by introducing the reader to 40 real-life trades or strategies that were carried out by named market participants. The 40 chapters cover different geographies and different markets, providing an unparalleled insight into how traders in the environmental markets work and think. Environmental trading developed in its current form in the early 1990s and the chapters cover these early beginnings through to the present day. Sections cover compliance and voluntary carbon; ethanol, biodiesel and feedstocks; biomass; environmental finance trades; water markets; and trading as a project developer.

40 Classic Trades in the Environmental Markets provides plenty of inspiration for current or prospective environmental market traders, project developers or analysts. It will also be valuable for academic researchers, business school case studies, and for anyone wanting to learn more about the individuals that are shaping some of the fastest growing and most significant commodity markets of the 21st century.

Owain Johnson is the Global Head of Research and Product Development, CME Group. He is the author of *The Price Reporters: A Guide to PRAs and Commodity Benchmarks* and *40 Classic Crude Oil Trades: Real-Life Examples of Innovative Trading*, and the co-author of *Treasury Bond Futures and Options.*

Routledge Classic Market Trades

40 Classic Crude Oil Trades
Real-Life Examples of Innovative Trading
Owain Johnson

40 Classic Trades in the Environmental Markets
Real-Life Examples of Innovative Trading
Owain Johnson

For more information about this series please visit https://www.routledge.com/Routledge-Classic-Market-Trades/book-series/RMCMT

40 Classic Trades in the Environmental Markets

Real-Life Examples of Innovative Trading

Owain Johnson

Routledge
Taylor & Francis Group
LONDON AND NEW YORK

Designed cover image: Getty Images - GelatoPlus, Modified by AI

First published 2027
by Routledge
4 Park Square, Milton Park, Abingdon, Oxon OX14 4RN

and by Routledge
605 Third Avenue, New York, NY 10158

Routledge is an imprint of the Taylor & Francis Group, an informa business

British Library Cataloguing-in-Publication Data
A catalogue record for this book is available from the British Library

ISBN: 978-1-032-41794-3 (hbk)
ISBN: 978-1-032-41792-9 (pbk)
ISBN: 978-1-003-35973-9 (ebk)

DOI: 10.4324/9781003359739

Typeset in Sabon
by SPi Technologies India Pvt Ltd (Straive)

Contents

Acknowledgements

This book obviously wouldn't exist without the 40 individuals whose stories follow: some old friends and some new friends.

Thank you for taking the time to talk me through your trades and your strategies and for being so open. It was a genuine pleasure to hear your stories and to record your highly entertaining and eye-opening experiences.

I'm also grateful to the many traders who for various reasons were unable to speak publicly, but who still took the time to provide suggestions and encouragement.

When I was starting work on the carbon section, I particularly appreciated the wisdom of Alice Leblanc, Josh Margolis and Laurent Segalen, while Matthew Stone was a great guide to biofuels.

I very much appreciate the kindness of Liz Bossley, Ilia Bouchouev, Michael Christensen, Juan Carlos Fonnegra, Brodie Govan, Henrik Hasselknippe, Russell Karas, Livia Li, Elena Lobodina, Dominic Sutton Vermeulen, Prof. Thomas Tanner, Rene Velasquez, David Whitehead, Jacky Zhang and Michelle Zhang who provided generous assistance as well as occasional introductions to their various circles.

I have learnt a great deal from my conversations about developing environmental markets with Anthony Miller of the U.N. Sustainable Stock Exchanges Initiative and his fantastic team. I have also benefitted a lot from chairing the discussions of the World Federation of Exchanges' Sustainability Working Group.

Kristina Abbotts and Christiana Mandizha of Routledge combine tremendous patience with positivity, and I deeply appreciate their support once more.

This book is dedicated to my family, who are remarkably understanding when I take on interesting projects on top of an extremely busy role at the exchange. Thanks for your support.

Introduction

I've spent most of my career working with traders and traded markets, so I am clearly biased in favour of applying market solutions to difficult issues.

That said, I genuinely believe that markets work as intended, particularly when properly managed.

Certainly, the 40 chapters that follow largely confirm that environmental markets can do exactly what the economics textbooks say they should: provide a cost-efficient way of bringing different parties together to allocate scarce resources and send price signals.

A belief that markets are useful would not be a controversial statement in sectors like foreign exchange, fixed income or in major commodity markets like crude oil, copper or wheat.

In those equally crucial areas of the economy, no one questions whether markets are the right way to allocate resources and exchange assets.

But championing markets can still feel like a provocative position in the environmental sector, where many outside observers assume that environmental markets simply unleash capitalist excess, replicating the dynamics that helped create the environmental crisis in the first place.

In reality, almost all major environmental markets exist only because governments deliberately create and regulate them to solve specific problems.

These markets do not run on autopilot: they require thoughtful, intensive and careful design to set caps, define eligible activities and enforce compliance so that market forces deliver efficient and, in many cases, more equitable outcomes than the alternatives.

Some activists would prefer environmental action to take place without markets, whether through taxes on carbon or other negative externalities, other forms of government intervention or companies voluntarily reducing harmful emissions.

Different approaches have been tried at different times and in different countries, but so far market solutions have emerged as the most cost-effective and politically acceptable way of delivering environmental improvements.

DOI: 10.4324/9781003359739-1

In many ways, modern environmental markets build on the runaway success of the U.S. acid rain programme of the early 1990s, which led to the development of the first large-scale environmental market (Chapters 1–2).

This early win helped drive the adoption of market mechanisms around the world and in different areas of environmental concern, from carbon to water to transport fuels.

Despite the doubts of some activists, introducing financial discipline and the profit motive through a market mechanism can at times prove transformational.

'To some of these folk, the idea that someone might make a profit from restoring the environment is a terrible thing', says George Kelly in Chapter 35. But he adds, 'without markets, without price discovery, and without transparent and effective market mechanisms, there would be no way of showing that relative value and so it would be harder for people to make the right choices'.

Price signals

Environmental markets are typically designed by governments, in the case of carbon allowances and water, or driven by government policy like subsidies or tariffs, which is the case for the biofuels and biomass markets. The voluntary carbon markets (Chapters 21–26) are a rare environmental market that has emerged without the explicit involvement of the official sector.

Whatever the original driver of market development, once the rules are established, the trading begins.

(Or at least that's when trading is supposed to begin; we will see a few examples where individuals, like John B. Henry, Garth Edward or Plinio Nastari, got tired of waiting around and kicked things off themselves.)

Trading activity is fundamental to the environmental markets' role in creating behavioural change in the real economy. Each trade – whether for carbon, biomass or biofuels – establishes a price signal that tells companies about the price of emitting pollutants or of using hydrocarbons, relative to cleaner alternatives.

The social benefit of these markets is clear; it is their raison d'être. At the same time, their link to politics and social drivers can also be their Achilles heel.

Environmental markets expose traders to different types of risk than other commodity markets because they are so much more dependent on political decisions.

The same political and legal choices that create these markets can also destabilize them if rules are changed abruptly, which is why robust, predictable regulation is critical to their effectiveness. Politically driven changes in market design or policy can completely disrupt potentially profitable trading strategies.

The chapters covering the journey to maturity of Brazil's giant ethanol market are some of my favourites and they demonstrate very clearly how traders had to be able to react quickly to changes in ethanol import tariffs and quotas in Brazil, Europe and the United States.

The carbon markets have also seen more than their fair share of policy-related disruptions.

The European Union (EU) decision to de-link certified emission reductions from the EU Emissions Trading System put an end to Stef Peter's innovative 'flex product' (Chapter 12) and to Torleif Haugland's initial methane elimination business (Chapter 38). 'I still have the scars from this period', he notes.

Similarly, the EU policy reaction in May 2022 to the Russian invasion of Ukraine drove carbon prices down sharply and unexpectedly, reminding Francisco Grajales (Chapter 9) that 'this market is driven by fundamentals and technicals only as long as there is political stability. Once there is social instability, you can forget about both fundamentals and technicals'.

Introducing the traders

So, who are the traders that develop and sustain these environmental markets by their buying and selling, their risk management and speculation?

As we will see, they are a disparate bunch. After all, there are very few schools or universities that prepare students for a career in environmental markets trading. Not many children tell their career advisors that they want to become an environmental trader.

The 40 contributors took a wide variety of routes into the market. Some came in through a traditional academic pathway, while others came in after gaining substantial practical experience.

There are plenty of traders here with deeply impressive academic credentials, such as Simon Crooks, who was a post-doctoral researcher in atmospheric science at Oxford University before he moved into trading (Chapter 23).

But equally, we will meet some highly successful traders whose strength and advantage derive from their expertise in the physical markets rather than from their education.

Dhimas Arif Wibowo, who now runs a successful used cooking oil (UCO) supplier and trading house in Indonesia (Chapter 18), started by collecting UCO in jerrycans in the evenings to supplement his earnings as a policeman. He says that many years later, he still remembers 'just how much a full jerry-can of UCO weighs'.

Similarly, legendary ethanol trader Nelson Ostanello was just 16 years old when he started work as an office boy at a sugar mill in Brazil (Chapter 13). Regularly changing departments with time, he eventually learnt every part of the ethanol business, which stood him in good stead as a physical trader.

In this sense, trading as portrayed in these 40 chapters is a genuine meritocracy.

It is easy to judge the success of an individual trader because his or her profit and loss account shows clearly whether they are profitable or not. There might be many ways into the markets but, ultimately, the only way to stay employed is to make money.

Although there is clearly no single entry point for traders, we can perhaps try to break down the contributors' backgrounds – with apologies for the generalizations – into four broad categories.

First, we have the serial entrepreneurs who simply enjoy spotting new opportunities and who want to get involved in new markets, whatever they might be.

Environmental markets tend to be 'new' in the sense that none existed before 1990, and they are constantly changing. That makes them highly attractive for innovators who like to break new ground. John B. Henry (Chapter 1), Richard Sandor (Chapter 2), Jeff Huang (Chapter 25) and Tom James (Chapter 29) would all acknowledge that they fall into that segment.

Second, we have those people who moved sideways from adjacent commodity markets, sometimes deliberately as a positive career move and sometimes more by circumstance.

Daria Dyncheva analyses voluntary carbon based on her prior experiences in the steel market (Chapter 37), while Juan Carlos Santacruz is an oil trader in Colombia who moved into carbon by developing the concept of carbon-compensated crude oil (Chapter 24).

Third, we have the natural traders.

These are people who realized fairly early on in their careers that they love markets, trading and commodities. They might have been fairly relaxed about which market they traded, but they have found themselves in the environmental markets, enjoy their roles and have stayed there.

For example, Mike Taylor (Chapter 11) asked a trading manager on Enron's natural gas desk what he thought the quickest path might be to becoming a trader. 'He told me that "the line starts way back there" if I was looking to trade natural gas or oil or power, but that I would be next in line if I wanted to go to the emissions desk'.

Fourth and finally, we have the 'believers'. These are the market participants who started out with a genuine interest in the environment and who turned to the markets as a way of furthering their aspiration to create change.

For example, Torleif Haugland had a distinguished career in environmental policy before seeing 'an opportunity to do something practical' (Chapter 38).

Many of these 'believers' were originally environmental activists, academic researchers, environmental lawyers or even, in the case of Jeff Cohen (Chapter 39), regulators.

True 'believers' like Tatiana Fayzullina, who 'couldn't imagine doing anything else' (Chapter 40), are fairly unusual in the context of other commodity markets. In most other markets, traders are usually fairly dispassionate about the underlying commodity that they trade.

Unlike in the environmental markets, most commodity traders' choice of underlying market was typically more accidental than strategic. Few of them burned with a passion for copper, soybeans or gasoline and grew up desperate to find roles in those markets.

In contrast, many senior environmental traders were originally motivated primarily by their strong environmental convictions, and their interest in markets or trading emerged later on.

Perhaps that is in part because many of these markets are so new that it simply wasn't realistic to set out to be an environmental trader.

As Claire Byers notes in Chapter 4, 'when I started out, no one would have gone into environmental products without actually being interested in the environment itself'.

The 'believers' are currently very well represented in these markets, but it will be interesting to observe how the balance between pure traders and believers evolves in the years to come.

As environmental markets become more and more mainstream, perhaps we should expect to see them treated more and more as 'just another commodity market', where traders are assigned to a desk more at random and less because of their personal interest.

Trader characteristics

Having talked about the differences between environmental traders in terms of their backgrounds and motivations, it is only fair to recognize their similarities.

There are some clear characteristics that are common to the 40 contributors, which would also be instantly recognizable in other commodity traders in energy, agriculture and metals.

Interpersonal skills and sociability are crucial attributes. Traders in general are gregarious; they like to exchange information and to test their ideas with their counterparts.

Unlike some of the more liquid commodity markets, most environmental markets are still not dominated by screen-based high-frequency trading. That means deals are often done in-person or by phone between counterparts who still know each other, putting a premium on the ability to build relationships.

The specialist nature of the environmental markets also means that many people spend their whole careers in the same market, developing very long-term connections. As Fenella Aouane notes in Chapter 30, 'so many people from the old days are back in the markets that some conferences feel like a school reunion'.

In such high-touch markets, maintaining a good reputation is crucial to long-term success. 'Of course, it's important to make money, but the most important factor if you want to enjoy a long career in the market is to maintain your integrity', says Ricardo Parada in Chapter 14.

High levels of energy, which might even be perceived as restlessness, are another characteristic that appears to be a prerequisite for success in the markets.

'Good traders are all curious', says Parada. 'They want to understand how things work and how they can change and improve things to make their business better and more profitable'.

A lot of contributors have changed roles or companies frequently, and several have even moved countries or industries. These are not people who like to stand still or to go through the motions day after day and year after year.

At the same time, though, the slower pace of the environmental markets often forces patience on these otherwise impatient people.

Traders who thrive on the adrenaline of constant dealing are unlikely to thrive in the environmental markets. Chelsea Bryant notes that, relative to other markets, 'deals are slower, bilateral negotiations are detailed, and the rules of the game can change mid-play' (Chapter 10).

For Ronnie Kristensen, 'intense trading doesn't really exist in the biomass market' (Chapter 28), and Philip Hardwick also talks in Chapter 31 about the difference between how outsiders might perceive his role – lots of shouting on noisy trading floors – and the reality of putting together complex environmental trades, where 'the final execution of the deal is actually just the last 30 seconds of a trade that might have taken a year to prepare'.

Legal eagles

Perhaps the final commonality between traders across the environmental markets is the ability to understand and profit from detailed regulations.

The pioneers operating in the early days of the markets were highly dependent on legal advice because the rules were being written along the way, while even today, the rules are constantly being updated and revised.

Several of our contributors came to trading from the legal or regulatory side, and the ability to absorb large amounts of technical guidelines can clearly provide an advantage.

'The fun part for me when I was trading carbon was immersing myself in the theory of the emissions markets and then being able to turn that knowledge into actual, rewarding trades', says Alfred Evans (Chapter 21), who adds that 'my best trading ideas came from nothing more than taking a lawyerly view of market structure and from my understanding of the way that different elements of the carbon market can interact with each other'.

Similarly, for Francisco Grajales, 'if you are serious about these markets, you really need to understand the legal side and you need to know the regulations'.

The same advice comes through again and again. Simon Crooks cautions that 'it doesn't matter what other people are saying, what matters is the official documentation. Read the rules!'

This emphasis on understanding the law and regulation is not the typical mindset in other commodities, where there is usually less direct government influence and intervention.

Perhaps a good parallel is physical operations. A lot of commodity traders caution that it's hard to be successful without properly understanding the physical operations that govern how material moves from one place to another.

Operations are the actual non-negotiable underpinning of these physical commodities, whereas government regulations perform the same framework role in many of the environmental markets.

In this context, hiring an environmental trader with a strong legal or regulatory background is no different from a more typical commodity desk hiring a talented physical operator.

'If you want to succeed here', warns Chelsea Bryant in Chapter 10, 'you must thrive on precision. You need to be willing to roll up your sleeves and dive into the fine print, tracking changes in policy at every level: federal, provincial, state, and even municipal'.

The downsides of trading

From the outside, trading sounds glamorous, and this is particularly true of trading in the environmental markets, which combine the excitement of trading with a greater modern-day social acceptability than, say, oil trading.

As we have noted, though, traders live or die on their results, and so the pressure on individuals can be enormous.

Young people in China perceive carbon trading as a 'cool' area, Liu Yu notes in Chapter 6, but at the same time he warns of the dangers of the profession:

> it is normal as a trader to feel very nervous at some times, or very happy. You have to learn to absorb these different feelings because trading can be very stressful and tense. This market can stop many people from sleeping properly.

As soon as one deal is completed successfully, the search for a new source of profits immediately begins. The market has a very short memory, and 'you don't hear "thank you" a lot in the trading business', Lex Batters comments (Chapter 34).

A few years ago, John B. Henry had to have all of his teeth redone because he had ground them down through stress, while during his trading career Ricardo Parada gained 30 kilos in weight and developed hypertension (Chapter 14).

As well as stress, many of the female contributors commented on the sexism that existed in the early days of the market and which has diminished with time, although without disappearing entirely.

Claire Byers caught pneumonia on a trading floor where the air conditioning was designed around the needs of larger middle-aged men, while Fenella Aouane became 'almost resigned to the fact that I was probably always paid less than guys that were doing the same job as me'.

It was certainly a surprise to me, while preparing this book, to see how limited the number of senior female environmental traders were, even relative to other commodity markets, which tend to be male-dominated.

This was especially puzzling given that the broader environmental sector – policy, advocacy, fundraising and project development – tends to attract a high proportion of women. Environmental conferences typically see women in the majority.

Perhaps the greater opportunities for women to attain senior positions in sectors adjacent to the markets means that female candidates with a strong interest in the environment have less incentive to pursue careers within the markets themselves. In contrast, women who are passionate about energy or metals may find working on the market side more congenial than pursuing paths in the upstream or mining sectors.

Conclusion

The following 40 chapters will describe some environmental markets that have worked fantastically well and delivered real improvements, as well as others that have functioned less well or are still works in progress.

The contributors will also reveal some highly profitable winning strategies as well as some trades that went horribly wrong.

These are the inevitable ups and downs of the markets, and particularly of environmental markets, which are young and constantly evolving. As Neville Atterbury notes about his career in biofuels, 'every year has been packed with a different kind of "new"'.

Environmental traders have to be aware of the normal forces of supply and demand, but beyond that they also need to keep their fingers on the pulse of the evolving political and social landscape.

Many traders are well paid, but this is far from 'easy money', as the discussions of the impact of stress reveal.

Whatever your views on the efficacy of the environmental markets and their ability to drive change and benefit the planet, I hope that these 40 chapters will leave you impressed by the ingenuity, hard work and creativity of the individuals who drive these markets.

Part I

Environmental market pioneers

Many people think that Europe invented the environmental markets, but in reality, the first pioneers came from the United States.

The U.S. Clean Air Act of 1990 introduced the Acid Rain Program, which led to the development of an allowance trading system for sulphur dioxide (SO_2) and nitrogen oxide (NO_x) emissions.

The acid rain market, so entertainingly described here by two of its prime movers – John B. Henry and Richard Sandor – was a tremendous success, driving down SO_2 and NO_x emissions in a highly cost-effective manner.

It was the positive example of the U.S. acid rain market that later encouraged the European Union (EU) to introduce a market solution to drive down carbon emissions.

The EU Emissions Trading System (EU ETS) has since grown into the largest environmental market on the planet, but its early days also had their challenges, as described here by three of the very first European market participants: Garth Edward, Claire Byers and Ingo Ramming.

DOI: 10.4324/9781003359739-2

Chapter 1

Trading away acid rain

A corporate lawyer turned serial entrepreneur, John B. Henry launched Crop Genetics International in the 1980s to develop, manufacture and market products to improve productivity and protect crops without the use of chemicals. John went on to develop the market for sulphur dioxide pollution allowances in the 1990s, serving as chief executive of Clean Air Capital Markets, an environmental investment bank. In 2000, John founded eLaw-Forum, which became DryStone, to make a market in legal services. He is a graduate of Harvard College and Columbia Law School and has served on numerous boards of corporations and of non-profit organizations, such as Harvard, the Smithsonian, the Stone Hill Theatrical Foundation and the Committee for the Republic.

I'm a 12th-generation Virginian and for 12 generations nobody in my family made any money. I'm the first guy in my family who created businesses and made a payroll.

The three generations before me were all church ministers, and I think my mother wanted me to go into the ministry as well. My parents were very moral people who, as the phrase goes, were rich in the things that count.

That legacy stayed with me in two ways: first, I always had to have an idealistic business. I found I've always had to do good in order to do well. I was going to use biotech to get rid of chemicals in the crop protection market, and then later I worked to bring free market principles to bear to clean up the environment.

Second, I used to wonder to myself why I was always selling all the time. Then, one day I realized I'd seen my dad selling Jesus Christ for 35 years. I basically grew up in a sales organization and that was the air that I breathed.

When I started looking into the environment, I was like an evangelist for developing a market solution. It was a real missionary sale for me because I had to create both the buy and the sell side and then try to bring them together.

DOI: 10.4324/9781003359739-3

Clean Air Act

The environmental markets in the U.S. began with the revision of the Clean Air Act, which President George H.W. Bush signed into law in November 1990.

The amendments to the Act were designed to curb four major threats to the environment and public health: acid rain, urban air pollution, toxic air emissions and stratospheric ozone depletion.

The most interesting aspect for me was that the amendments established a national permit programme that was designed to speed up the implementation of environmental improvements.

The folk from the advocacy group, the Environmental Defense Fund (EDF), had pushed the government to introduce a market solution because they were interested in lowering the cost of reducing pollution.

At the time, there was a huge focus on acid rain, which was largely caused by sulphur dioxide (SO2) emissions from coal-fired electricity plants.

One way of reducing SO2 emissions was to build a scrubber, which is a chemical plant that is attached to the power plant and filters out harmful pollutants. Another solution was for power plants to burn lower-sulphur coal from the Powder River Basin in Wyoming.

The concept behind the government's introduction of permits was that you could cut the cost of environmental compliance in half if you could ensure that investment capital was flowing to wherever it was most cost-effective to reduce emissions.

The idea was that those utilities that could clean up their emissions for less would be able to sell their SO2 permits to generators where cleaning up would have a higher cost. That way, the U.S. would be able to eliminate acid rain as quickly and as cheaply as possible.

This new market concept looked like an interesting opportunity to me.

My first company was an agricultural biotech company, and, after that experience, I was looking for a business that didn't have any technology risk in it. In trading, you had sales risk, but at least you didn't have to deal with technology risk.

Building the market

I worked with a really good environmental lawyer who was very smart and who understood the inside and outside of the statute, which was complicated, and I set up an environmental investment bank called Clean Air Capital Markets.

We figured out which utilities were likely to have excess permits and which firms were likely to be short of permits, and we built a model to figure out what was the cost basis of reductions.

The Clean Air Act created what we would call 'paper flow' by telling the utilities they had to reduce their harmful emissions. That meant I didn't have to go out and sell them on the idea that acid rain was killing fish, but I did have to persuade them about the benefits of a market solution.

The U.S. government didn't create an environmental market. It simply created the preconditions for a market. I had to make the market actually work by going out and persuading people that this was real.

I would take my knowledgeable and very expensive environmental lawyer with me on the road, and we would go and do sales calls on the utilities.

We needed to be very convincing. Back then, the utilities were full of what I would call C-students. Legal, insurance, pharmaceuticals: those are all A-student markets, but the utilities were full of C-students. It was a regulated industry, and whenever you regulate an industry, you drive the smart people out.

It was a tough sell. These were engineers in the Midwest who didn't go to fancy schools. I'm pretty conceptual myself so I can see opportunities, but these were guys that just thought in terms of generating electricity rather than about trading permits or anything non-tangible.

I got the heck kicked out of me by some of those utilities. I'd be on planes flying back from midwestern cities, looking out the window at night and wondering how the hell I was going to pull this off.

In retrospect, I feel like I almost willed that market into happening because I just wouldn't take no for an answer.

Closing the deal

Eventually, I got Wisconsin Power and Light on board as a seller, and I started to pick up some other potential sellers. But, for the life of me, I couldn't find anyone prepared to be a buyer.

I've always been bold, and I've always had confidence, even when I didn't have any real basis for it, but at this point I also got lucky. As Mark Twain said, 'to succeed in life, you need two things: ignorance and confidence'.

I had gone to Harvard with Boyden Gray, who was a leading architect of the 1990 Clean Air Act. We were close friends and we used to socialize together in Washington, DC.

Now Boyden was personally invested in making the Act a success, and he was a good person to know because he was working at the time for President Bush.

I went to Boyden, and I laid out the issues I was having with finding a buyer for the SO2 permits. I asked him if he could speak to his boss, the president, and maybe together they could put some pressure on the Tennessee Valley Authority (TVA) to step up as a buyer.

The TVA is an electricity producer that is owned by the federal government, which meant that the ultimate boss of the TVA was President Bush.

Boyden brought the president onside and Bush basically ordered the TVA to buy some SO2 allowances. They flew the head of the TVA up to Washington,

DC, and they told him to buy those allowances right there on the lawn of the White House.

The TVA would never have agreed to be the first buyer without political pressure. I was lucky beyond belief that I had a good connection that was able to lean on the TVA.

I didn't have a buyer, so I had to create a buyer. I truly believe that if I hadn't been close to Boyden Gray and persuaded him to apply some pressure, the market could have been stillborn.

Fortunately, the TVA bought some allowances, and the first-ever environmental permit trade was done and dusted.

Publicizing the trade

After I broke the market open, that deal was all over the media; it was even on the television. It was quite dramatic. During the COVID-19 lockdown, I came across the clippings of newspaper and magazine coverage of that first trade and it was a big folder.

That first deal opened the doors and reassured the other utilities that this was a real market and that they should get involved.

After the TVA transaction, I think I did probably between $100 and $200 million of deals. I got some of the really big guys as clients, so I had a lot of market power. I was acting as the agent on some big volume tickets, and I had very high margins, so I made some serious money for a while.

Those high margins were justified. I wasn't just acting as the trading agent, I was also basically selling a lot of intellectual property because I was also educating people about trading. I had a lot of expenses, some serious costs.

I was babysitting the market to get it going so I had to do a lot of very sophisticated presentations and I was paying huge fees by the hour to my legal expert.

But then Cantor Fitzgerald came in and ruined the market. They commoditized it by breaking up the big tickets into small volume deals. The margins also collapsed: I had been able to make $10 an allowance and they took it down to 10 cents.

Cantor took all the margin out of the environmental markets and so I moved on. In retrospect, perhaps I gave in too soon, but I already had a new business idea in mind: I wanted to make use of the internet, which had just gotten popular, to create a market in legal services.

Maybe I was just ready to pivot to a new challenge. I like doing bold things: if someone else has done it, I don't want to do it.

I did well in the environmental business for a while, but I didn't tear the cover off the ball, and I ultimately failed to turn the distinction of being behind the first environmental trade into a business that was self-sustaining in the long run.

Now I've built a very big and self-sustaining company in the insurance space, and I guess I'm prouder of that than of anything.

But if I had only been about making money, I don't think I would have done as well in business as I have.

Perhaps it's my family heritage, but I really like the idea of doing good through business.

The idea that I was helping the planet by bringing the free market to bear on solving environmental problems, well, that really spurred me on, even when the C-students at the utilities were giving me a hard time.

As an entrepreneur, I took enormous risks throughout my career, and I survived them. But I wouldn't recommend it and I wouldn't have lived my life the same way over again, knowing what I know now. A few years ago, I had to have all of my teeth redone because I had ground all of them down through stress.

I have a lot of confidence, but it wasn't always well founded: I was way over my skis a lot of time and I was fortunate that I took crazy risks and survived and did well.

This was a statutory market that was created by an Act of Congress, but I don't think it would have gotten off the ground, if I hadn't been there and been so crazy.

I had to be a true missionary because I was bearing all of the sales risk. In this case, the product was there in theory, but it wasn't really there in practice. Until we got that first trade done, the theory was all great, but the experience was missing.

Environmental markets are tough because they are a concept sell, which is very difficult.

A conceptual market is kind of like conceptual art. There's art that's really beautiful that you want to display on your wall, and then there's also concept art.

You know concept art is important, but you wouldn't necessarily want to own it. Very few people can sell conceptual art or conceptual markets; it was a heavy lift, it really was.

My entrepreneur coach has this theory of unique ability, which is where you discover what you can do that others can't do.

I'm in my seventies now, and when I look back at that time, I think I was very lucky because there wasn't always a firm basis to my confidence, but then I also think I made my own luck, and I maybe did something that other folk couldn't have done.

I was the right guy for a moon shot. I loved big ideas, I loved a concept market and I loved to be an evangelist. And who else would have had the connections to get the head of the TVA onto the White House lawn to do the first trade?

The EDF later estimated that due to the trading scheme, SO2 emissions fell faster than predicted and at one-fourth of the projected cost. Using a market mechanism proved to be a resounding success.

There were very few people who would have been in a position to make that first environmental trade happen. I'm pleased to have been the right person in the right place at the right time.

Chapter 2

Developing environmental auctions

Dr Richard Sandor has been called the 'Father of Carbon Trading' for his work in developing financial markets for the environmental sector. As a professor on sabbatical from the University of California, Berkeley, in the 1970s, Dr Sandor became the chief economist and vice president of the Chicago Board of Trade (CBOT), where he pioneered the world's first interest rate futures contract, the Treasury bond futures contract. For that work he was called the Father of Financial Futures. Dr Sandor serves as chief executive of Environmental Products LLC, which since 1998 has designed new markets and provided investment advisory services. He was chair of CBOT's Clean Air Committee, and later co-founder of the Chicago Climate Exchange, the European Climate Exchange, the Chicago Climate Futures Exchange and the Tianjin Climate Exchange in China. In 2007, he was named as one of Time *magazine's Heroes of the Environment. Dr Sandor has served on numerous boards of directors, has taught at several leading business schools and has published numerous academic papers as well as his bestselling book, Good Derivatives: A Story of Financial and Environmental Innovation.*

There are few things more embarrassing in life than throwing a party, only for nobody to show up. That was the worry that kept me awake at night in March 1993.

We were about to host the world's first-ever environmental auction on the Chicago Board of Trade (CBOT), and we weren't sure how the reception was going to be.

The sellers were locked in: the U.S. Environmental Protection Agency (EPA) was offering 50,000 sulphur dioxide (SO2) allowances to U.S. utilities as part of its Acid Rain Program. We just didn't know what the response from the buyers was likely to be.

I had helped to persuade all of the parties, including the U.S. government, that it would be a good idea to auction the permits. My name was all over this project so if it didn't take off, I was going to look like a total jerk.

DOI: 10.4324/9781003359739-4

Everyone involved was biting their hands, and my anxiety levels were at a peak. To make things even more intense, I had also agreed to trade a large over-the-counter SO2 options deal. Apart from the reputational side, my business was going to suffer if the auction failed.

Commoditizing air

It had been a lengthy journey to get to this point. Four years earlier in 1990, I received a call asking me to rejoin the board of the CBOT, now part of CME Group, which at that time was the largest commodities exchange in the world.

Some years earlier, I had come up with CBOT's ten-year interest rate futures contract as well as options on bonds so I had built a reputation as an innovator in the financial markets.

At the same time that I received the call from CBOT, I was working on a position paper on acid rain for a group of lime producers.

When you pass flue gas through lime, it chemically combines with sulphur, which prevents harmful emissions. The lime producers were looking at the implications for their business of efforts to combat acid rain.

The guy that commissioned me to write the paper had said, 'hey, you commoditized interest rates. Can you also commoditize air?' My response was just to say 'sure'.

I talked to Billy O'Connor, who was the chairman of CBOT, and I told Billy that there was going to be an emissions trading programme, and that he should take my word that this was going to be big. I told him I wanted to form a new board committee, which I named the Clean Air Committee.

At my first board meeting back at CBOT, Billy announced the new committee and said, 'Doc is going to head it'. (A lot of people call me Doc because that was the acronym on my trading badge.)

Jim Thompson, who was Governor of Illinois at that time, jumped on the idea and three or four other independent directors came onboard as well. They loved the idea that developing environmental products could be a public-private partnership initiative.

A couple of months later, Jim Thompson called me and said, 'come on, let's go to Washington, DC, and see the EPA'. That's when I was introduced to Bill Reilly, the head of the EPA, and to Michael Boskin, who was chairman of the President's Council of Economic Advisers.

The first thing I told Bill was that there was a problem in the pending clean air legislation. I told Bill Reilly that the current setup provided for asymmetric information, which would make it tough to get this market off the ground.

I had discussed the issue with Billy O'Connor, who summed it up by saying, 'I'm not going to trade this market because I don't know what the emissions are going to be'.

The EPA needed to put continuous emission monitors on the smokestacks because otherwise the speculators were not going to trade since only the utilities would know how much the supply was going to be.

Bill told me not to worry and that he would take care of it. He put out a technical amendment, which is the easy way to fix legislation.

We also told Bill that CBOT would be interested in running an auction for the EPA and that we would do it on a pro bono basis.

Then we went to see Michael Boskin, and we said 'look, the Chicago Board of Trade and Governor Thompson are excited about this pending legislation. We think the government really needs to support this programme because we think it's a game changer'.

Market development

Bear in mind, all of these conversations took place decades ago. We had a lot to discuss because back in 1990, a market-based solution to public problems was not exactly a normal occurrence.

We pushed on with discussions and preparations, even though the registry wasn't set up and nothing was properly ready.

I got even more excited and I ended up deciding that I wanted to do some trades myself. I agreed to an OTC trade in SO2 options for 30 years out, which was absurd in retrospect.

I also started putting together some other structured trades, which ended up being the first trades submitted to the registry, so I had taken on quite a lot of personal exposure to the SO2 market.

In the meantime, my friend and mentor Ronald Coase had won the Nobel Prize for Economics in 1991 for his work on social costs in the economy. I'd kept Ronald informed throughout about the concept of the SO2 market and the potential auction.

At that point, it was all starting to come together. You had a Nobel Prize being awarded in this exact area, you had acid rain legislation and you had somebody like me, a professional inventor, who got a lot of things wrong but got some things right as well.

The CBOT eventually won the right to conduct the auction on a pro bono basis, and the auction was scheduled for March 1993.

Hammer time

Then the nerves began: we had spent years preparing for this moment, and yet we couldn't control the outcome.

Fortunately for everyone involved, the auction went off very well, and the only surprise was the number of bids. Despite all of my worries, we ended up receiving more bids than anybody had expected.

There were 150,000 allowances for sale and the auction grossed around $20 million from average bids of somewhere around $130 per tonne. The auction bids and the participation levels were far higher than anticipated but the price was lower than most observers had expected.

I wasn't that surprised that the price came in lower, although I was positively surprised about the range of bids.

We designed it as a discriminatory auction, which means each successful bidder is awarded at the price level at which they bid. That's a different format to the classic auction where each successful bidder is awarded at the same clearing price.

In our auction, if you bid $250 and you were successful, you got awarded at that level.

We designed the auction that way very deliberately but the format generated a lot of criticism. I think the criticism was misplaced. Our design was meant to provide price discovery; it wasn't really meant to be the most efficient auction mechanism.

I wanted to see the range of bids. We had written an SO2 futures contract and so we thought it was important that potential market participants could see the different price levels in the spot physical market for permits.

Some economists complained that it wasn't efficient and that we should have awarded all of the winning bids at the same clearing price. But I'm in the price discovery business and those of us in the know were very happy with how it worked.

Potential future traders would want to see the range of potential prices, rather than just a clearing price.

Before the auction, estimates of the potential price of allowances ranged from $300 to $1,000 a tonne, so the auction average of $130 looked cheap to some.

In my opinion, the lower price was not surprising at all. The threat of legislation and the cap had induced early action from power producers. The utilities had been preparing for the cap for years. A lot of them had already built scrubbers and were installing them, so I wasn't surprised that their demand was lower.

Polluter pays

A lot of the criticism of the lower auction price was not based on economic factors but more on a moral basis.

My response at the time was that people don't complain when food prices are low. Surely, it's good for everyone if you can achieve good outcomes at a low price?

The rhetorical answer from some folk was, 'well, you're letting the polluters off easy', to which my response was that 'the goal was to stop acid rain, it wasn't to punish the polluter, right?'

I mean we're getting moral at that point. My stated view was, 'that's a question for a Sunday. Monday through Friday, we work to get rid of the problem. On Sunday, we can discuss punishing the polluter'.

We have a different objective here: Monday to Friday, we are trying to get rid of pollution. As to who the sinner is, well, that's a weekend problem.

Emissions trading is nothing more than an expression of the economist David Ricardo's concept of 'gains from trade'. Environmental markets are Ricardian markets: they demonstrate the theory of comparative advantage.

The first cuts should come from the people who can make them at the cheapest level. It's Ricardian economics: it's that simple.

I used to tell people at the time that before the EPA's Acid Rain Program, we were effectively paying people to pollute because there was no constraint on pollution.

Developing a market allows you to pay them for not polluting. There are incentives, and that's the key. What you learn in Chicago and from price theory is that incentives matter.

Kyoto and beyond

That auction was hugely significant. In terms of environmental improvements, governments had overseen the phasing out of lead in the 1980s, but a market-based approach like SO2 emissions trading was unlike anything else that had ever come before.

I know personally that the concept really resonated because in the beginning of 1997, I was on a panel at the White House that Al Gore chaired. Everybody was kind of dour about the prospects for the environment.

I got up and said, 'I don't get this pessimism'. Gore snapped to attention, and I said, 'look, if the incentives are right, people can clean up the air. Markets can replace taxes and subsidies if you give them a chance. We did it for acid rain and you can do it for carbon'.

I stayed friends with Gore after that and that same year he went to Kyoto on behalf of President Bill Clinton where he pushed for trading. The Kyoto Protocol stated that emissions trading had a role in combatting climate change. Without U.S. support, I think it would have gone nowhere.

The growth of environmental markets stems from that first auction and its success, and the subsequent private trades.

I moved on, and after Kyoto, I did some more structured trades and then I started the Chicago Climate Exchange and later on its affiliates. I got to work with the United Nations and with a lot of people in Brussels and the U.K. on the original EU Emissions Trading System (EU ETS).

All of that was fascinating work and it all stemmed from the success of the original acid rain auction.

Benefits in kind

The auction was a total home run from the point of view of a public-private partnership that happened at virtually zero cost.

The EPA estimated that the Acid Rain Program had something like a 50:1 cost-benefit ratio. The programme cost something like $23 million per year to run. It generated around 50 times that figure in benefits, by reducing healthcare costs from lung disease, missing workdays, and some 37,000 deaths.

Those figures don't even include the intangible value of the programme in terms of scenic beauty or protecting rivers and lakes.

CBOT stepping in at that particular point really woke everybody up. I was on the EPA's Acid Rain Advisory Committee, and there were lots of well-intentioned environmentalists involved, but they didn't understand finance or registries.

I told people that CBOT was pricing the world's food supply through its wheat, corn and soybean benchmarks, so I didn't see why we couldn't also price clean air and turn the environment into a commodity.

The involvement of the world's biggest commodity exchange gave the auction additional credibility with the Senate Finance Committee and the Senate Agricultural Committee. They had to take environmental markets seriously when they were being endorsed by the exchange that handled all the trade in stock indexes and interest rates.

In the period following World War II, many British inventions were commercialized in the U.S. But this was an example of the opposite happening. The environmental markets were invented in the U.S. but they were truly commercialized in Europe.

U.S. financial innovation flowed from the U.S. to the U.K. and Europe.

People think that the U.S. squandered that lead and that it has abandoned environmental markets, but people don't realize that the open interest across the U.S. environmental markets is currently over one million contracts, which is bigger than open interest in gold.

Game changer

That one auction changed the nature of environmental finance and trading. It set the entire stage for the commoditization of public goods, and helped lead to the development of carbon trading and of water trading.

The use of an auction mechanism became the standard for all of the national carbon emissions auctions, such as the German auctions. It was *the* model.

Using auctions is still part of the permanent landscape for the environmental markets decades later. The architecture of an auction provides valuable price discovery; well-designed auctions are fair, transparent and reputable.

The whole concept of auctions doesn't just work from a theoretical point of view; it has also proved over the years to be very practical.

On a personal level, this was also the first time in my career that my kids were interested in, or even understood, what their Daddy did.

It turns out working on the environment is a lot cooler than in areas like bonds and bond options, five- and ten-year rates and the yield curve.

The financial side didn't go over too well at home, but it was definitely a bit different when they realized that Daddy was working on climate change...

Chapter 3

Valuing a new market

Garth Edward first studied at the University of Oxford and National Taiwan Normal University before completing a master's degree at the University of Cambridge. After graduating, he joined the United Nations Environment Programme in Nairobi and then New York. In 1997, Garth was hired by Natsource LLC to set up its carbon brokering business. He then joined Shell in London in 2001 as environmental products trading manager, a role he held until he moved to Citigroup in 2008 as director, global environmental products. Between 2010 and 2016, Garth traded LNG and environmental products for PetroChina, and he then traded LNG for French utility ENGIE in Paris between 2016 and 2020. In 2020, Garth moved to Singapore to work for Aramco Trading Company, as LNG trading manager, and from 2022, he also established and took on emission book lead functions.

When I switch on my trading screen nowadays and I look at the activity in the European Union Emissions Trading System (EU ETS), it is very clear that the ETS has become a proper *bona fide* serious market that is trusted both by governments and by the largest firms.

The ETS has transitioned from touchy-feely aspirational talk to actually deliver economically and commercially, and I would argue that the ETS delivers environmentally as well.

I was heavily involved in all of the discussions and preparations that led to the development of the EU ETS, and then in 2003, I executed the first EU allowance trade in the market when I was the environmental products trading head at Shell.

That trade is something that I look back on with pride. The ETS has become a really significant market and it was a meaningful achievement to help get it started.

When I joined Shell in 2001 in London, I was tasked with setting up their environmental products trading desk from scratch.

The firm had some indirect exposure to emissions markets in general through its power and renewable business. Shell could also see that it would

DOI: 10.4324/9781003359739-5

be covered by a broader European emissions trading system so it wanted to be prepared.

I guess, looking back, it was a relatively cheap option for Shell to hire someone like me that they could put on the trading floor and then see what happened.

We started out trading renewable energy certificates (RECs) and renewable obligation certificates (ROCs), as well as nitrous oxide (NOx) and sulphur dioxide (SO2) permits in the U.S.

We agreed some of the earliest iterations of carbon deals, which were of course completely unstructured and most of which were unguided by any regulation of any kind at that point.

As one of the 'standard bearers' of European industry, we were also very active in the various early regulated European iterations of emissions trading, such as the U.K. and Danish systems.

At that point, there still wasn't a formal European Union scheme in place because the European ETS wasn't scheduled to come into effect until 2005.

Preparing to trade

As Shell's representative, I was deeply involved in discussions with the European regulators and government officials who were setting the policy agenda and drafting the practical legislation ahead of the introduction of the ETS.

By 2003, the discussions about policy and the final rules had become sufficiently advanced that we felt we had a good level of clarity about where the ETS was headed.

Both I and my colleagues at Shell felt that we had enough confidence about how the rules would play out that we could make a trade.

The motivation was, I suppose, to transition from all the talking to the walking; to move from policy to reality.

As a trader on a trading desk, at some point in time, you have to generate some profits. After all, traders don't get paid for attending meetings.

At some point we had to convert all of these discussions about the shape of the ETS into a real, profitable business. That applied not only to ourselves at Shell but to other firms in the market.

I knew exactly where to look for a potential counterpart for a first trade. There were probably 15–20 companies that were always involved in the discussions about the ETS: they were the big power companies, the big oil companies, some European banks, and to a certain extent the cement, glass and steel producers.

We all knew exactly who each other was because we had sat together in so many meetings. I called up Seb Walhain and his team at Belgium's Fortis Bank (*see Chapter 4*). We discussed the concept of getting a first trade done for quite some time, and then we began to draft a contract.

There was some uncertainty about how we could structure a deal without everything being finalized on the ETS side. This was 2003 and the first compliance year wasn't until 2005 so at that point in time there were no operational registry systems. Then, since no permits had been issued, we couldn't make or take physical delivery.

Eventually, we agreed on a forward trade that was based on our understanding of the rules at that point in time.

Pricing the trade

The next key question was obviously what price we could land on for the first trade.

Assessing fair value in any carbon market is always a challenge, and that is particularly true given the market hadn't yet been fully defined.

Of course, the most rational way for a trader to make a call in any commodity market is to take a view on the balance of supply and demand.

In emissions, that means trying to estimate the marginal cost of creating the marginal emission reduction or of buying the marginal allowance. But the ETS originally provided a free allocation of permits, even to power generators, so in that context the marginal cost of abatement was unclear at the inception of the scheme.

Because we were looking to trade before the scheme had even launched, there were no benchmarks we could lean on, no real vision of supply versus demand, and no real sense of where the marginal cost could reach.

There is only so far you can get anyway with supply-demand analysis in the carbon markets, when prices and activity are so highly dependent on the rules that governments set. Any changes in the way that an official scheme operates can have a huge impact on prices, irrespective of perceptions of fundamentals.

We tried with Fortis to come up with a price that was 'reasonable'.

The Danish and U.K. schemes were in the background of people's minds, but bear in mind that the U.K. scheme had traded in an incredibly wide range. The U.K. scheme got up as high as £20–30 and then went effectively to zero because it was structurally massively oversupplied.

Those schemes provided some experiences that were in our minds but they didn't really provide much of a particularly clear sense of where the starting price should be for the ETS.

Getting started

It was important not to be massively wrong on the first trade. That was a critical concern. In a high-profile company like Shell, you don't want to make a mistake and create a huge exposure for the firm or something like that.

A major mis-step so early on would have meant 'game over' for me or for the carbon desk. If it had gone wrong, the company probably wouldn't have done anything more in the ETS or a long time.

We tried to be as careful as possible. We introduced different fallback mechanisms into the contract with Fortis to ensure that each side was covered in the event of unforeseen changes to the ETS before launch.

We also agreed to limit the risk by limiting the size of the trade. Neither side wanted to trade huge volumes when no one was entirely sure how the scheme would play out.

Eventually, we landed at a trading level of around €5 per tonne and we signed the deal with Fortis. Of course, that €5 looks very cheap now when today we are trading in the €70s, but remember that the ETS has also traded down as low as €1–2.

At that point, with no other benchmarks or true reference points, we both felt that €5 was a reasonable starting point.

We ended up being pretty close to how the market played out. The ETS did indeed trade at and around €5 for quite a long time when it launched in 2005. That price didn't reflect any supply-demand fundamentals at that stage; it was just where buyers and sellers thought the price was reasonable.

Nowadays, we are in a very different world. The ETS is more mature and you can actually talk in terms of true fundamental analysis and a 'rational' price for permits.

In the modern ETS, traders typically take a view on the marginal cost of abatement, effectively trying to understand what is the first tonne of carbon that can be reduced. For example, the marginal cost of abatement will likely reflect the cost for European power generators of switching from coal to gas.

That means that you could argue that the emissions price is largely set by the difference between the cost of generating power from coal while buying carbon emissions certificates (the 'clean dark spread') and the cost of generating power from natural gas while buying certificates (the 'clean spark spread').

That's a very rational approach, but of course in the early stages of market development, it didn't yet apply. Particularly in that first phase when power generators had a free allocation, it wasn't understood ex ante how the ETS would impact power prices, for example.

Of course, it turned out that the European utilities would end up making enormous windfall profits because the power price embedded the full opportunity cost of EU allowances, while the power firms actually received the allowances for free.

European electricity prices increased but utilities' cost base didn't and so obviously the impact on their net revenue was enormous – firms received billions of dollars of benefit. This impact was not well understood beforehand by anybody, including the power companies themselves.

Varied approaches

Different carbon markets clearly require different approaches, as do different stages of market development.

The voluntary carbon markets, for example, have no true parameters of supply and demand so making a call on fair value is really entirely up for grabs. There's not a rational price that can be assessed on fundamentals since the price is primarily based on buyers' willingness to pay and buyers' appetite. That buyer sentiment is very hard to model or to assess.

The Chinese emissions trading programme is another very significant market but it can't be traded in the same way as the European ETS because it has one major structural difference: the Chinese programme is based on intensity-based emissions rather than absolute emissions.

There was a big policy debate in the very early days of establishing emissions trading systems about whether the best model was an absolute cap or a relative cap.

The ETS ended up going with an absolute cap and that's been the bedrock of the whole system from the beginning. China's policy choice was to go with intensity-based targets, which change every year depending on economic output growth.

Both are legitimate approaches, but the weakness of an intensity-based approach is that effectively the supply-demand balance changes every year, which means that the forward curve is unknowable and doesn't exist.

This is a shame because it is the forward curve that provides the price signal that allows firms to allocate capital appropriately to emissions-reducing technologies and so on.

Trade rationales

Whatever the carbon market, where possible I try to focus on the supply-demand balance, while also taking any potential rule changes into account.

After all, you have to have some rationale behind taking positions. That still doesn't stop you from being wrong from time to time, but at least you know your position came from a logical starting point.

One of the pleasing aspects of the emissions markets is that there are occasions when it's been possible to call the market rationally and legitimately.

One example was the price of certified emissions reductions (CERs). It was known for a long time that the volume of CERs that was being produced could not be consumed fully in the EU ETS and hence supply would clearly exceed demand.

Nonetheless, there was still a long period when CERs were trading at above the €10 mark, even though it was clear that these levels could not persist. In the end, that's indeed what happened: CERs got crushed, prices went to zero, and then CERs were removed from the EU ETS.

Emissions trading is interesting intellectually because sometimes, if you get your analysis right, you can understand what should happen.

These are opportunities in the carbon markets that probably don't really exist in something like the oil market, where there are so many more external factors in play.

In the emissions markets, if you understand the fundamentals and also the way the rules work and how these interact with fundamentals, you can try to spot disconnects and opportunities.

In a way, I have been searching for profitable moments like that throughout my career. I've been fortunate that I have found them a couple of times and every day when I switch the trading screen on, I continue to keep my eyes open for the next opportunities that might emerge.

Chapter 4

Trading the first EUA

After completing a degree in natural sciences at Cambridge University, Claire Byers went to work for Shell as a geologist. She left Shell to undertake a master's degree in environmental technology at Imperial College, London, after which in 2000 she joined Ecofys International as an environmental consultant. In 2002, Claire was hired as an environmental products trader by Dutch utility Nuon, later moving as manager of environmental products to Belgian bank Fortis where she co-founded the carbon banking concept. In 2006, she left Fortis to found environmental consultancy Sigma Global, which she co-led until 2012. Claire has worked for campaigning group Project Everyone, and after completing a further master's degree in sustainable agriculture and food security from the Royal Agricultural University in 2021, she was appointed business development lead for agroforestry business TreeSource.

I joined the Dutch utility Nuon in 2002, and quite soon afterwards they moved my colleague, Seb Walhain and me – together we were the entire environmental products team – onto the trading floor.

I'm sure that when we arrived there were a few sneers from the traders in the more liquid markets who were making lots of money. They were probably saying to themselves, 'what the hell are you two doing here with your made-up market that doesn't even exist yet?'

After all, this was a few years before the European Trading System (ETS) came into force for carbon and so we were mainly looking at financing renewables projects, and buying and selling renewable energy certificates (RECs).

In those days, our job was more about keeping an eye on government policies, doing some supply and offtake contracts for renewables, carrying out project risk assessments, etc. – there was no real tradeable market.

In general, we found that most of the other commodity traders weren't particularly mean to us because these were really intelligent people who wouldn't dismiss a new market out of hand.

Some of the other traders were actually really interested in how carbon trading might impact their oil or coal positions, although there were clearly

DOI: 10.4324/9781003359739-6

others who thought that carbon was some kind of a Mickey Mouse market based on a commodity that didn't really exist...

Everyone knew that the political will was there at governmental level to develop carbon trading, but there were plenty of questions about when that might happen and whether carbon would ever become a major market.

You can imagine that it is a pretty weird feeling to sit on a trade floor where there are lots of thrusting young things trading super liquid markets if you are largely reading policy documents and hoping to do a deal every six months or so.

We were obviously desperate to get something happening because there were entire days when we weren't trading, or even talking about trading. For us and for our credibility on the floor, it was a case of, 'we can't wait for the politicians much longer, let's make a market'.

Agreeing the first deal

Before the EU launched the ETS, the UK started its own emissions market, which later folded into the broader EU scheme. Looking at how the UK market worked at least helped us get to grips with how the ETS might play out, even though Nuon didn't really have any major exposure in the UK.

The ETS was set to launch in January 2005, but already by February 2003, we had decided we didn't want to wait any longer for the scheme to launch and so we went ahead and looked for a potential deal.

My boss at the time, Jogchum Brinksma, was really open to doing new and innovative things and was quite rightly keen to make a name for himself and so he was prepared to drive the trade forward.

With our fantastic legal adviser Douglas Gessell, we came up with a contract that reflected our understanding of the ETS insofar as it had been defined.

Obviously, we had only limited ideas at that time about how national allocations would work and fungibility between different environmental certificates hadn't been fully defined. Would an Emissions Reduction Unit (ERU) would be worth the same as a certified emissions reduction (CER) certificate or the same as an EU allowance (EUA)? It was anyone's guess.

Nobody knew much. The legislation introducing the ETS was in place, but few of the finer points of the market structure had been spelled out. We knew, for example, that CERs were going to be accepted in the ETS, but not to what extent in terms of volumes or at what price level.

One of the few facts we did know for sure was that an electricity company like Nuon was going to have a deficit – a shortfall in EUAs – and so we thought it would be a good idea to buy some certificates in advance from a firm that would receive an allocation under the ETS.

Fortunately, one of those European firms expected to receive allowances once the ETS was up and running was my former employers Shell. Shell's environmental trading manager Garth Edwards was also extremely interested in innovating and in getting the new carbon market going (see Chapter 3).

Shaping the deal

The discussions moved quickly, although there were obviously a lot of operational and legal hurdles to clear.

We didn't even know how allowances were going to be exchanged so we weren't clear how we would ultimately take delivery of the EUAs from Shell. We had some concept that there would be an ETS registry, but we didn't know whether it would be a tradeable register or whether an exchange would emerge.

Usually, in trading, the sticking point in any negotiation is 'what's the price?' But in this case, the future price of EUAs was a complete unknown.

Price is usually a function of supply and demand, but in this case, there was only limited information about how the allocations would be made and how easy it would be to trade them, so estimates for the supply-demand balance varied wildly.

We got around the issue of price risk by agreeing the trade for just 5,000 tonnes which was a very small amount, and which meant that at least there were not megabucks at stake if the eventual price moved wildly against either Shell or ourselves.

We also made sure that we included a clause in the contract that, if for any reason, the ETS didn't go ahead or was radically different to the format we were expecting, then the two parties could agree to make the deal null and void.

The idea was not to make money. That was absolutely not what this trade was about. The price and the volume were effectively nominal. They were numbers picked out of thin air to get a deal signed.

Our motivation on the environmental products team was purely to get the ETS properly started and to send a message to other potential carbon traders that this was going to be a real market.

Positive reaction

As the first deal concluded under the upcoming ETS, the trade was publicized quite widely. A number of articles were written, and we were asked to speak about it at a lot of conferences.

Once the first trade had been concluded, it became clear that it would be crucial to develop a standardized contract and so there was a whole swathe of work undertaken around that (see Chapter 5).

Our next task was to get out and make contact with the big industrial companies who didn't have trade floors.

The industrials knew that their allocations were valuable, but they didn't have the facility or the knowledge to trade the EUAs that they were receiving. Bringing them to market ended up being quite a focus for us: we had to go out and do some education to drum up business.

Sometimes in those days we would see the price of EUAs surge, despite the fact there were a lot of certificates that were theoretically available. What was happening, though, was that the companies holding them weren't coming to market. They were either unaware of the price, taking a conservative approach and holding on to their assets or simply not set up to trade.

In the early days of the ETS, it sometimes felt the market would never be liquid. There seemed little incentive for the industrials to come to market when there were so many uncertainties. We were at the well-informed end of the spectrum but even we couldn't trade on the basis of non-existent details.

At the beginning of 2004, two of us moved from our now six-person environmental products desk across to Fortis, a Belgian bank. Banks were getting more interested in the environmental markets: they figured they had sophisticated trading floors and they understood risk, commodities and trading. They had all the infrastructure and great lawyers.

Bank customer teams were also starting to look at using environmental products as part of their financial product suites. There was just so much more range of opportunity in a bank in terms of offering services to clients.

Moving to a bank seemed like a natural progression, and Fortis were really quite bullish about entering new markets, as a lot of financial institutions were in the early 2000s. There's something quite romantic and exciting about a new market, and Fortis were really keen to get in there and get trading going.

Chilly reception

We had a lot of successes at the bank and did plenty of interesting business, including starting the groundbreaking European Carbon Fund in collaboration with Société Générale, but to be honest, my overriding memory of that trading floor was how extremely cold it was.

I was one of the very few women on the trading floor, and most of the other traders were older guys who had a little bit more padding than me and didn't mind that the air conditioning was on 24/7.

Meanwhile, I would be sitting at my desk wearing a woolly hat, a scarf and a coat. I used to go and visit the legal team in their offices, just to get some warmth.

I actually ended up with two weeks off work suffering with pneumonia. Who gets pneumonia in their office? Back then, people were a lot less aware than they are today, and there were few other women on the trading floor to also complain.

It might sound petty, but the temperature was one of the nails in the coffin for me leaving the trading floor.

Later on, I did a master's degree in sustainable agriculture and food security, and now I work outside a lot with forestry. I think it's taken me a long time to realize that I originally wanted to study geology because I enjoy being outside and walking around hills.

I should have figured out a lot earlier that I loved working with nature, then maybe I would have looked for a job outdoors earlier, rather than spending so many years sitting in a Shell office looking at seismic surveys of the North Sea, or sitting in my scarf and hat on a freezing Dutch trading floor.

Making a difference

When I look back at my career in trading, I was never particularly interested in commodity markets for their own sake. The interesting part for me was getting the market started, figuring it out and problem solving.

Outside of managing my own position, a price fluctuation of a few cents on any given day, couldn't have interested me less, and ultimately, that didn't make me a particularly enthusiastic trader. Ultimately, I'm interested in the environmental markets because they were set up to make a difference in terms of actually avoiding climate catastrophe.

It does make me smirk when I read articles that say trading environmental products today is like the Wild West. It's always been the Wild West! We've always faced problems, and we've always had to come up with solutions on the fly. Every time a new environmental product emerges, it will always present new problems that need solving.

When I started out, no one would have gone into environmental products without actually being interested in the environment itself. It would have taken someone with huge foresight to plan to go into trading because, despite the provisions set out for carbon credits in the Kyoto Protocol, there was nothing to trade at that time. Back then, no one saw the environment as a route to getting on the trading floor.

I really believed in the power of the market when we started, and I still believe that environmental markets can be a good way to harness capitalism for environmental needs.

But over the years I think I've become a bit more cynical. It's just so difficult to create a market that adequately accounts for its inevitable externalities, and there are so many companies that are trading away every day without their activity improving the environment.

Ultimately, I think a heavy tax on carbon would have been more effective, but that is so politically unpalatable that it's not even discussed. I'm still confident, though, that the ETS has done some good: it's clearly better than nothing and the logic behind it is very sound.

Nowadays, I'm interested in more holistic solutions. Carbon is really important, but it is only one aspect of restoring and improving our environment. Supporting biodiversity is arguably even more crucial.

A biodiversity market is emerging slowly, but there are significant hurdles to creating robust and credible rules, without also making the market rules extremely complicated and impractical.

Ultimately, with carbon trading and now with biodiversity, we're trying to fit nature into our capitalist systems, and, almost by definition, they don't fit together.

You can't properly value every single element of nature and then trade each aspect separately in different markets. Nature is much more valuable when the complexity and interdependencies of entire ecosystems are appreciated. With nature, the whole is always greater than the sum of its parts.

Chapter 5

Trading the first ISDA-backed EUA

Ingo Ramming began his professional career in 1996 as an interest rates structurer for German bank Dresdner Kleinwort, and after a brief period working at energy trader Enron, he returned to Dresdner in 2000 as head of interest rate and hybrid structuring. Ingo moved to London in 2005 and was tasked by Dresdner with the set up of Carbon Trade & Finance, a joint venture with Russia's Gazprombank to invest in projects in Russia and CIS, which he run between 2006 and 2013. With Commerzbank's takeover of Dresdner Bank, he was made co-head of commodity solutions, before being appointed head of corporate and investor solutions in 2017. He held this role until 2022 when he moved to Madrid, where he serves as head of carbon markets for Spanish bank BBVA. Ingo has also held a number of senior external positions, serving as co-chair of the EU ETS working group of the International Emissions Trading Association (IETA) between 2013 and 2019, as a member of the supervisory board of Deutsche Börse Commodities, as a member of the exchange council for the European Energy Exchange (EEX) and as a board member for carbon credit transaction network Carbonplace.

If you want to give your colleagues in risk and legal a really good laugh, then I recommend that you ask them if you can start trading a commodity that doesn't physically exist and where the rules for the underlying trading scheme haven't yet been confirmed.

That's what I did in 2004 with my colleagues at Dresdner Kleinwort when we requested approval to start trading carbon emissions even before the European Union Emissions Trading Scheme (ETS) had started.

As I'm sure you can imagine, I heard every possible variant of comment about 'hot air'. That was not really a surprise: Back then, ESG was not a topic, and the idea that carbon dioxide (CO2) emissions were a product that could be traded was a brand new concept.

DOI: 10.4324/9781003359739-7

There was a lot of bantering around, and a lot of jokes, but I also found that there was also a remarkable amount of openness within the bank to the idea.

I had re-joined Dresdner from Enron in 2000 with a mandate to run interest rate structuring, but also to broaden the business by looking at new markets.

Our first experiment was with weather derivatives because we were receiving quite a lot of requests for temperature and rain transactions, so we did a couple of weather deals in 2000 and 2001.

By the time I came along to suggest carbon trading, the bank was comfortable with weather derivatives, which definitely helped my case.

Although I guess the weather was a bit simpler to understand than carbon emissions. After all, everyone knows what rain or wind is, but carbon emissions are a much less tangible proposition.

Internal support

There were definitely some initial concerns about my plans, and to be fair my colleagues were right to be concerned.

Our track record and the support of my boss Thomas Röder and the bank's sustainability team, especially Armin Sandhövel, gave us a good level of credibility internally, especially with the risk board, but ultimately the job of the back office and of a risk manager is to ask the proper questions and to challenge the front office.

If my colleagues hadn't asked good questions, then possibly we would have made simple mistakes in certain aspects of how we set up our trading plans.

From a product trading perspective, sometimes you think, 'OK, let's just do it' so it's helpful when someone internally comes along and says 'OK, but explain exactly how and explain what will you do if certain things don't happen' and so on.

The fantastic thing is that no one ever wanted to block us from trading carbon emissions. There was no internal resistance; on the contrary, everyone was keen to figure out how we might make carbon trading function efficiently.

The questions we received were all great: what are the tax implications? how can we physically transfer carbon allowances? how does the bank open an account at a registry? what would we do if the ETS wasn't launched as expected?

The bank's willingness to consider something like this also may reflect a different era in the capital markets. All of this happened before the financial crisis, when there was perhaps more openness to trying new things and developing new side businesses.

Better Hesse

Ultimately, my role was to convince my colleagues that carbon emissions were a new asset class that would actually be tradeable, that it was real and that future growth could be expected.

I was building on work that my colleagues in the bank's sustainability team had already done to help set up the Hesse Tender in 2001. This was a pilot project in Germany where companies could submit their project ideas to reduce CO2 emissions and the required carbon price. It was like the Kyoto Protocol's Clean Development Mechanism or Joint Implementation.

The auction cleared in December 2002 at €6.58 per tonne, and it was the first time a carbon reduction credit was priced in Germany.

(The credits had the option to convert them into EU allowances, but were used after the issuance primarily for offsetting CO2 emissions and the first CO2-neutral claims.)

The Dresdner sustainability team had seen some of our press releases about our weather transactions and so they came over to the trading floor and said 'look, we have developed something, but how can we make it work better, and can you help us to make it tradeable?'

Of course, that sounded crazy and exciting. We had a lot of discussions and there was a lot of reading required on my side to get up to speed.

Finally, we as a trading desk acquired credits through the Hesse Tender, on the understanding that if the European ETS actually happened then we would be able to exchange them for European allowances.

That was a start, but then we had to think about how we could make this market scalable. We didn't want to just do a ceremonial trade and a press release; we wanted to do something that would actually help to develop the market and give it a chance to scale.

Master piece

What we quickly realized was that the market was missing a trading framework. In other markets, the International Swaps and Derivatives Association (ISDA) publishes a master agreement that everyone uses as a standard trading contract.

A master agreement means that counterparties don't need to negotiate every aspect of a deal, every time that they do a new trade. This makes trading much more efficient and therefore more scalable.

Obviously, at that time, ISDA didn't have anything in place for the carbon market.

I found a colleague in legal, and we decided to give it a go. We would try to create a document that the market could use to underpin carbon trading.

We managed to create something acceptable and in the process of developing the master agreement we also worked through a lot of the issues that our colleagues across the bank had raised in terms of liability, operations, delivery, tax treatment and so on.

Once we had the ISDA master agreement in place, we were comfortable to begin trading and we went ahead and agreed the first-ever ISDA-backed emissions trade.

Our counterparty was the Dutch bank Fortis, and the deal was brokered by Benedikt von Butler from Evolution Markets, one of the early stars of the environmental markets.

Remember that we did this trade in June 2004, before the European ETS had even started. The scheme was expected to launch in 2005, so we agreed a forward transaction with Fortis whereby we would deliver EU allowances in December 2005 at a fixed price.

Reaction times

There was a big reaction to the news of the trade. We even got coverage in the *Financial Times*, which showed us that there was a good level of interest in the carbon markets and that the ETS might get some decent traction.

But did we expect at that time that the ETS could become a market with a €750 billion turnover by 2022? Of course not!

What did give us confidence about the market's future was that carbon emissions were an issue that virtually all of the bank's corporate clients on the electricity and the industrial side would have to address. There was a real economic base underpinning the carbon market.

Our weather business back then was very much based on one core user base, which was power utilities hedging against colder-than-expected winters in Germany.

In contrast, although power utilities were of course by far the biggest carbon emitters, there was a much broader client base exposed to emissions. That suggested that carbon trading could develop into more than a niche sector product, which made it very interesting.

The focus on climate change and the sense of urgency was significantly less in 2004 than it is today. Now there are relatively few people that challenge the scientific consensus on climate change, but it was very different back then.

But even given the lower environmental focus of those days, it was clear that there was something real happening. This was clearly a sector that would matter, and therefore our view was that we should play a role in developing the market, and then if it took off, we should actively participate and try to gain a fair market share.

Standard bearer

After the success of our ISDA bilateral deal with Fortis, we went on to develop a master agreement for emissions as part of the Deutscher Rahmenvertrag, which is the German framework that underpins derivatives.

This led us to complete the first cash-settled European emissions trade in December 2004, which opened up the market to investors that were not directly covered by the ETS, and then in 2005 Dresdner issued the first retail instruments for German private investors that were linked to emissions rights.

Getting the appropriate trading documentation in place moved emissions away from a niche market where every deal required a long-form confirmation. Trading documentation creates scalability by reducing transaction times and administrative work.

And every time new documentation was published, or Dresdner announced a different type of first-ever trade, we were also sending a signal to the broader market. 'Look, we are in, and we want to broaden this market. This is important to us and to our clients'.

Channel crossing

It took a lot of hard work from a lot of people to get to the point where we could conclude our first carbon deal. Later on, of course, everyone internally was quite happy and carbon trading established itself as a pretty good business for the bank.

When we worked on our first carbon deal, we weren't looking to do a quick one-off trade and then run away. We wanted to develop something for the medium and long term that would provide the bank with a sustainable business.

The beauty of that time was that we were able to try things. Not everything worked out, but more than enough things did. We never reached critical mass with weather derivatives, for example, but carbon trading became a success.

At the end of the day, carbon trading just looked interesting to us. We had the curiosity to pursue it, and luckily in this case curiosity didn't kill the cat. Far from it!

Part II

Trading compliance carbon schemes

Compliance carbon markets, also known as mandatory carbon markets, are government-regulated trading systems designed to limit greenhouse gas emissions from designated sectors.

The most significant compliance markets are the European Union Emissions Trading System (EU ETS), which we encountered in the last section, China's national system, and the state-level programmes in North America.

The following chapters explore the evolution and practicalities of these compliance carbon markets, and reflect different trading approaches.

It is perhaps unsurprising that traders of compliance schemes need to pay a great deal of attention to any potential changes in public policy and to prevailing political sentiment.

In China, state-owned firms need to trade profitably without losing sight of their broader social responsibilities, while we see examples in both Europe and North America of the opportunities and the threats that emerge from changes in governmental approaches.

The development of compliance carbon schemes created a new commodity asset class that has attracted a range of different trading participants, some of whom are attracted by the lack of physical storage costs attached to holding carbon allowances.

DOI: 10.4324/9781003359739-8

Chapter 6

Balancing trading profits with social impact

Liu Yu graduated from Tsinghua University with a doctorate in engineering. He has worked in enterprises affiliated to China Huaneng Group Co. Ltd, one of China's largest public utility groups. In 2019, he joined Huaneng Carbon Asset Management Co. Ltd, where he currently serves as chief executive. The firm holds a leading position in the carbon trading industry and was the first company in China registered using the term 'carbon assets'. Liu Yu's team provides professional support related to all aspects of carbon for China Huaneng Group. He also led the first trading team among China's power utilities to undertake proprietary carbon trading and financial operations, creating multiple first-of-their-kind carbon financial businesses in the Chinese market and becoming a major figure within the industry. Based on the Chinese government's 'carbon peak and carbon neutrality' goals, Liu Yu has organized research and development into an integrated energy service business model for power generators. Utilizing a digital smart energy management platform, he has explored the incremental market in energy services for power utilities, providing strong support for China Huaneng Group's push into its next phase of growth beyond its already successful core business.

When you work at an important state-owned enterprise, the ideal trade is one that achieves both good economic benefits and good social benefits, fulfilling the social responsibility of a public company in China.

One notable example took place in late 2021, when China's national carbon market launched its first compliance cycle. It was both the first year of the whole national carbon market, and also the first year that power plants had to fulfil their carbon emission obligation.

Over 2,200 power plants participated, the majority of them for the first time, meaning that most were inexperienced in trading.

Huaneng Group is one of China's five largest state-owned power generation groups, and we were in the fortunate position of having some surplus carbon quotas that we decided to sell during that period.

DOI: 10.4324/9781003359739-9

The market proved hard to analyse due to the abundance of regulations and a constant stream of news. It felt like every day there was different information coming into our trading desk, although some of the initial market discussions were a mixture of misunderstandings and rumours.

The lack of precedents created a challenge for me and my team: we needed to analyse the market situation properly if we were going to arrive at the correct trading strategy.

Setting the strategy

Trading in this new market required an innovative approach, particularly as we were trying to achieve two aims simultaneously.

Of course, we wanted to sell at optimal prices that could help us achieve high returns and boost the overall group's profit and loss account. But, at the same time, we were also conscious of our responsibility as a significant state-owned enterprise.

For example, we needed to execute our trading strategy in a way that did not make the carbon market fluctuate too much or become too volatile. The Chinese government was obviously keen to see this new market develop in a stable and sustainable way.

This emphasis on market stability can make the market appear less dynamic, but it also reduces the risk of sudden shocks that could undermine confidence or disrupt compliance.

Beyond that, we also needed to make sure that we provided sufficient liquidity to the new market to ensure that the power plants could find a seller when they wanted to buy. At first, many of the other utilities were worried whether they would be able to buy enough quotas.

There was what you might call a 'social liability' that required the larger state-owned enterprises like ourselves to make sure that there were enough allowances available in the market. After all, no one wanted to see firms default on their obligations.

At Huaneng Carbon Asset Management, we used our trading skills to support orderly market development and we prioritized strategic sales to make sure that buyers could find the allowances that they needed.

But at the same time, we also managed to time our trades so well that we achieved the highest market prices in the country for that year in several of our transactions. Our trading activities generated significant extra revenue for the broader firm.

Even though the absolute volumes may not have been very large, the fact that we were able to sell at the best prices at that time, in my view, reflects our trading team's strong analysis of market conditions and our skilful execution of specific trades.

This was a double win: we achieved both strong economic benefits and positive social outcomes at the same time, fulfilling the social responsibility of this important state-owned enterprise.

It was really classic trading, and I'm happy to say that the trading team's success during that important first year of the scheme was recognized internally, drawing praise from group headquarters.

Dealing with neijuan

Although our trading went very well overall, there were obviously many ups and downs during that period. In times like those, a trader's emotions tend to move in tandem with the fluctuations of the market.

It is normal as a trader to feel very nervous at some times, or very happy. You have to learn to absorb these different feelings because trading can be very stressful and tense. This market can stop many people from sleeping properly.

Everyone needs to develop their own ways to deal with stress. In China, we talk a lot about the concept of 'neijuan', which English translates as the anthropological term 'involution'.

Neijuan is when relentless competition and pressure lead to exhaustion and stagnation rather than progress and improvement. It literally means 'curling or rolling inwards', suggesting that extra effort and competition may not yield increased rewards.

In China, in many industries, the work pace is quite intense. Living in China, especially given the national context and its special stage of development, means that from the old to the young, everyone is quite used to high pressure.

So, the first point is that everyone here has more or less become used to, or has adapted to, this overall atmosphere of 'involution'.

Second, I do experiment with different ways to relieve stress. Some friends have suggested I try yoga or meditation, but I haven't actually started yet.

Instead, I try to find time for exercise, like playing ball games, running or cycling, to relieve stress and also make the body more resilient to this 'involution'.

Social experiences are also important. For example, taking the team to a bar or to a restaurant together, whether after a business trip or working overtime, works well. Spending time together outside the office is a good way to relax, to unwind and to build team cohesion.

The next generation

My current role means that, as well as navigating the technical and financial complexities of emissions trading, I am also responsible for helping to shape the culture and capabilities of a new generation of carbon market professionals.

Many young people in China are optimistic about the carbon market, especially given China's dual carbon targets for 2030 and 2060.

Some think carbon trading is a 'cool' area to work in. They may not say those exact words when I am interviewing them for roles, but it is clear that young people today look for jobs in a different way than we did: they want to find something interesting or cool, not just something stable.

A passion for the environmental markets is a great start, but when I am looking for new talent, there are a few criteria that I apply.

First, young people entering this field must have an innovative mindset and an exploratory spirit, because there aren't many mature systems or much experience to draw on.

Second, they need to understand the essence of carbon trading. Carbon is obviously different from traditional markets like oil, largely because it is more policy-driven, but at its core it is still a financial market. That means that I am looking for strong market analysis and judgement skills.

Third, trading requires a genuine interest in financial markets. The carbon market is new, and its future development will require the introduction of some new financial tools, perhaps including derivatives. From the perspective of a power generation enterprise, this development would give us more confidence to participate and create greater value.

If a candidate has all of the skills that I have described, then we can guide them and teach them some techniques for analysing the market and policy that will hopefully make them into good traders.

Future market growth

When I look back on my own career, which began in 2007, I am struck by how profoundly the Chinese energy sector has transformed in less than two decades. There is no doubt in my mind that the next two decades will be equally transformative.

In my view, there is only one direction of travel for the Chinese carbon market and that is a robust growth trajectory. Arguably, the Chinese carbon market is already one of the largest environmental markets in the world because it covers over 40% of China's total emissions.

China's power generation sector alone emits over 5 billion tonnes of carbon annually, so according to the ministry of ecology and environment, we are already the world's largest scheme in terms of carbon emissions covered.

But our market is still at a relatively early stage and there are many specific policy issues, which are still being piloted, that need to be resolved.

The logic of carbon asset management here is distinct: while the European Union Emissions Trading System (EU ETS) operates as a cap-and-trade market with a strong financial component, China's ETS is a rate-based, multi-sector tradable performance standard.

This means that instead of absolute caps, the system sets carbon intensity benchmarks for each sector. For example, a coal-fired power plant is allocated allowances based on its emissions per megawatt-hour, not on its total emissions.

This approach reflects China's unique industrial structure and the government's desire to balance emissions reduction with economic growth.

One of the open policy issues is the speed at which new industries will be included in the ETS. So far, it includes only the power sector, but the scheme will expand to include cement, steel, and aluminium. The addition of those sectors will mean the scheme covers nearly two-thirds of the country's greenhouse gas output.

We are also discussing the best way to allocate quotas. The current system provides free allocation based on historical emissions and output, but there is growing pressure to introduce more auction-based mechanisms to improve price discovery and market efficiency.

Allowing financial institutions or investment firms, rather than just compliance entities, to participate as buyers and sellers is also something that many in the industry, including potential participants from abroad, are waiting for.

These are the key issues that need to be addressed for the next stage of China's carbon market development. Once we answer these kinds of questions, the Chinese market will absolutely enter a new stage of development.

I can only speak for myself not the whole industry, but I am optimistic about the future of our carbon market. If the issues that I mentioned can be resolved, then the future can be realized. But whether it will take three, five or eight years, that is hard to judge right now.

The government's approach is pragmatic: start with a simple, stable system, then gradually introduce complexity as participants gain experience and the market infrastructure matures.

My journey through China's carbon market has been both demanding and rewarding. I have witnessed the market's birth, participated in its early development, and contributed to its ongoing evolution.

The challenges are real, but so are the opportunities.

As China continues to refine its carbon market and deepen its commitment to climate action, I am proud to be part of this historic transformation and I am optimistic about what the future holds for both my company and the market as a whole.

Chapter 7

Carbon cash and carry

David Besançon studied sciences at France's École Polytechnique before taking a master's degree in engineering at the École Nationale des Ponts et Chaussées. In 1994, David joined JP Morgan's equity derivatives trading team in London, before moving to a similar role at Dresdner Kleinwort in 1999. He worked in Citibank's Global Hybrids Structuring Group in 2003–4, after which he moved to investment bank Natixis, where he rose to become global head of commodities trading, a role he held until 2018. Since his retirement from Natixis, David has worked as an industry consultant, focussing on commodities optimization and trading, originally with Vesontio Solutions and then since 2020 with Boston Consulting Group.

The lifeblood of banking is capital. Any trade that raises capital, or at least is capital-neutral, and makes money at the same time is the best possible scenario for a bank trader.

Structured products are designed to do just that. They are very commonly used in finance because they are a way of raising capital for the bank, while offering market exposure to the bank's customer base.

The simplest form of structured products is when a bank offers its customers an investment that is based on the future performance of an asset or an index, with a capital guarantee.

Banks like to offer capital guaranteed structured products because customers buy the investment by paying upfront, which usually gives the bank access to fresh capital.

Imagine that a customer wants to buy a capital guaranteed structured product linked to the one-year performance of a particular stock index. He or she invests $100 with the bank, and if the index goes up by 10%, then in a year the bank will pay the customer $110. If the index goes down, the investor receives back the initial investment, $100.

The customer is happy because they can access potential growth through the structured product, while knowing their investment is protected by a highly rated institution. Meanwhile, the bank charges some fees for arranging

DOI: 10.4324/9781003359739-10

the investment, and, importantly, during that year, can use part of the original $100 as capital.

When I was at the investment bank Natixis, we offered trading and hedging services to our large corporate customers, which meant we touched most of the commodities – energy, metals and agricultural.

When the European Union Emissions Trading Scheme (EU ETS) was launched, we obviously started to get involved in that as well, particularly as we had a lot of airline customers, who were very obligated to redeem EU Allowances (EUAs) to comply with carbon emissions regulations.

Market structure

The emissions market was relatively easy to enter for banks because it was a commodity market that wasn't physical in nature.

The new rules that were introduced after the financial crisis of 2008 have made it very difficult for banks to trade physical commodities. The regulatory capital requirements to trade most physical commodities are punitive (except for some metals) so most banks had exited this type of activities.

Emissions represented an exciting new opportunity because the allowances are not physical so banks can hold them, without needing to allocate huge amounts of capital or to pay physical storage fees.

There was also much less potential for fraud in official carbon emissions schemes than you typically get in the physical commodity markets at that time, which always make banks super nervous, because the allowances were all linked to official government registries.

We first handled some simple emissions hedging flows, but very quickly opportunities emerged as a massive contango developed for allowances. Contango is a market structure where prices are much cheaper today than they are expected to be in the future, as indicated by the forward or future prices.

The key to a successful 'contango trade' is being able to take the material at today's (cheaper) price, store it, and then deliver it back later at a future price, fixed today, that is higher than the original price plus the storage costs and the cost of capital. The difference is your margin. This type of trade is also called 'cash and carry' for this very reason. These trades also present limited market risk since the economics are locked in at inception.

For this reason, commodity traders are always watching out for those times when a contango develops. In the oil markets, for example, traders quickly look to find tanks or idle vessels to start storing oil or refined products when markets move in contango.

Traders watch for the shape of forward prices, assess the viability of the investment and as soon as it is viable they acquire the commodity and the storage capacity, while securing the financing.

When we saw a steep contango emerge in the emissions market, we realized this could be a good opportunity for some of our customers since we could offer a capital-guaranteed high-yield investment product based on emissions allowances 'cash and carry' trade: the client would bring the capital, the bank would structure, execute and carry the trade. The profits, net of the bank fees, were given back to the client.

We immediately offered the contango structure trade out to various clients. We saw strong interest first from the private banks. They were very keen because interest rates were so low at that point, below 1% in Euro and U.S. Dollar, whereas we could offer them a capital-guaranteed structured product based on the contango in the emissions market that would pay around 2–3% p.a. interest with their original investment guaranteed, which was a much better investment proposition than any regular term deposit.

Structural integrity

Once we received an initial investment, we would immediately lock in the market structure by buying the prompt EUAs and selling EUA futures. There was almost no risk involved because it was a simple 'cash and carry' structure done on exchange, which removes credit and fraud risks.

An emissions market in contango is about as good a scenario as you can get as a bank commodity trader: trading is risk-free if the hedging is done right, there's no risk of fraud and there's no physical commodity exposure.

Everybody is happy, which is not something you can say too often in trading.

The broader market is happy because you are bringing in more liquidity by offering exposure to emissions to customers like private banks that wouldn't otherwise be active in that market.

The clients (investors) are happy because in a super low interest environment, they are making more money than on other investment alternatives with similar risk since they have a capital guarantee from an AA-rated bank.

The bank is happy because we are helping clients, without needing to use capital since it is brought by the investors and charging some fees from the transactions.

What's not to like?

Portfolio optimization

The simple emissions 'cash and carry' was a very successful trade, but as a trader you should be always looking to optimize your global portfolio and to create additional opportunities.

We obviously priced every deal individually, but we were also aware of our overall portfolio, which we were trying to manage on a global basis rather than piecemeal.

For example, we were typically short to the airlines because we were supplying them with certificates that we were looking to buy back more cheaply in the market by either carrying some of the risk or building an offsetting position from our other corporate customers, possibly with the flow from the structured products side.

We would always look at our position on a consolidated basis. That wasn't the main driver for doing individual deals, but the portfolio effect could often be very helpful. If you build up a portfolio with shorts and longs everywhere, then that sometimes opens some interesting optionality.

Our value-at-risk (VAR) was never huge because we were trading spreads positions (time-spreads or basis risk from proxies) or else trading back-to-back with customer flows or hedging in the market. The principle was to always stay within your risk mandate and limits while positioning according to our vision of how the markets will play out and playing with the curve or exploiting some optionality.

Re-structuring

Markets obviously don't stay in contango forever, and once the difference between current and future prices is less extreme, then the contango trade doesn't work anymore and you can see a lot of quick restructuring.

Investors in our structured products either let them expire and simply didn't renew their investments or cashed them in at higher market prices.

As trader, though, we weren't losing money on previous trades, even when the contango came to an end, because we had locked in all the economics. We had received the cash, and the hedges were all in place.

If any client wanted to unwind and get their money back early, then we were always able to quote a bid and an offer for the current market level.

An emissions contango 'cash and carry' product is relatively easy to manage. You might even consider it basic for a bank that is used to creating and trading structured products.

That structure is always sat there on the shelf waiting for the right market conditions to emerge.

It's so easy to operate that once a few banks started to offer it, everyone else – including hedge funds doing it for their own account using leverage – jumped in. The margins went down slightly due to the increased competition, but then again, the cost of execution and capital requirement was minimal for the banks, so these types of trades continued to be done until the contango disappeared.

Obviously, trading emissions was positive for any bank's image, but the important thing was trading on behalf of the clients with limited risk, while making some money for providing the service.

Building bridges

I had trained as an engineer, and I had a passion for building things and solving problems – I still have that passion – so I went into civil engineering. I thought I would build bridges and roads, help mankind and leave something permanently useful behind.

But I then did a couple of internships in the construction sector and saw people cutting corners in many areas at that time, which didn't suit my idealistic student vision at all. I needed to find something else, so I switched to industrial engineering.

I liked that branch better – it was a lot about physics of material and fluid mechanics – but I also would have needed to do a long internship in an industrial plant in the middle of nowhere in France when I had a girlfriend in Paris...

So, when JPMorgan, who were actively recruiting engineer profiles since they could count and understood the maths of fluid mechanics and diffusion statistics on which modern quantitative finance was based, offered me an internship in the very centre of Paris, I jumped on it. The bank gave me a part-time role on a trading desk, and that was it: I was forever lost to engineering and dived headlong into finance, then derivatives trading.

I worked in Paris, London and New York for JPMorgan, Dresdner Bank, Citibank and then Natixis, specializing in equity and hybrid derivatives. I moved into commodities in 2009 after the global financial crisis, initially heading structured trading for commodities, later becoming head of trading for that group.

Commodities were complicated, but also super interesting compared with trading financial products like equities and bonds since it is not one but many markets that you must understand, as well as the physical and geopolitical aspects.

Trading commodities can be a real challenge: there are lots of data points, the structure of the forward curve is completely different because it represents perceived supply versus demand in the future, while in equities or rates it results from a pure arbitrage quantification that is relatively easy to compute.

Crossing bridges

Natixis had deep strength in developing structured products for equities and interest rates that we brought across to the commodity business.

There used to be a lot more innovation in the equity and bond markets, typically because they are dematerialized by nature and more straightforward to transact than commodities, where the data can be messy or sparse while the markets can also be heavily interconnected.

A lot of the technology and know-how in structured products was created in the equity space so expanding that into commodities unlocked a lot of opportunities. Mixing the two was innovative at the time, of course; nowadays that's mainstream.

Not that it was an easy transition: modelling is completely different for commodities where there are correlations everywhere and there is more impact from geopolitics.

The data for commodities doesn't fit easily to financial models. Traders like some degree of certainty, even if there is always stochasticity in options pricing. But the data for commodities is sometimes so challenging (for example, correlations can flip so easily) that it can be difficult to put a firm price on some transactions. That means there's more risk, coming from many sources.

In emissions, for example, analysing the supply-demand balance was always a big problem because sometimes the European Union would release more allowances, i.e. unexpectedly releasing additional supply, and the market would completely collapse.

You rarely see the same impact of a single decision maker in other commodities today. Admittedly, OPEC decision could really move the oil market when its member controlled most of the world supply but has much less influence nowadays. In a market like copper, the supply is diversified across different countries so that if one country changes the tax rules or closes a few mines, the impact is less because supply is a bit more spread out.

In European emissions, on the other hand, there is just one single source of supply, which would decide sometimes to increase or reduce quotas to adjust convergence with policies objectives.

That exposure was not always comfortable at first. It took some time to understand the market dynamics better and to manage the risks better, but essentially you can't model political decisions, which should be classed more as random events and are best apprehended through risk scenarios.

Increasing sophistication

My trading philosophy was around bringing what I'd learned as an engineer and a quantitative structurer in the financial markets across into the relatively less sophisticated commodity markets.

A lot of my commodity trading colleagues came from the physical markets, but when derivatives grew in importance in the 1990s and 2000s, it created a whole new way of looking at the market.

You can still make a lot of money in the physical markets, especially if you have access to logistics and actual supply information, but in my opinion one key to success is to combine physical knowhow with sophisticated paper trading, backed by powerful analytics.

The junction of those two approaches is where the magic happens: after all, derivatives unlock leverage, forward trading and a lot of other benefits.

That's exactly what we experienced in the emissions contango trade, which is a relatively simple structure that generated significant benefits for everyone involved and which can be used whenever the market conditions are appropriate.

Chapter 8

Arbitraging compliance auctions

A native of Québec City, Francis Lessard graduated from Canada's Université Laval with a bachelor's degree in mathematics and economics, and a master's degree in economics. He first joined Canadian power utility TransAlta in 2016 as an environmental trading analyst before becoming an environmental products trader in 2019. Then, in 2021, Francis joined European utility Uniper in Calgary as a senior specialist in environmental products. Uniper subsequently appointed him manager of North American environmental products. In 2024, Francis moved to energy trader Dynasty Power as managing director of environmental products.

Sometimes I ask myself if I am trading in the wrong markets.

After all, I studied mathematics and I would consider myself an analytical, number-minded person, but there's not always that much information to analyse in the environmental markets.

It's not like the power markets where there is so much data to work with: real-time, daily curves, forward curves, supply and demand forecasts.

In my experience, at least 75% of power traders and analysts will have math, finance or quant experience. But it's different in the environmental markets, where the traders will often come from a legal or regulatory background.

Let's be honest, that's because it's not absolutely necessary to have a numerical background to succeed as a trader in my markets, although strength in analytics does give you another tool in your toolbox, and I would say my analytical style has helped me out a lot.

But a lot of quants just focus on the numbers, and if you rely purely on data and analysis to trade the environmental markets, then you will mess up many times.

In these markets, you can't ignore policy and you can't ignore gut feelings. Sometimes there's no real reason why the market is going up or down; maybe there hasn't been any news for a few days or maybe there's no real reason for someone to hold onto a position.

DOI: 10.4324/9781003359739-11

In times like that, it's really difficult to use data or technical analysis to make money as a screen trader. You need instead to listen to your gut feeling, which is something that comes with experience.

Capital inefficiency

The regional governments behind the key north American compliance carbon markets – California, Québec and Washington – typically sell their carbon allowances through an auction mechanism, with the auctions taking place four times per year.

Those auctions are what we call the primary market. There is also a secondary market that operates all year round, where firms that don't necessarily participate in the government auctions can trade allowances that have been delivered or will be delivered through the primary auctions.

A lot of firms prefer to trade in the secondary market rather than participate in the auctions because it's so costly to participate in the auctions.

Participating firms need to post collateral equivalent to the entire volume of allowances for which they are bidding. That means that if a company wants to bid for 1 million allowances at around $40 per allowance, they would have to post the full $40 million upfront.

Of course, there's no guarantee you will win the entire 1 million allowances, you might just win half that volume. That means you might have posted $40 million to buy just $20 million of allowances, and that money is trapped for the best part of two months.

Financial traders, for example, guys at hedge funds, can't typically allocate that much capital to a single auction. Unless you have a very low cost of capital, participating directly in the auctions is prohibitive.

At the same time, though, the auctions are the fundamental price discovery mechanism for the north American carbon markets so, as a trader, I absolutely want to express a view on how they are going to settle.

Auction winner

The most efficient way to trade around the auctions is by using a mechanism developed by the ICE exchange, which is called the current 'auction clearing price' (ACP).

The ACP allows you to buy or sell a carbon allowance future at exactly the settlement price of the quarterly auction.

Depending on levels in the market and when you're buying or selling the ACP, you usually have to pay between 50 cents below or 50 cents above the auction settlement price, although the most common market is from 10 cents below up to 30 cents above. That's the additional cost that a trader pays in order to be guaranteed that they will receive a futures product at exactly the auction price.

Trading the ACP has been working quite well for me over the last four or five years.

I will typically have a view on where the auctions are likely to clear, but at the same time I won't want to tie up $10, $20 or $40 million in capital.

My strategy is to buy the ACP and simultaneously trade the outright futures product for the same month. If the next auction is in May and I am bearish about the results of that auction, I would sell the May future and buy the May ACP.

Similarly, if I think the auction is going to clear really high, I sell the ACP and simultaneously buy the equivalent month's future.

I'm essentially participating in the auction virtually, using derivatives that are much cheaper to trade than locking up capital in the auction process.

During the first quarter of 2024, Washington held its usual auction, but the auction took place amid a lot of regulatory uncertainty. There was even a ballot initiative under discussion that might repeal the entire compliance carbon market and send prices to zero.

Given that context, I thought there was a strong possibility that the Washington auction would settle low, so I put on a bearish trade by selling the future and buying the ACP. The auction ended up clearing $8–9 below the market price at the time so that worked out very well indeed, especially as we usually trade between 50,000 and 500,000 certificates.

This strategy has been pretty successful for me. It's a relatively easy way to gain auction exposure without tying up capital. It makes such sense to me that I'm surprised it hasn't caught on more. But for some reason it hasn't, and the ACP contract isn't used that much.

Perhaps the reason for that is that some traders can't live with the temporary fluctuations in their profit and loss accounts.

The time difference between the actual auction and the auction result is seven days. That means that even though you have a matched position – you have sold one instrument and bought the equivalent instrument – there are seven days where you will experience a lot of volatility because your future position will still move up or down, while your ACP position is fixed.

If the market moves up or down by $1, in theory your position is offset, but for seven days your risk team is going to see mark-to-market exposure. Let's suppose you have taken on $1 million in exposure, and the market moves down by 50 cents during that week, you would look like you have lost $500,000.

That perceived volatility might put some people off from trading the strategy. But in reality, even if the auction results are not yet published, the auction price has already been set and the positions match off so any moves during those seven days are really just temporary noise.

Speculation and accumulation

This trading strategy is not a long-term fundamental view; it's more of a view on short-term cash flows and on market patterns.

I am also acutely aware that the auctions cut through any speculative froth in the market. It's obviously easier for speculators to move the market when it's typically trading 3–4 million allowances per day, rather than when there's an auction of 55 million allowances on a single day.

The north American carbon markets are not particularly liquid, and they are relatively small, so news items can move the market up or down by 50 cents quite easily. In early 2024, we have even seen daily moves of the order of $2.

The natural buyers of allowances are not really part of that volatility; they tend to buy their allowances through the quarterly auctions, which put a soft floor on the market price.

As a trader, you need to differentiate between what the speculators are doing day to day, and where the natural buyers will come in. Where the auction will settle is not always in line with the current price in the secondary market.

My strategy aims to profit from any incongruity between where the secondary market is trading and where the auction ultimately settles.

Auctions can sell 55 million allowances in a single day, so at a rough price of $40 per allowance, it would require a large capital injection to drastically move the auction settle. The speculators in our small market certainly don't have the firepower to drive the auction far away from the level set by the natural buyers.

There are clearly long-term policy fundamentals that establish the general direction of the markets over the long run, but in the short run prices are often driven by capital flows. There are a lot of speculators with no fundamental view at all. They simply trade technical signals, or on their gut instincts, and many are able to do decently well out of it.

Speculators try to translate small news items into price movements, but sometimes the moves are overdone.

Every financial trader is trying to find some small clue that gives us a reason to buy or sell. Sometimes, if we are all heading in the same direction, we create a much bigger price move than is justified.

But the auctions always bring the market back in line. Even if the secondary market trades up to $50 tomorrow, if the following day an auction clears at $42, then the secondary market will rapidly come back to $42. The auction establishes where the natural price should be.

Liquidity challenges

The North American compliance markets are liquid by environmental standards but when the market crashes there is often no way to sell and when the market moves up there is no way to buy.

As a trader, it's obviously critical to have a correct view of where prices are going, but even then it can be really hard to execute a strategy, particularly if you want to take larger positions.

Some people are happy trading to make $500,000 per year but if you want to make $10–20 million a year, then for sure you need to develop larger positions and to do that you really have to go against the trend of the market.

Let's say you have a bearish view of prices. You might need to wait until the market is moving up or a lot of people are buying at the same time because otherwise it will be hard to sell significant quantities.

There are small periods of liquidity and large periods of illiquidity on either the downside or the upside. You have to pick your times very carefully if you want to take larger positions.

For example, I thought that the market would go down the other day, but I wasn't able to sell in any size until it had already gone down by 35 cents.

There were three bids for 1,000 allowances showing on the screen when I first looked. I really wanted to sell around 50,000 allowances, but I couldn't find a bid of that size anywhere. The moment that someone else sold those 3,000 allowances the market dropped 35 cents straight away.

That meant I effectively missed out on the value of those 35 cents because I couldn't sell enough at the right time, even though I was confident in my call.

On the opposite side though if my goal had been to buy, it would have been easy. The market was so lopsided that I could have bought 500,000 allowances at a time when I could not find a way to sell 50,000.

As a trader in the environmental markets, you typically have to be correct twice to make money: you have to get the price direction right but also understand what is happening in terms of liquidity.

The environmental markets are not like the established commodity markets where you can get in and out of large positions all day long.

You really need to pick your moment to enter and exit trades. If you've been trading these markets for a long time, you start to learn which periods in the year have more natural buyers and more activity.

Only way is up

Liquidity is slowly improving, and in general I think the North American compliance carbon markets are poised to grow. At the same time, some of the renewable certificate markets may shrink as prices fall in line with the increasingly lower costs of developing renewable energy.

When I first started trading these markets, some solar renewable certificates were trading above $300, whereas now there are solar programmes coming in lower than $50.

Meanwhile, in the compliance markets, we are going to see a growing tension over the next few years because, by design, the supply of certificates is scheduled to be reduced every single year.

That means that there will be fewer allowances issued, just when we are also seeing more and more institutional players and money managers looking to jump into these markets.

These new players will drive up liquidity, but they will also drive up volatility. That is the kind of scenario that provides a lot of trading opportunities. I suspect that some traders will make a lot of money in these markets in the next few years.

Personally, I've already had a good ride. I don't come from a wealthy background, I come from a regular blue-collar family where I'm the first person to go to university.

I never really planned out my career too far ahead, but I like what I am doing, I enjoy these markets and I am happy with where I am. This is a good place to be because I am sure that the next few years will be a fun time to be a trader in these markets.

Chapter 9

Trading the human factor

Francisco Grajales Cravioto first studied industrial engineering at the Universidad Iberoamericana in Puebla City, Mexico, before completing a master's degree in environmental engineering at the KTH Royal Institute of Technology in Stockholm, Sweden. Francisco joined Finnish utility Fortum as a climate change and emissions trading analyst in 2000, before moving to Washington, D.C. to work at the World Bank between 2004 and 2006 as a junior professional associate. In 2006, he was appointed assistant fund manager for the Econergy International Corporation, and in 2008, he moved to Germany as the senior environmental commodities originator for Swedish utility Vattenfall, evolving into a trader position.

I take a holistic approach to carbon trading.

By that, I mean I am not married to a specific strategy. My view depends on how the market is behaving and how I think it will respond to policy changes or prices.

There is nothing wrong of course with taking a different approach: I have seen plenty of traders that are solely fundamental traders or are purely technical traders.

Some traders have been using technical strategies successfully in other commodities, and then they apply the same strategies when they end up in carbon. Some of them do very well but some of them struggle.

It's the same with fundamental traders: the carbon markets sometimes follow fundamentals, but sometimes they move on technical factors. Then sometimes they don't follow anything at all: there are price moves on the back of rumours about policy and public perception, which I would call moves on market sentiment.

People often play down the human side of the carbon markets, which I think is a mistake.

Politicians and public perception have a huge influence on the market because they can create changes in policies or in market rules.

It's clearly very important as a trader to watch out for any structural modifications, and the likely timing of any changes. Some of those modifications

DOI: 10.4324/9781003359739-12

won't necessarily reflect fundamentals, but will be driven more by public opinion.

Technical knock out

Everyone's trading style is derived from their professional background. I feel fortunate that I came to trading from the technical side, but I was also exposed to fundamentals and to the political side.

I finished my university degree in Mexico in 2000 and I wanted to study for a master's in environmental engineering. In that era, there weren't that many courses covering the environment so I looked around to see which universities offered environmental engineering.

I ended up doing my master's degree in Sweden because Sweden was one of the most advanced countries in terms of environmental law and policies.

During my studies, I fell in love with environmental economics and markets and the question of how to put a price on externalities. After graduating, I became an emissions trading analyst for the Finnish utility Fortum, which was about to be covered by the European Emissions Trading Scheme (ETS).

I really enjoyed the sector but it was too early in a way; there weren't many jobs in emissions and I didn't see a clear path for myself, even though I was already captivated by the topic.

I saw a great opportunity to work at the World Bank and, even though I was not trading, that was when I learnt all about the contracting and negotiations around emission reduction projects, which were at that point in time destined for the Clean Development Market (CDM).

I had two great years at the World Bank and then I got hired by an investment fund that was involved in renewable energy projects. I was involved in over-the-counter trading, drafting contracts, buying CDM certificates.

These were very helpful experiences because, if you are serious about these markets, you really need to understand the legal side and you need to know the regulations.

Then I started working in origination for Vattenfall, after which I moved onto the trading floor. In 2010, after Vattenfall acquired the Dutch utility Nuon, we integrated the two teams, which bolstered our emissions trading experience.

From then on, we actively traded CERs and EU allowances (EUAs), and fortunately I just grew alongside the company, and now I am the lead trader of EUAs.

My background enabled me to learn the whole value chain of carbon: from the projects, legal requirements and origination that create the supply, all the way to the final consumption of credits or allowances, which in my case is by a power utility.

Working across the whole life cycle of carbon has given me a very good view of the market.

Human resources

Perhaps because I have worked in so many parts of the carbon cycle, I am always highly aware of the human element, particularly when it comes to taking a view on the longer term prospects for the market.

When the EU ETS reforms were approved in 2021 and the politicians signed off on a more ambitious 2030 target to reduce emissions, sentiment changed overnight. The market had been very down for many years because of oversupply, but with the new reforms it felt like everybody wanted to jump in.

The conventional wisdom was that Europe had finally committed to a strict market regime, which would be undersupplied in the future, meaning that prices could go as high as €200 per tonne.

Everybody jumped on the bandwagon, and it lasted for maybe a year and a half. We went from €20 to €100. But the one thing they all forgot was that at the end of the day, high carbon prices will impact consumption by pushing up prices, which ultimately are paid by the end consumer.

That is not only true of EUAs but of any environmental commodities. Everybody says they want to save the planet; but there is a certain unwillingness to pay. At some point, the consumer will say, 'sorry, at present I care more about my situation now'.

Just as prices were rising, we suddenly had the Russian invasion of Ukraine, which sent energy prices soaring. There started to be rumours about a potential European political response. But most people didn't believe it because the same politicians had just approved the ambitious reforms in 2021.

My view was that politicians can ultimately change whatever they want. Whatever the law says, it can always be amended if people start protesting or going out onto the streets.

We started hearing rumours that the authorities might do something to reduce the price of carbon, which was heading to €100.

I felt the market was not sustainable from a social/political point of view, although technically and fundamentally it could have been. Of course, technically you can say 'yes, it looks bullish long term and we're going to €150 if you run the Fibonacci extensions'.

My view was that everything looked very bullish and fine on paper, but the reality was that the Commission was already looking at ways to control the carbon price.

Short rations

I was definitely in the minority. I heard the argument a lot that the Commission wouldn't change the rules just a year after agreeing the 2030 target.

My answer was always, 'I don't care. Something has to happen'.

I started going short and short and short.

I expressed my bearish view in different ways: I primarily took out several put-spread option positions. I would buy the €70 put and sell the €50 put. That made the trade cheaper and gave it a good payout ratio.

With that structure, you make money all the way from €70 to €50. Your profits are capped below €50 so you don't make any more money at that point, but you can make a really good payout profile with that kind of structure.

I traded several structures: €70–€60, €70–€50, and so on. I generally focussed on the December 2023 contract – the current year's December contract – rather than on the spot.

Normally, in EUAs the liquidity is very thin after two years forward and even one year ahead is not great, so the best liquidity is in the current year's December contract.

I placed my trades through two or three brokers and I put the positions on over several weeks. Whenever the market went against me, I would maybe add a little bit more size to my position because the options I liked, which were way out of the money, would become cheaper when the market moved higher.

With an options structure like that, you can hold a position for a really long time, knowing that your loss is capped. You can have a drawdown but you aren't going to experience real pain.

That's good because if you are holding the position over the long term, you need to absorb a lot of fluctuations that can go against you.

Another good thing about the options is that they only create a big exposure once you get close to expiry. When the expiry is still a long way off, they don't consume much risk capital.

I never touched my options position; I just waited for it to move to expiry.

But I was also optimizing with futures and doing some short-term trading. Some weeks I might take a long position to take advantage of a temporary move, but, given my bearish views, I would try to stay short overall.

Let's say that for every four weeks, I might have been long one week and short the others. I was always wanting to position for an overall downwards move.

Commission payment

Fast forward a few months, the Commission approved the famous RePower package in May 2022 when they said they would bring more carbon supply to the market to raise money to help with the extra cost of energy prices in Europe.

People still didn't believe it. There were many traders who were long carbon, particularly on the fund and investor side.

A lot of firms had bought in at €80 and ridden the market up to €100, so had done very well and were in denial. But one year after we hit €100 we went to €50.

My options for December 2023 were in the money, as were some options I had traded for early 2024, so I just took the profit by letting them expire.

EUAs are a very volatile market with huge intraday moves, so I have learnt to be strict about taking profit when I can. There will always be other opportunities to try again with another strategy or two or three.

As well as the volatility, I was also thinking, 'OK, the market has dropped from €100 to €70 to €60. That's already a lot. How much more downside can we have?'

It becomes a question of risk versus reward. I could gain €10 more from a move from €60 to €50, but how likely is that? Or could the market move back to €90?

As a trader, you have to estimate how much there is to gain from going short. If there's a lot, then go for it, but you have to have a sense for the downside limits. For example, the market probably won't go to €10 or €5, that's almost impossible.

Human factor

For me, this was a lesson that this market is driven by fundamentals and technicals only as long as there is political stability.

Once there is social instability, you can forget about both fundamentals and technicals. At that point, it's all about what society as a whole wants and the influence of broader society on political decisions. RePower is the perfect example of that phenomenon.

Environmental commodities affect the way we live and the way we behave. Unless people are committed to real sacrifice there will always be a price for environmental commodities where people are saying, 'no more, I can't afford it any more'.

If governments really agreed to set the price of carbon where it would make a profound difference, say, close to €1,000, then people in Europe might not be able to take holidays by plane; they might not be able to afford to have a car.

At some point, people who are being forced to only travel by bicycle or train, will no longer be willing to make that sacrifice. The price of carbon has to reflect that willingness to pay.

I don't know where that boundary lies, but we can see that obviously even prices of €100 or €150 made people nervous. In this case, the impact was exacerbated by the energy crisis, but the lesson is that people are not always willing to absorb the cost of environmental commodities.

That's one of the lessons I've learned in my 20 years of experience. It's very easy to just say 'yeah, it's a tradeable commodity and we can look at fundamentals and technicals'. But there is always a human aspect to any environmental commodity.

Chapter 10

The power of linkage

After graduating in mathematics from Canada's University of Alberta, Chelsea Bryant began her career in 2007 with actuarial firm Towers Perrin (now WTW) as an investment consulting associate, before moving to global consultancy Mercer in 2010. In 2012, Chelsea transitioned to the energy industry, joining Canadian firm TransAlta, then later TC Energy, trading over-the-counter (OTC) environmental markets. From 2017 to 2020, she helped launch and lead the Canadian subsidiary for ClimeCo, a US-based environmental advisory, credit development and trading firm, ultimately leading their global Carbon Advisory practice. In 2020, she joined Radicle, the largest developer of Canadian compliance-grade environmental commodities, as a member of the Senior Leadership Team in the role of managing director of global markets and strategy, leading trading, sales and marketing for the organization. Radicle was acquired by Canadian financial institution BMO in 2022, and Chelsea has stayed on at the firm, holding various management roles, across trading, environmental products and carbon advisory services, with her current role as managing director, global markets. She is currently based in Austin, Texas.

One of the most memorable compliments I've received in my career came from a lawyer who told me I had "the perfect blend of paranoia and meticulousness to be an excellent lawyer." That may sound odd, but it's exactly the mindset you need in environmental markets.

Many of these markets trade OTC through bespoke, individually negotiated agreements. Success comes from paying close attention to details, understanding and interpreting regulatory nuances, and navigating constantly shifting political landscapes.

If you want to succeed here, you must thrive on precision. You need to be willing to roll up your sleeves and dive into the fine print, tracking changes in policy at every level: federal, provincial, state and even municipal.

DOI: 10.4324/9781003359739-13

Everything matters: programme design details, interactions between different systems, incentive structures and even community-specific impacts.

Environmental commodity markets are shaped by layers of policy that overlap and interact in ways that can be unpredictable. It's a chessboard with dozens of moving pieces, and to stay ahead you must be thinking several moves in advance. That need for a broad, forward-looking perspective is what makes these markets so fascinating.

The pace of environmental markets is unlike traditional commodities. Deals are slower, bilateral negotiations are detailed and the rules of the game can change mid-play. It takes patience, creativity and a tolerance for political risk that goes beyond traditional markets. But once you learn to navigate these complexities, it's addictive.

Cap-and-trade linkage

In October 2013, the U.S. state of California and the Canadian Province of Québec signed an agreement to link their cap-and-trade programmes via the Western Climate Initiative (WCI).

When linkage took effect on 1 January 2014, carbon allowances from either jurisdiction became interchangeable across the combined system. After linkage, a California or Québec allowance was fully fungible, identical in both value and compliance use.

At the time, I was working at Canadian energy firm TC Energy, which owned and operated assets across Canada. As a large industrial emitter, TC Energy had an environmental commodity trading desk alongside its power and fuel desks. Some of TC Energy's power assets were either in WCI jurisdictions or sold power into them, so we were watching the California-Québec linkage very closely.

One particularly interesting detail was that once linked, the jurisdictions agreed to hold joint auctions of carbon allowances starting in 2014, rather than operating separate ones as they had done before. But in the few months between the linkage announcement and the January 2014 start date, each side would continue to run its own independent auctions.

It was a fascinating dynamic: auctions taking place independently with a contemplated future combined market already on the horizon.

During this period, the auction floor prices that were publicly announced for Québec and California differed due to exchange rate movements between the Canadian and U.S. dollars. By late 2013, the Canadian dollar had weakened considerably against the U.S. dollar, which meant that when expressed in U.S. dollar terms, Québec's floor price sat below California's.

It created a quirky market moment: hypothetically the same carbon instrument in a few months, yet for that short pre-linkage window they had different floor prices.

Hypothetical arbitrage

Looking back to the pre-2014 period, the gap in USD-equivalent auction floor prices between Québec and California created a hypothetical arbitrage scenario and raised an interesting theoretical question: if the Québec stand-alone auction settled at or near the floor price, could an entity conceptually buy and hold those credits until the two systems linked and prices converged?

Of course, nothing is ever as simple as it sounds. These programmes were structured in a way that established restrictions on which entities could participate: only registered participants with assets or compliance obligations in the relevant jurisdiction could make a meaningful purchase of credits.

To even consider taking advantage of any potential price difference, a company would need to both have the ability to purchase credits in the Québec auction and hold these credits through to linkage of the two systems. And there was always a risk that if linkage was delayed or disrupted, the opportunity could disappear entirely.

Public data from that period showed that very few companies were registered in Québec prior to linkage. Not every organization with regulatory exposure has a trading desk, and even among those that do, it would depend on an individual company whether they were open to trading around their natural compliance position in a specific market segment.

A different type of market

In traditional commodity markets, arbitrage disappears rapidly. If a commodity trades cheaper in one region than another, traders rush in to close the gap.

Environmental commodity markets don't necessarily behave that way. Restrictions on who can participate, combined with the ever-present risk of policy changes, can allow price differences, or arbitrage opportunities, to persist far longer than in other markets.

Environmental market linkages like this example can create rare, time-sensitive opportunities. But before taking on any position, it's essential to study the linkage agreement in detail. You must be confident that the credits will be truly fungible once the systems connect, so that prices can converge if the market linkage goes through successfully.

The potential value of an arbitrage also has to be weighed against the cost of carrying that position until linkage. Financing a strategy like this only makes sense if the expected price difference is large enough to justify the time and capital involved. In this example, the two currencies had diverged significantly, creating a wide hypothetical spread.

Another important distinction is the relative size of each market before and after linkage. Lower-cost credits from one jurisdiction can flow into the newly combined system, with downward pressure on pricing depending on the relative size of the lower cost market segment. Ultimately, it's the larger of the two markets that will have the greatest influence on where the new equilibrium settles.

The Ontario surprise

Linkage brings opportunity: a larger market with more participants, greater liquidity and more diversified policy exposure. But with those benefits comes a new risk, the potential consequences of market de-linkage.

Take Ontario: the province had linked its emissions trading system with California and Québec in January 2017. But following elections in June 2018, Premier-Designate Doug Ford announced that his very first act in office would be to dismantle the province's cap-and-trade system entirely.

At the time of Ontario's election, allowances from Ontario were fully fungible with those from California and Québec. Once the new Ontario government cancelled the programme, any Ontario allowances held in Ontario compliance accounts were immediately frozen and then invalidated, becoming worthless.

For Ontario entities that had already sold and transferred credits into the linked system, the impact wasn't the same. Regulators completed a review and confirmed that Ontario-originated credits accounted for only about 2% of outstanding total supply in the linked California-Québec system, and did not invalidate these credits.

At that time, I was working for ClimeCo and we were deep in the weeds of navigating policy risks and opportunities across a wide range of environmental markets. We had discussed this possibility, but it was still shocking to watch it unfold in real time.

It was a stark reminder for environmental markets: policy risk is real.

Mitigating de-linkage risk

For firms active in linked environmental markets, political risk isn't an abstract concept, it's a real factor that can undo years of planning in a single policy announcement.

A linked market can be powerful, but it also means that when one jurisdiction abruptly changes course, accounts can be frozen, rules rewritten and value erased almost overnight. It's not always clear how to protect against these types of tail risk events, but there are some strategies that can conceptually soften the blow when political risk looms.

When there's clear de-linkage risk, like an upcoming election, leadership change or new policy on the horizon, a firm could structure positions to reduce exposure.

One illustrative example is to take forward exposure of the fungible instrument that is not at risk rather than holding a spot position. This can be structured as a stand-alone forward or a roll: deliver a spot credit now in return for delivery of a forward credit that remains valid, irrespective of de-linkage, after the event risk has passed.

This is a theoretical way to step out of the line of fire while still maintaining market exposure. However, it's important to review the market pricing dynamics of spot versus forward levels of these respective instruments to determine the cost of any hypothetical strategy.

Transactions can be structured to anticipate political instability: if one programme collapses, you could potentially design delivery so that the credit is substituted with another valid instrument. A transaction like this may be structured OTC or by using an exchange-traded futures contract, if it exists, depending on the contract specifications.

Ultimately, every firm manages risk and exposures differently. In the case of the Ontario cap-and-trade programme, some firms were negatively impacted when the new government cancelled the system abruptly and provided no compensation to market traders and speculators.

In environmental markets, policy isn't just background noise. It's part of the price of admission.

Finding my place

I didn't start out in environmental markets. With a degree in mathematics and an economics minor, I thought I'd be an actuary. That was the plan, until I discovered the broader world of investment consulting, where we advised large pension plans, endowments and foundations on liabilities and risks and opportunities.

That work opened a door I hadn't expected. From there, I found environmental markets almost by accident.

Back then, these markets weren't widely discussed in North America, but I remember having interesting conversations with investment managers who were starting to explore sustainability-related funds. It was a niche, almost experimental topic.

When I moved to TransAlta's commercial team, with a large renewable energy portfolio, I had the opportunity to learn more about this emerging space. Then at TC Energy, I fully transitioned into trading bilateral OTC environmental markets, and I fell in love with this nascent asset class. Every step pulled me deeper into a field that is constantly evolving and always engaging.

Today at BMO, I spend my time navigating the complexity of environmental commodities and systems and decarbonization projects. These markets aren't just about analysing numbers. They require interpreting policies, understanding participant behaviour and finding opportunities across a vast myriad of different programmes.

No two deals are typically alike. Each one can be bespoke. It's a space where you build relationships, explore white space and trust your instincts. It's challenging, creative work. And because these markets are always changing, you're always learning and evolving.

If there's one lesson environmental markets have taught me, it's this: opportunity lives at the intersection of patience, diligence and insight. Where others may see complexity, I see possibility. And that's the power of linkage: scale, liquidity and stability.

Chapter 11

Trading California carbon during COVID-19

After a brief stint in Microsoft's treasury function during college, Mike Taylor joined energy trader Enron in 2001, as an analyst on the emissions trading desk in their Houston office. In 2004, he consulted for Charles River Associates and then in 2005 he joined NRG Inc as a senior emissions trader. The following year, Mike moved to Louis Dreyfus Highbridge Energy to start up their emissions desk. Mike was appointed senior vice president for carbon and emissions trading at Element Markets in 2008, a role he held until late 2015, when he left to found broker and consultant Emission Advisors, Inc. The firm was acquired by Aegis Hedging Solutions in 2021, and Mike stayed on at Aegis as director of emissions trading for two years. In 2024, Mike founded Emissions Experts Inc, a brokerage and consulting firm. A graduate of Louisiana State University, Mike is also the author of the bestselling book Reduce Carbon Compliance Costs: Strategies for Facilities in a Carbon Cap and Trade Program.

When I was given a full-time offer to join Enron after a summer internship, I wanted to know which team I would start with. They told me, 'well, we can either assign you a spot or you can go find someone who will hire you'.

I took that as a sign I had better manage my own destiny, especially as I was surrounded by some very driven, motivated and even aggressive people.

I asked a trading manager on the natural gas desk what they thought the quickest path might be to becoming a trader. He told me that 'the line starts way back there' if I were looking to trade natural gas or oil or power, but that I would be next in line if I wanted to go to the emissions desk.

That sounded pretty good to me and so I ended up joining Enron's emissions trading group. That was my introduction to these markets. The company declared bankruptcy a little while later, but I found another job and I have stayed with emissions trading ever since.

It was a great experience. I was getting invited at the age of 24 to speak at conferences as a so-called expert. It was such a new and developing space that I didn't have to compete with 10- or 20-year veterans because the environmental markets in the U.S. had not been in existence for too long.

DOI: 10.4324/9781003359739-14

It was easier back then to be a big fish in a small pond. Of course, now that pond is more like an ocean.

CARB diet

The way the emissions cap-and-trade programme works in California is that the California Air Resources Board (CARB) allocates some free allocations of carbon emissions to various industrial sectors, including fuel suppliers. CARB also holds quarterly auctions that release an additional supply of allowances into the market.

The first-ever quarterly auction back in 2012 sold allowances for $10 per tonne. CARB then established that each year the auction floor price – the minimum level CARB would sell at – would increase by the prevailing rate of inflation plus an additional 5%.

By early 2020, the auction floor price had reached $16.68. That was a very important number for the market. Every trader knew that the state of California would not sell allowances below that price at auction.

If the over-the-counter (OTC) market were ever to trade below the $16.68 floor price for any extended period of time, then CARB's auctions likely wouldn't be fully subscribed and allowances would not enter the market. Participants would not buy allowances at auction if they could buy them cheaper in the OTC market.

At that time, the OTC market was trading in a $17–18 range, which wasn't too far above the auction floor of $16.68. A lot of the trading shops took on additional leverage to buy allowances because we were trading so close to the auction floor: they figured being long was a one-way bet.

Inflation was running at around 2% and CARB adds an annual 5% uplift so a lot of traders felt that if they bought at close to the floor price, they would essentially be guaranteed a 7% return every year.

There were lots of speculators in the space looking at the next decade through to 2030, when there were more supply cuts planned in the programme. Everybody had a forecast where prices were rising and so lots of people loaded up on allowances.

To be fair, it wasn't a bad strategy. The market had generally been gradually rising since its inception, and the OTC market had rarely traded below CARB's auction floor price.

Pandemic panic

Of course, everything changed when the COVID-19 pandemic hit in March 2020.

Almost overnight, there was lots of uncertainty and the environment switched to risk off. The lockdown had begun, so obviously emissions from transportation were plummeting in California. At the same time, trading firms were just selling everything.

This was March 2020 and so we had just had CARB's February auctions and there were another two months until the May auctions. Some financial trading firms started to say, 'I can't wait that long to see if prices will recover', so they began to sell out.

As prices fell, the ICE exchange started to get nervous that a lot of these companies were extremely leveraged. The exchange was worried about defaults and so it sharply raised the margin requirement, which is the deposit level that a customer has to hold in order to maintain a trading position on the exchange.

Margins very quickly rose from around 1.5% of the value of the allowances to north of 10%. Before the pandemic, if you'd bought $100 million of allowances on the futures market, you only had to have $1.5 million in capital, but now all of a sudden you had to have $10 million to maintain your position and to cover the daily mark-to-market losses.

A lot of these trading firms didn't have that much available liquidity, especially during the first two weeks of COVID-19 when everybody was battening down the hatches.

It became a vicious circle. As prices fell, margins increased and that forced still more selling because some guys couldn't meet their margin call. Their positions were liquidated by the clearing members who stand between the traders and the exchange, and that selling activity drove prices lower still.

The clearing members were liquidating entire trading books in some cases. They were just merciless: they just wanted to get out of positions at any cost so they would hit bids and hit still more bids.

It was hard to find buyers in March 2020 and prices crashed from $18 all the way down to $11. The trading shops had reduced their risk appetite, and the compliance entities in California didn't need to show compliance till November so they were holding off.

Nobody really needed to buy in March and so we traded right through that crucial $16.68 auction floor price that everybody had kind of treated as a default floor for the whole market.

It turned out to be wishful thinking to think of the auction floor as an overall market floor.

Sure, buyers would eventually need additional allowances to meet compliance requirements so prices would eventually have to rise above the floor in order for the auctions to restart. But given the much lower demand, we could technically have stayed below the auction price for another two years and still have been in compliance.

Catching the knife

Panic was fairly widespread at this point, but I could spot an opportunity emerging at these levels, so I went to some of my customers to try to persuade them to cover their 2020 compliance obligations early.

My first port of call was the oil and gas firms, but of course that March, oil prices were also plummeting – famously turning negative in April 2020 – so a lot of them were just trying to keep the lights on.

They told me, 'Mike, we're not spending any money to buy for compliance purposes when we don't even know if we're going to be an ongoing concern. We may not be in business when the November compliance date comes around'.

Plenty of guys told me they were busy trying to figure out if they could make payroll next month rather than worrying about their compliance profile.

My counterargument was that if you go out of business what does it matter if you have one more contract out there? But, if you are still in business next year, then don't you think it's a good idea to have locked in a price that was guaranteed to be below the auction floor price?

I had come up with a structure whereby, rather than trying to make a bet on the spot price, we would instead buy allowances on a forward basis. My idea was to buy December 2021 allowances, so 21 months further out, which would lock in part of the current low levels.

The forward structure of the California market is largely based on the cost of capital, and at the time interest rates were also plummeting to basically zero, so there was only a 3% premium for 2021 versus 2020 allowances.

I told the compliance entities,

> look, if we're at $11 right now, or even at $12, don't forget that the floor price will be $16.68 for the May auction and, if inflation is running at least 1%, then that means that the floor price for the 2021 auctions will be at least $17.68.

I told my guys that I could get them locked in at $13–14 for December 2021 delivery. My argument was that the only way prices would be below that is if the programme imploded or went away altogether.

It was statistically very, very unlikely that prices could stay below the auction floor price for seven straight quarters.

Locked and loaded

Even once I had some of the guys interested, they would tell me that they didn't have capital to invest, even to back a sure thing, given the pressure everyone was feeling.

Fortunately, I was able to find one or two counterparties with flexible credit arrangements who didn't require significant margin or pre-payment. At that point, I could tell the potential buyers, 'I'm not even asking you to spend any money today, I'm just asking you to sign a contract that locks in a price below the government auction floor'.

After all, that is something that has only happened once before in the history of the California programme, and prices stayed below the floor for just about a month.

Eventually, I won some folks over, and our clients locked in delivery for December 2021 at $14–15. They were all delighted when the auction rolled round in mid-May and we were back at the floor price of $16.68.

But if got even better for them. The California market staged a full recovery, and when they took delivery in December 2021, prices were up as high as $30.

Some of our clients had bought a million tonnes, so savings of $15–16 meant that they saved $15–16 million each. In the environmental world, that's a whole lot of money.

I had made a big call and I had called it right. That paid off for our clients and for my firm, Emission Advisors. Our revenue grew by 388% between 2016 and 2019, and in 2020 we were named on the Inc 5,000 List of America's Fastest-Growing Private Companies.

Precision timing

In the chaos of the early days of COVID-19, it wasn't easy to make that call that the market would recover so strongly.

In March 2020, prices were gapping down in 50¢ increments when we had been used to a bid-ask spread that was 3¢ cents wide. When you were looking at the screen, you felt like your heart was dropping out of your body.

People were losing money; trading liquidity was drying up and the pain just kept coming day after day after day. After two weeks, you start to wonder is this ever going to stop. How low can we go? Is the California programme going to cease to exist?

A lot of people had assumed that the market would never trade below the auction floor price so when it went under, they started asking if prices could go all the way to zero and whether California would abandon the programme?

One of the things I did before I recommended that my clients lock in was to call my government contacts and ask if there was any talk of pausing compliance, or cancelling the programme, or allowing firms to defer their compliance.

The only change I heard was that the authorities were considering extending 2019 verifications by an extra month because people weren't able to travel. Nothing substantial. Every official I spoke to told me that the pandemic wasn't going to cause them to throw out all of the climate change goals and programmes that had been worked on for decades.

When I heard that, I was sure the market was definitely going back up. The government was committed to the programme and once all the traders with weak balance sheets had been washed out, we'd be left with traders and compliance buyers with strong balance sheets.

Sure enough, once all the forced selling was done, the offers started to tick back up and we had our first compliance entity come in and buy half a million allowances, which is a pretty large trade. By May 2020, the world was adjusting, and we realized that, although COVID-19 was here, business wasn't going to stop.

Firms that were planning to bid in the May auction started buying in the OTC market and prices ticked up to $15.50, then $16, $16.10 and $16.20. We were back around the auction floor price of $16.68 by the time the May auction occurred.

After the trading community saw that compliance buyers were back in the market, they felt more confident and some of them who had sold at $16–17 flipped around and started buying as well.

In the end, there were just 44 trading days when we were below the auction floor price, between mid-March and mid-May.

We had timed it perfectly to lock in for 2021. There were actually only ten days when the market was below $15 and most of the rest of those days, it was below $16. That was a very short period of time to lock in those huge savings.

Irrational markets

The economist John Maynard Keynes said that 'markets can remain irrational longer than you can remain solvent'. That's what happened. In March 2020, it took just two weeks of an irrational market for a lot of firms to become insolvent.

These were often guys who had got into the market in 2018/19, and were new to trading emissions, rather than guys like me who had been in the industry for 20 years.

My edge was that I had realized that the auction floor price wasn't a floor for the whole market, but it was a very strong fundamental signal.

My view of emissions trading is that you need to understand whatever programme you are working with from a fundamental perspective. There are 430 pages of regulation governing the California scheme. I have read the rules cover to cover multiple times because my reputation is on the line if I don't clearly understand the market.

As a trader in the environmental markets, you have to have a little bit of a different lens when you are looking at intrinsic worth. In the pandemic, if you had been able to buy oil at minus $40 per barrel, you would be confident that someone would ultimately pay you for that oil because it has a utility value.

It's very different when you are dealing with an electronic carbon allowance, which is not going to help you heat your home or to feed your family. People like to say that gold is always going to be a store of value, but is a carbon allowance? After all, it's an electronic allowance that could disappear tomorrow.

There are obviously supply-demand fundamentals in the environmental markets, but you also have to look deeply into the regulations. Emissions compliance markets move with the stroke of a pen.

Then, if you truly understand the market and the market shows you a great opportunity, you need to be ready to pounce on it. My aim is not to scalp pennies; I'm trying to make dollars, and that's what we achieved in 2020.

Chapter 12

Trading the EUA-CER spread

Stef Peters graduated from Delft University of Technology in the Netherlands with a master's degree in mechanical engineering in 1987. He held a number of positions in the electricity sector before joining Norwegian utility Statkraft in 1999. During his 24-year career at Statkraft, Stef held a number of senior roles, serving as head of renewables, head of origination for Continental Europe, head of global carbon and from 2013 head of global environmental markets. Stef retired from Statkraft in mid-2023.

One thing I have learnt is that when you are running a trading and origination team, you can't just rely on just one business line – just like you shouldn't rely on a single pick when investing in the stock market.

You need to make sure to have at least three different business activities. Some of your business lines will disappear over time: governments can change the rules of the game, or competitors can catch on to your strategy and your trading margins disappear.

The key is to put enough effort into finding and developing new businesses. If done well, some of these new businesses will in a few years turn into your new cash cows.

Second, always look for free or cheap optionality in your deals, if possible, even if far out of the money. Optionality can be the difference between a nice deal and an exceptionally good deal.

Lastly, a good team should be much more than the sum of its members. A substantial element of the incentives should be based on total team result, which can also finance new business development.

By following this philosophy, I managed to have a successful, profitable and above all very pleasant career in the environmental markets, with a great company, Statkraft.

DOI: 10.4324/9781003359739-15

Ticket to Kyoto

In the early 2000s, when I had just started working for Statkraft, we developed a very profitable business from sourcing, transporting, importing and trading green certificates.

We were taking advantage of a temporary surge in demand in the Netherlands where tax rebates were coupled to green electricity use.

We didn't expect this system would last long. Basically, these tax incentives didn't achieve their goal of increasing local Dutch renewables generation, as most of the green certificates were imported from abroad.

By 2003, we started looking for alternatives before the system would come to an end.

The first alternative market we looked at was the U.K. Levy Exemption Certificate System (LECS). Like the Dutch system, LECS also allowed for the import of green certificates. We expected this system would also not last long, but we ended up being successfully active there for more than ten years.

The second alternative for us was a potential new carbon market.

The Kyoto Protocol hadn't been ratified yet – that took until 2005 – but it was in the ratification process, and it looked highly likely to us that the global carbon markets were going to further develop, and potentially become very big.

My perception was that the carbon certificates that Kyoto envisaged – certified emission reductions (CERs) and emission reduction units (ERUs) – would look a lot like green certificates and so I had one of my analysts look into the Kyoto Protocol thoroughly and we took some external advice.

We also looked into the European Trading System (ETS) that was to come into force from 2005 onwards. Our conclusion was that both the international and the European carbon markets could be very interesting for us.

Statkraft, as a large hydro power producer, hardly emitted any carbon emissions so it was not easy to receive the mandate from headquarters in Oslo for emissions trading, but step by step we got there.

The first trading period for European Union Allowances (EUAs) was three years from 2005 to 2007 and the second period was five years from 2008 to 2012. The third was eight years from 2013 to 2020.

Like most players at that time, we initially focussed on sourcing CERs from various projects, mainly in Asia or Africa. We then started to see interesting trading opportunities emerge in the interplay between the European ETS and the Kyoto-based CERs.

For example, in the second trading period of the European ETS, companies that had to meet compliance standards were obliged to surrender a certain amount of EUAs to cover their carbon emissions.

European rules allowed companies to hand in (cheaper) CERs instead of EUAs to meet their requirements, up to a certain maximum level, on average around 13% for the EU, but with different levels per country.

In 2008–9, there still weren't many CERs available because a lot of projects had only just begun operations, so the discount between EUAs and CERs was limited. Our belief, however, was that at some point in the future larger volumes of CERs would come to the market resulting in a widening of the price gap between CERs and EUAs.

We considered taking a trading position on the spread (long EUAs, short CERs) for 2011 and/or 2012, but this would be risky, and we would need a lot of risk capital if the widening of the spread took too long. After all, markets can stay irrational much longer than we can stay liquid.

Keeping your options open

We didn't take the outright spread position but considered other ways of acting on our core assumption. In the end, we came up with what we called a 'flex product' that we marketed to European firms that fell under the ETS.

Our concept was that we would guarantee to any European firm that we would make sure they would have enough allowances to cover their compliance requirements, and we would guarantee to cover their requirements at a cheaper price than the level at which EUAs were trading.

Let's say a big customer needed five million EUAs for 2008–12 and went out to the market for the cheapest offer. We would offer to supply them at a €1 discount to the EUA market price, but in exchange we would decide whether to deliver purely EUAs, or some blend including CERs and/or ERUs.

We would always make sure that the customer would meet his compliance requirements, but we would own the optionality regarding the mix of certificates.

In addition, we had the optionality regarding the date of delivery of the certificates, as long as we met the compliance deadline of 30 April of the following year. Often, we were allowed to deliver until a week before the deadline.

This option was very valuable because EUA as well as CER/ERU prices could be quite volatile, especially close to the end of a calendar year and close to the compliance deadline of 30 April.

We developed contracts that described in detail the types of optionality, but also gave very strong guarantees to the compliance companies that Statkraft would compensate them if we could not deliver for any reason, except for force majeure.

Win-win deal

In this deal structure, Statkraft basically had two types of optionality: *which* products to deliver and *when* to deliver. This was clearly very valuable to us. But we also added large value to our customers: they had substantially cheaper compliance, and as far as I know were always pleased with the deals.

The customer couldn't lose; they were saving money and any compliance risk was taken away by us as we managed it on their behalf.

Most customers would anyhow never have been able to exploit these optionalities themselves. It was too complex and too risky for them to try to arbitrage different types of certificates and different time periods. Even if they had wanted to, their compliance people would never have allowed it.

Why were those implicit options so valuable to us?

Well, we had already done many comparable deals resulting in a large portfolio of purchases and sales. For example, many of our long-term CER purchases had clauses where we had the right but not the obligation to buy CERs at fixed prices if the CDM projects overperformed by delivering more CERs than we contracted.

We could sell options in the market and collect the premiums. Or we could just sit on the optionality and wait for developments in the markets.

I believe I'm quite analytical, and I'm always looking to add value for both sides of the deal. If somehow there's no value for one side, then the deal is most likely never going to happen. Theoretically, the deal can happen of course if one side is less sophisticated, doesn't fully understand the deal and is willing to pay too much. But in general, these are not the type of deals you want to do.

Value needs to get added somewhere within a trade, otherwise it's just a zero-sum game, where one of us wins, and the other side loses. Looking for win-win isn't too difficult as long as you try to understand the position and potential needs of your counterpart.

Our strategy was successful for a couple of years but came to an end in 2013 when no CERs were allowed in the EU ETS anymore. CERs had become more of a voluntary offset instead of a compliance unit, with totally different rules.

Sporting chance

In my early days at Statkraft, the people I hired were sort of younger versions of myself: analytical, commercial and with an interest in (complex) content. Experience in energy or environmental products was not immediately needed. Quite of few of these 'analysts' later become successful traders and originators.

When my team was growing, I obviously also had to hire people that were more different from myself and who also dared to disagree with me, to keep me sharp.

When hiring people, and I've maybe hired more than 50 people onto different teams over the years, the first thing I looked for is whether the person is smart, and preferably *really* smart.

I'm looking for analytical people, who are also truly interested in the subject matter so that they can really have fun doing their job. And when asking a commercial question and looking in their eyes, I would like to see a dollar sign.

Money shouldn't be the only objective because that doesn't tend to work in my opinion, but you do need to understand why we are in business. You shouldn't go into trading just to make money though. Personally, I like the winning, to be successful, to prove we're right.

Developing business and executing deals feel fantastic when it all works out. Having a passion to understand the market deeply is the difference between the traders that win and those that lose, I believe. The money will follow automatically when you're fully committed and having fun.

As a manager I've always been responsible for the strategy, the hiring and the creation of one team, which, cliché, should be more than the sum of the individuals. Of course, I also needed good people in my team to compensate for some of my weaknesses!

When I was hired into the Amsterdam office of Statkraft in 1999, we were a little group of only ten people. Six of those were from the mothership in Oslo and four were Dutch hires. It turned out that all four Dutchies had in common that they were sporty, and at high levels in their chosen sports.

Was there an assumption that the mentality of fanatic ambitious sportspeople would be useful for success in business? Or was it just because our Norwegian boss at that time was, like many Norwegians, very sport-minded?

Strangle-hold

The benefit of doing your homework and thoroughly understanding the rules of the ETS was very clear when we did an EUA options strangle trade in the autumn of 2005.

Options strangles are when a trader buys or sells both a call option (the right but not the obligation to buy at a certain level) and a put option (the right but not the obligation to sell at a certain level) with different strike prices but the same expiration date.

The strike prices of the put and call options are typically a long way out of the money, meaning they are not close to current market prices and are therefore cheap to trade.

Our options strangle was for the end of the first EUA compliance period of 2005–7. That period was 100% decoupled from the next compliance period and was set to end on 31 December 2007, although compliance companies could still hand in allowances until 30 April 2008. (Unlike later phases of the ETS, firms were not allowed to transfer EUAs from that first period to the next phase.)

My view was that on that day – the final day of reckoning – there would either be a shortage of EUAs or there would be too many EUAs. If I were correct, then on 30 April 2008 either the price of EUAs could fall to zero or it could surge to high prices, determined by the cost of power plant fuel switching from coal to gas.

Someone in the market was prepared to sell put and call options. The way you calculate the value of options is through the Black-Scholes model, and the sellers were asking a price that was 50% higher than Black-Scholes was indicating.

You could argue that they were charging a high price, but in my view, it was actually insanely cheap because they were thinking purely in terms of Black-Scholes rather than understanding that the compliance period had a hard stop, and the outcome was going to be entirely binary.

I wasn't trained as a trader because I started my career as an engineer, but plain common sense told me that even if I had to pay more than twice the value indicated by Black-Scholes, those options were still worth buying.

I bought the first clip through a broker, and then managed to acquire a second clip. When looking for more, the seller got nervous and said no more.

Those were great deals. The first phase finished with a surplus of certificates and so the EUA price went to zero. The call options were obviously worthless, but the puts were big-time in the money.

That trade again proved my point that environmental markets are by definition *artificial* markets, where you have to understand the rules and regulations, which often are totally different from real physical commodity markets.

Environmental traders need to understand the policymakers that created and maintain these artificial markets. If you trade the European ETS, then you should follow officials in Brussels closely. Show up at events and listen hard, especially to relevant policymakers, and also read between the lines, for potential trading directions.

Environmental markets can be very useful to achieve certain environmental goals; they can also be lots of fun, but they can also disappear with the stroke of an official's pen. That's why a good environmental trader needs to avoid becoming dependent on a single strategy.

Part III

Trading ethanol

Ethanol is a clear, colourless liquid commonly produced through fermentation, where yeast converts sugars found in crops such as corn, sugarcane or barley into ethanol and carbon dioxide. It can also be synthetically produced by hydrating ethylene.

Ethanol serves multiple purposes, including use as a fuel additive, solvent and in industrial applications. Environmentally, ethanol is valued as a renewable biofuel that can reduce greenhouse gas emissions compared to fossil fuels when blended with gasoline.

Ethanol is actively traded in global markets, with Brazil, the United States and the European Union among the largest producers and consumers.

The ethanol trade typically involves moving physical products within regions and internationally, and traders therefore need to have a strong grasp of physical operations as well as keeping an eye on the shifting supply-demand balance and on government regulations, such as blending mandates and import tariffs.

DOI: 10.4324/9781003359739-16

Chapter 13

Trading the early days of Brazilian ethanol

Nelson Ostanello joined sugar and ethanol producer Usina Açucareira Ester in 1975 and stayed with them until 2002, holding a variety of increasingly senior roles, including commercial, administrative and financial manager. He then moved to Coimex Trading where he served as commercial manager, responsible for the ethanol division in Brazil, between 2002 and 2005. Nelson was hired by Bauche Energy Brasil Trading in 2005 as the commercial director in charge of their Brazil ethanol business. In 2010, Nelson was appointed chief executive of Greenergy Brasil Trading, where he was responsible for the firm's Brazil office, its ethanol and diesel trading and its regional investments. He retired from Greenergy in 2024. Nelson holds a bachelor's degree from PUC Campinas, with a further degree in business administration from the Universidade São Francisco and a master's in business administration from the Fundaçao Getúlio Vargus, specializing in agribusiness.

When I was 16 years old, I started work at a sugar mill in Brazil. I started at the bottom as an office boy but I slowly built up my career and by the time that I finally left Usina Açucareira Ester, I had worked as a senior manager, division chief and financial manager.

My background meant that I spent time in every different sector of the office and I learnt how every part of the company functioned. But once I went to the commercial division, I knew that was where I wanted to be.

I ended up spending most of my career on various trading desks, trading ethanol and sugar and later on refined fuels as well. After I started buying and selling, I realized that was the part of the business that I loved most.

That's not because of the money that traders can make. In my view, money should be considered a consequence rather than an aim in itself.

What I always enjoyed was the opportunity to do deals – to buy from one company and sell to another at a profit – as well as the chance to learn. I was also fascinated by the logistics of physical trading, which can be very complex, particularly in the export market.

DOI: 10.4324/9781003359739-17

I have spent nearly 50 years in this industry now, but I don't think I ever stopped learning and growing.

My mother had started working at Usina Açucareira Ester before me. She was a very humble employee who cut the sugarcane in the fields. Before she eventually retired, I was managing my mother, which was a strange feeling.

The big short

My trading career spans a key period in the Brazilian ethanol industry. When I started out, it was way before the present boom in Brazilian ethanol.

Brazil was a significant net importer of ethanol throughout the 1970s, 1980s and right through to the beginning of the 1990s.

We had a seasonal short in Brazil because we are between crops during our summer. We were importing significant volumes every year during the summer months.

We bought a lot of ethanol for the Brazilian market from Russia and South Africa. We just had to be careful when we bought from Russia because summer in Brazil is winter in Russia, so we needed special heated vessels to carry the Russian ethanol.

Trading in the 1970s was very different to how it is today.

Firstly, we were very dependent on the government for everything. We needed licenses from the government to operate and licenses to import material. Then we needed quota allowances that let us sell ethanol to Brazil's state-owned energy giant Petrobras.

We have live data now, and you can almost know everything that is going on, but in the beginning, it was terrible. Can you imagine how it was back then? It was completely different: we didn't have the internet, we only had a phone, or we used telexes to do deals.

After telexes, we switched to faxes. We thought that was big progress but I guess there are younger traders now who have never seen a fax machine in their lives.

Even getting our Russian counterparts on the phone was a drama, between the difficulty of getting an international line and the large time difference.

You could never get prices on time. I remember that to check the sugar price, I would have to buy the newspaper the following day to see what the price had been the previous day.

Nothing worked efficiently. One time we bought a vessel from Russia to discharge in the north of Brazil. When the vessel arrived, the draft of the vessel was too deep because it was fully laden and so it couldn't enter the port to discharge.

I needed to receive the vessel outside the port, then discharge some of the product into a barge so that the vessel would be able to reach the berth and discharge the rest.

I had to go onboard with the surveying company to talk to the captain, but we ended up sitting around for hours waiting for the federal police to show up and inspect our vessel.

The police showed up very late because it turned out that another vessel had brought a lot of Brazilian girls onboard to have a party. That party ended up costing the charterer an extra fee for the delay in unloading. People in the industry weren't always very professional at that point.

The giant stirs

Everything changed in 2002–3, when Brazil experienced serious overproduction of ethanol for the first time ever.

That represented a huge change for the market, after we had been so short earlier in my career. We needed to develop new storage tanks quickly to cope with the extra supply, but most importantly we needed to find new export markets.

It was at that point that I moved across to Coimex Trading, who had already begun exporting Brazilian ethanol in a very minor way, maybe 78,000–79,000 cubic meters over an entire year.

My principal job at Coimex was to expand our trading activities and to export more ethanol from Brazil to the world.

We started to export our product to Europe. The majority went to Sweden, where for a time they were running the buses in Stockholm using our ethanol.

Then after that, we discovered the Japanese and South Korean markets. We worked with the big Asian trading houses like Mitsui, Mitsubishi and Samsung to sell high-grade ethanol for pharmaceuticals or for food manufacture, including saké production.

The problem we faced, though, was that these exports were reasonably high value, but very low volumes.

Our exports to Japan, for example, used chemical vessels. We never sent a full vessel to Japan or Korea because our buyers used to take 10,000–12,000 cubic meters at a time, when filling even the smallest full vessel required at least 40,000 cubic meters.

There was nobody in Japan or Korea big enough to take a single cargo, but we needed to find destinations that could take full vessels if we were going to clear some of our new surplus.

That's how I ended up doing the first Brazilian ethanol export deal with India.

Full Brazilian

I could see the potential demand from India so I visited the country a couple of times and I started working with a good friend in Mumbai who had a lot of local clients.

We quickly realized that, as in northern Asia, there was not going to be any single Indian customer that would be willing or able to take on a full vessel.

I didn't want to give up on the plan of placing a full vessel though, so we started to look at whether we could put together a consortium of Indian buyers that would justify placing a 50,000 cubic meter vessel.

That turned out to be infinitely more complex than we might have imagined.

If I tell you that we ended up selling to 66 separate Indian clients from the same vessel, I'm sure you can understand why this was not an easy deal to put together.

By the way, India is eight or nine hours ahead of Brazil in terms of time zone, and we were doing everything over the phone.

Every one of those 66 Indian clients needed to open letters of credit with us. We were incredibly fortunate in terms of performance: of all the 66, we only had to use the letter of credit for one buyer.

On the supply side, we had to buy from up to 15 different Brazilian mill suppliers to fill the vessel. That sounds like a lot of counterparties, but compared to the Indian side of the deal, the Brazilian side was relatively easy.

After all, we knew how the guys worked here. We understood the millers, we understood the port. Basically, we knew everyone in Brazil, but that certainly wasn't the case in India.

That was the first ethanol vessel to move from Brazil to India, and it was one of the key signposts that Brazil was going to become a serious player in the ethanol markets, as an exporter rather than as an importer.

It wasn't an easy deal, with so many counterparts involved. To pull something like that off, you need a lot of hard work but also very good luck.

We were fortunate because the ethanol price had gone up between the time we bought and the time we sold, and back then the profit margin on cargoes was good enough to compensate us for all of the effort involved in getting the deal done.

It's much more difficult nowadays to make serious money trading physical material because the margins are much lower than they used to be. In Brazil, we have exchanged high margins but low volumes, for low margins but high volumes.

Solving the U.S.

We had successfully opened up the Indian market, but the next major export market we needed to crack was the U.S.

The big problem we faced there was that the U.S. imposed an import tax on Brazilian ethanol of around $150 per tonne. That level of duty made exporting directly to the U.S. impossible.

Our breakthrough was to leverage the Caribbean Basin Initiative, which was an incentive that the U.S. provided that allowed some Caribbean countries to export certain domestic products to the U.S. without any duty.

Coimex decided to develop ethanol dehydration plants in Jamaica. Our first plant was a joint venture with Jamaica's state oil refinery Petrojam.

We brought in hydrous ethanol from Brazil, removed the water from it in our dehydration plant in Jamaica and then exported the material to the U.S. as anhydrous ethanol.

As a Jamaican-produced product, the anhydrous ethanol was not subject to that almost $150 import duty that our original Brazilian ethanol would have attracted.

There was a huge amount of money involved in that operation. There was a big capital outlay in developing a dehydration plant in the Caribbean, but then the savings on exports to the U.S. were also very sizeable and made the whole investment worthwhile.

We also kept optimizing the logistics to the point that we were able to discharge the hydrous material in Jamaica and then immediately load the anhydrous material onto the same vessel, which took it to Houston in the U.S.

The efficiency of the Brazilian ethanol market had come a long way from my early days.

Seeking arbitrages

I spent almost five years as commercial manager of Coimex, building out the firm's export business and inaugurating the Jamaica plant.

By the end of my time at Coimex, we were a very sizeable exporter: in my first full year alone, we grew the ethanol export business more than ten-fold to almost 1 million cubic meters, which is quite amazing in retrospect.

After Coimex, I joined Bauche Energy as commercial director in charge of Brazil ethanol, and we went on to build two more plants in Jamaica to follow the same playbook.

But no trading strategy lasts forever and eventually the U.S. cut the Caribbean subsidy. Fortunately, even without that advantage, the plants in Jamaica stayed profitable and provided us with additional optionality.

Bauche merged its ethanol division with British biofuels firm Greenergy International in early 2010 to form Greenergy Brazil, and I took over as chief executive.

Our main driver at Greenergy was to continue to grow Brazilian exports, in particular to Europe or the U.S., either directly or via our facilities in Jamaica.

The market is hugely more efficient and more mature now than in the early days. Information on prices and volumes is more transparent, and it's harder to find an edge.

I loved pioneering new routes for our exports. Opening up India or discovering that our route to the U.S. lay through the Caribbean were great deals.

But just because the market has changed doesn't mean that there aren't still trading opportunities and arbitrages.

For example, despite Brazil's new status as an export powerhouse, we imported ethanol from the U.S. to northeast Brazil just a few years ago because the crop there wasn't too sizeable and they were short in that region.

After all, alert traders will always find fresh opportunities.

Chapter 14

Trading ethanol into Brazil

Ricardo Parada Pimenta graduated from Brazil's Mackenzie Presbyterian University in 1979. By 1984, he was manager of the ethanol department at Cotia Trading in São Paulo. Ricardo moved to SAB Trading in 1987 to run ethanol origination, sales and distribution worldwide. He was hired by Coimex Group in 1998 as head of sugar and ethanol in São Paulo. He then moved to Geneva in 2000, as Coimex's commercial director, with the mission of expanding the firm's presence in the global sugar and ethanol market. Ricardo joined Bauche Energy in 2005 as commercial director and board member in Geneva. Then in 2010, he was appointed as CEO of North Sea Global Ethanol (NSGE), leading the Brazilian and the Swiss teams. At the end of 2011, he left NSGE to become an independent consultant, working for Lukoil, Glencore, Alcosuisse, Jürgen Schmidt, Chemium and VA&E. Ricardo joined Marquis Energy between 2016 and 2018, after which he returned to independent consultancy.

My career in the ethanol market started in 1984 so I have been in the business for over 40 years now. But I fell into it almost by accident.

I had graduated as a civil engineer but when Brazil went through an economic crisis in 1984, I lost my job. I was unemployed for six or seven months when a good friend of mine offered me an opportunity to work at his company, helping to manage ethanol shipments on the ground.

I love ships, so for me this activity was a mixture of work with pleasure. I absolutely loved going to visit the ships and terminals, talking to the officers and crew and also meeting the ship owners. It was a period of learning but also dealing with different situations. This was fascinating and it was something new for me.

In 1986, the first fuel-grade ethanol shipments occurred from Brazil to the U.S., after exporters discovered a narrow loophole that allowed Brazilian ethanol to enter in the United States without paying import duty, i.e., paying just the ad valorem.

DOI: 10.4324/9781003359739-18

Unfortunately for Brazil, this did not last too long. Due to a very strong lobby of U.S. producers, an excise tax replaced the import duty, favouring the U.S. production.

After a few years working on the operations side, the firm transferred me to the commercial sector, which again was something completely new for me. My technical background was a great help in understanding logistics, but I think my curiosity was the most important characteristic that helped me be successful in the market.

Even when I was visiting the ships to check that the tanks were clean and that everything was fine, I was curious to understand how the commercial relationships worked, how the ships fixtures worked and so on.

I found that I was maybe more curious than the guys that were already working in the commercial department. I ended up discovering a lot of things that our company was doing wrong and I recommended we should make some changes, so that we could maintain and increase our business.

Curious and curiouser

Good traders are all curious. They want to understand how things work and how they can change and improve things to make their business better and more profitable.

Curiosity can even save your life.

During my learning period visiting ships, I have made several friends. One of the friends was a surveyor for SGS and we were often assigned to visit the same vessels. One day, we went down together into the ship's tanks, which were huge, maybe 3,000–4,000 cubic meters.

We climbed down a retractable ladder to check if the walls were clean – we call it a wall-wash test – and then when we were coming up, he told me to wait, saying: 'never be the first person to enter a tank or the last person to leave a tank'.

Once he had stayed behind in the tank to make some notes and calculations, and when he followed the others up the ladder, he realized someone had closed the hatch and he was trapped. Ships have their engines running 24 hours a day so no one could hear him shout.

At that point, he was expecting to die because they were planning to start pumping in the ethanol and filling the tank.

He was saved by the curiosity of a sailor who walked past and noticed that there was a tray of samples by the hatch but that no one was around.

The sailor took the initiative to open the hatch and my friend was rescued. Without the sailor's curiosity, he would have died. I think about that story all the time and it motivates me to keep demonstrating curiosity by asking questions and learning.

Ethanol shortage

Brazil had begun to export ethanol, but in 1996–97, we experienced a shortage of ethanol, which led to an inversion of the typical flows.

It got so bad that ethanol cars were stopping on the street due to short supply of the fuel. We immediately turned to imports to meet the shortages.

Then, even after the situation improved, we started to consider ethanol imports as an economic alternative that could at times compete on price with Brazilian domestic supplies.

I was the only trader in the company that focussed on imports, and it was a stressful role. People played a lot of tricky games in those days. You had to be very careful with competitive movements.

One of the regular trade flows was to load Russian ethanol in the Baltic Sea from either Kotka or Hamina in Finland, then to bring the cargo across the Atlantic to the U.S. Gulf, load additional U.S. ethanol, and then bring the whole blended cargo to Brazil.

The Russians called their ethanol 'technical grade' because it was synthetic ethanol produced from ethylene and was 92% ethanol by volume. This product was then blended with U.S. corn ethanol, which was 99% by volume, making a final blend at 95% by volume, which was the strength required to meet Brazilian specifications.

Of course, you can't just focus on the strength, you have to consider other impurities, but in general the blend – and the trading strategy – worked well.

Risk versus reward

These operations generally allowed our company to make money but sometimes we lost money because there were enormous possibilities that things could go wrong.

We were buying 120,000 tonnes per year from Russia, but there were still times that, when the train arrived at the Finnish border, the Russians would not allow the trains to proceed unless they would get an extra 'fee'. The Russians are always the Russians...

The extra fees could be anywhere up to $100,000, depending on the humour of the particular Russian. We would generally pay the 'toll' and then we'd look to find a solution with our trading partners, either to share the additional costs, or else if the Russians were asking $100,000, maybe we could bargain them down to $50,000.

Those were hard times because I would go to sleep expecting the ship to be loading and heading to the U.S. within a week, only to wake up and find the shipments were still held up because there were discussions on the border.

Sometimes we would meet our Russian counterparts to try to build the relationship. We would meet in Paris because they loved to come to Paris, but they usually just wanted to get drunk and chase girls so the meetings weren't particularly productive.

Another time, we lost a very significant sum of money because our product was changed in the shore tanks. Someone transferred in somebody else's material and we ended up spending a fortune on arbitration.

There were plenty of moments of high tension. I gained 30 kilos in weight and experienced a lot of hypertension. I managed to lose 25 of those kilos later, but I still suffer from the hypertension.

When you are in a stressful trading role like that, you think that there can't be anything worse. But in reality, it can be a lot more stressful if you don't have a job and you still have to pay your bills.

The one reassuring factor in all of this was that we were buying fuel-grade ethanol so the chances of having a problem with impurities were very slim.

Winning cargo

Of course, there were also times when everything went perfectly.

Perhaps my classic trade was when I ran the same strategy – Baltic loading of Russian material, U.S. blending, and then import to Brazil – and there were times when we made as much as $500,000 profit in one vessel.

That was really something: you don't make $500,000 every day so that was a very special deal.

On a typical cargo of 10,000 cubic meters of Russian and U.S. ethanol, we could normally make a maximum of $100,000.

For the bigger profits to happen, the logistics of the loading and blending all had to run smoothly, and then the vessel had to be at the right place at the right time. That used to happen when there was a severe lack of availability, which ensured that we could achieve a great price.

Perhaps we were lucky with the margins made on those cargoes but we definitely could not miss taking our chance, after we had persevered with pioneering the Baltic-U.S.-Brazil route, despite its many challenges.

Turning to alcohol

Apart from bringing in Russian and U.S. material, the other great import play for traders was the trade between South Africa and Brazil.

I'm sure you wouldn't be able to guess the ethanol content of the blend that was being imported from South Africa.

Remember that we were bringing in 92% ethanol from Russia and 99% from the U.S.? Well, the ethanol that people were bringing in from South Africa was between 10% and 12%.

That sounds crazy, but buyers in Brazil weren't really buying true ethanol from South Africa. They were really buying alcohol (not ethanol) so we didn't particularly care about the ethanol content.

What was important was the alcohol content, and that was around 95% because the material was largely composed of isopropanol (C3) or isobutanol (C4), which are just alcohols.

Believe it or not, there was a period when cars were running in Brazil on a blend that was 12% ethanol and 88% alcohol, whatever it was, usually isopropanol or isobutanol.

This product was blended with 90% gasoline upon its arrival in Brazil, so it was very difficult for the authorities to identify what type/grade of alcohol was blended with the gasoline. This flow worked incredibly well, especially in the northeast of Brazil.

After all, the price one would pay for alcohol was pretty much lower than the price one would pay for ethanol itself. If the ethanol price were $400 per cubic meter, one might be paying $180 for this kind of blend.

Traders dealing with South Africa made a fortune – an absolute fortune. Eventually, the Brazilian authorities discovered what was happening and they blocked the blend, but for one or two years, it was a massive trade flow.

Political drivers

Ethanol is a very political market. That means sometimes it's very unpractical in pure commercial terms, but that's just the way it is.

Trade tariffs and domestic mandates drive a lot of trading activity. One of the reasons why I have stayed so long in this market is because there are always new opportunities opening up, often because of political decisions.

Whenever the U.S. changes its tariff regime, for example, that creates either problems or opportunities for Brazilian ethanol because import duties are such an important variable in this market.

Similarly, there are moments when the Brazilian government introduces a 20% import duty on ethanol and that immediately kills all of the ethanol exports from the U.S. to Brazil.

Other political decisions by the Brazilian government also have a significant impact. A few years ago, the government mandated an increase in the ethanol blend into gasoline from 27% to 30%.

The issue was that the new mandate was introduced at the same time that prices in the sugar market were very high. Sugarcane is the raw material for both sugar and ethanol so producers preferred to focus on sugar, leading to ethanol shortages.

The ethanol market changes very quickly, which is something that of course motivates and challenges everyone that is active on it.

Reputational risk

When I ran the trading desks and the commercial side of all of those ethanol firms where I have worked, my core obligation was to guess what exactly the market would be doing five years ahead, and then lead and prepare the company to go through this forthcoming period.

That's obviously not an easy task but the length of my career shows that I enjoyed some success.

Trying to predict the direction of a market is a huge challenge. I think sometimes we can compare this with a ship sailing to a certain direction.

You are sailing your ship, but then you realize that maybe you didn't choose the optimal route to your destination so you have to correct the route. You can do that relatively easily on a ship. The necessary course correction may cause you to lose a day or two of travel time.

But when you talk about a commercial decision, sometimes there is no easy way to reverse out of a position, and that might lead to situations that can certainly cost you your job.

Trades can go well, like making $500,000 on a single vessel, but they can often go badly for various reasons, and there are times when you can lose almost the same amount.

Of course, it's important to make money, but the most important factor if you want to enjoy a long career in the market is to maintain your integrity.

I consider myself to be a professional and I will continue to stay professional and not try anything that crosses the line or is wrong.

A lot of people in this industry cheat. I've seen people cheating in front of me or climbing on my back to try to benefit themselves, but each time it just confirms to me that the best policy is to take care of your own business in the most correct way.

Thanks be to God; I have spent 40 years in the market and my reputation remains unquestionable. That's something I learnt from my father who never cheated in his life.

When my father died in a hospital in Santos, Brazil, in 1996, every possession he owned in the world was with him in that hospital bed. It was a difficult moment, but he kept his integrity and self-respect to the end.

People, and especially traders, will do a lot to get rich, but I learnt from my father how to do things correctly. I have had some success in this market, but even when I have had difficulties, I am proud that I never changed my behaviour.

Chapter 15

Trading ethanol as an index

After graduating from the university of Toronto, Douglas Dias joined Canadian bank CIBC as an analyst in 1998. He went on to work as a project manager for industrial giant GE, before leaving to undertake an MBA from Wilfrid Laurier University in Canada. In 2003, Douglas was appointed director of commodities for Canadian food business George Weston Limited. In 2008, Douglas moved to renewable fuel supplier Greenfield Global as the vice president for sales and market development, later becoming executive vice president and co-managing director, renewable energy.

I have always been a fan of looking at the commodity business through the lens of an index.

Before I even moved to Greenfield, in my previous job in the food industry, I had dabbled in creating a bakery cost index that would include wheat, vegetable oil, any sweeteners, natural gas and diesel for transportation.

Our bakery business was exposed to that basket of commodities, so I worked on representing all of those costs as a single index. Indexes can be a very effective communication tool for businesspeople who understand dollars but aren't necessarily specialists in commodities or futures.

Viewing commodities as a composite index became popular in the mid-2000s when index funds started to adopt what are now the S&P GSCI Index and the Bloomberg Commodities Index (BCOM). The GSCI and BCOM are very general commodity indexes, but indexes can also be useful for individual commodity firms to identify their specific economics.

Indexes aren't always perfect. There are a lot of nuances, like foreign exchange, basis risks and market dislocations, but indexes are a great way of capturing broad risks and telling a story.

When I came to Greenfield, I wanted to create an index that would sum up the economics of converting grains to ethanol.

One of the advantages of an index is that you can convert all the factors into common units. For my stakeholders, if they see corn is up 4 cents, gasoline is down 2 cents and ethanol is up 3 cents, how are they supposed to net that out when different commodities trade in different units, like bushels and gallons?

DOI: 10.4324/9781003359739-19

What my index was trying to capture was what we now call the 'crush margin'. That term was traditionally used for the profit to be made from crushing oilseeds into oils and meal, but it has also become a popular way to describe the profit from converting grain and corn into ethanol.

Secret crush

Back in the day, Greenfield was structured to have a grains team and a gasoline team. That was the typical structure for an ethanol and biofuels business, you would have an inputs team who were all experienced grains traders, and then you would have the output side who were trading with petroleum companies and who had more of a skillset in the gasoline mix.

Greenfield ended up hiring me because they had encountered some difficulties managing these correlated asset classes as though they were separate. I was hired to bring the two sides closer together, so I thought the best way to do that would be by focussing the whole team on the 'crush margin'.

We built our own internal crush index, which was a custom index using our own specific ratios of inputs and outputs. The index required a lot of tinkering, but we ultimately developed something that I could show to my Risk Committee.

We could also measure the volatility of the index, which is a key concern for the committee, because our financial forecasts are directly underpinned by how that index turns out over the course of a fiscal year.

Risk management techniques can put some boundaries around potential deviations from the typical volatility range, but ultimately an ethanol producer is exposed to that index.

Unlike investors in general commodity indexes, ethanol producers don't get in and out of the business: we have plants, we have employees and we are always running at full rate. The only way to get more capacity is if you build more capacity, and the only way to reduce capacity is if you make the decision to shutter a plant, which no management team would do willingly.

The game is that you are exposed to this index over time quarter after quarter after quarter. Management has to make sure that the index stays in an acceptable range.

Hedging the index

Once we had the index in place, we could go to potential trading counterparties to discuss risk management.

I spoke to a few firms and said, 'as an ethanol producer, I'm long this crush margin index so as a hedger, I would like to sell this index from time to time'.

I was asking to trade a structured product that would tie together the energy, which was our revenue side – ethanol – with the corn and natural gas, which was our cost side.

There were only a very small number of people who were willing to talk to me about the concept and an even smaller number of people who were willing to trade the index.

The trade was a better fit for a private company with some risk appetite because even if our counterparty's ultimate intention was to lay off all the risk, they wouldn't be able to do so instantly because in ethanol, for example, you only had three to six months of liquidity. Beyond that, the bid-ask would widen significantly.

These are the risk factors that you have to account for in structuring the product. My counterparty had to figure out what they would do if they couldn't lay off their risk in time and then something happened.

There was also a lot of spaghetti involved because I wanted to settle on a monthly calendar average but that was a challenge to map into futures because of all the different settlement periods.

In the end, Ilia Bouchouev's structured desk at Koch Supply & Trading was prepared to take the trade on. They had the appetite for risk as well as very advanced analytics.

The initial trade worked well, and so we kept experimenting and trying to get more sophisticated to track our risks more closely.

The first step was to create options on the crush margin. Buying and selling a simple index is fine, but there are times in the markets when margins take off to the upside and then you wish you hadn't put your hedge on in the first place because of the opportunity cost.

You might tell yourself it was a cashflow hedge; it all made sense, it's all right-way risk, but that still doesn't necessarily feel good.

Increasing sophistication

Options represented a great solution to this problem of 'hedger's remorse'.

I loved to use options to buy a floor on the index. The likelihood was that my options would end up out of the money, but they would allow us to ride the spot markets higher, while still giving us a put option that allowed for prudent risk management.

The progression from simple options trading was to create option 'collars'.

We began to trade structured products with knock-in and knock-out features, whereby an option came into existence or ceased to exist when the index reached a certain price level. A collar structure made sure that we hedged some of our risks without having unlimited opportunity cost.

As well as getting ever more sophisticated on the structuring side, we also experimented with different flavours of index.

We tried Chicago ethanol versus corn, New York gasoline versus corn. We tried flavours that included a natural gas leg, and flavours that accounted for co-products. When you make ethanol, you get animal feed co-products so you can calculate a ratio of your gross corn input versus your net corn, which is corn minus co-products.

Our increased sophistication came partly with time and partly thanks to the School of Hard Knocks. When you have to stand there and explain to the Risk Committee why you didn't get the benefit of a market move because of the various features you had in your hedging instrument, well, then you just put on the next layer and the next layer.

The longest trade we ever did was for 12 months but typically just to get tighter bid-ask spreads, we focussed on two or three quarters forwards.

That worked because most boards look at risk management within the budgetary year. You're telling a story to your financial stakeholders, your shareholders, your bankers and you ought to be able to explain any deviances from the story you told them at the beginning of the year.

Structural integrity

Given how complex some of our trading became, you might ask why we didn't just put on some simple corn versus ethanol hedges.

The answer is that back in 2009–10, we often didn't have any direct exposure to ethanol prices. That sounds strange for an ethanol producer, but back then the ethanol benchmarks from price reporting agencies like Argus, OPIS and Platts were still brand new.

Our buyers weren't comfortable signing a one-, two- or five-year offtake agreement linked to those benchmarks. They were concerned someone could game the index or that halfway through the supply agreement the index could cease to exist.

A lot of times, our buyers preferred deals based on the NYMEX RBOB gasoline price. They knew there was a basis risk to the actual ethanol price, but they felt 'well, at least both sides can hedge with gasoline if they want to'.

Eventually the liquidity in ethanol benchmarks was sufficient that everyone migrated in that direction, but we probably had three or four years where I had major supply agreements that sold ethanol on a gasoline basis.

The second disadvantage to just using ethanol is the issue of who is a natural buyer of forward ethanol? An ethanol producer is a natural forward seller but who is the natural buyer? Everyone on the buy side prefers to float because their strategy is to pass the ethanol price through to consumers at the pump.

Gasoline companies figure if they buy forward there is a risk they will be offside versus their competition. The ethanol market suffers from a lack of natural buyers and an abundance of sellers, which means that the term 'structure' is really priced for insurance rather than trading.

If you do want to hedge some volume you will always find a counterparty – a market maker who is willing to trade – but that's going to come at a pretty steep discount compared to if you have the balance sheet to wait and see what happens.

A bespoke solution generally matches better. We've seen this in the development of the ethanol market, and we will likely see it again in the development of new environmental markets like sustainable aviation fuel (SAF).

If anyone wants to hedge SAF, it will likely be through a structured product, at least for the initial phase of market development. That's largely because there are so many different production pathways. You can make SAF from vegetable oils, waste oils, animal fats or alcohol ethanol. You also have different conversion ratios depending on your plant.

You could say that there should be one price for SAF that clears the market in a given jurisdiction and that would be based on the marginal cost of getting the last gallon to the marketplace, but markets can be sloppy.

It would be hard for a bank to support a SAF project without substantiating the offtake agreements, and, as we saw in ethanol, it is tough to pitch an illiquid SAF price benchmark.

If someone in these new markets wants to either manage their risks or to have a bankable formula that project investors can wrap their heads around, then I would always recommend looking at an index.

Speculation versus accumulation

Greenfield's index trades were entirely for risk management purposes.

Over my career, I have gravitated to the opinion that speculating and managing risk are separate roles that should be held by separate people.

The mandate of risk management is to protect the shareholder by preserving the value of our assets and preserving our cash flows. The aim is to reduce the volatility of outcomes.

In contrast, the mandate of a speculative trader is to optimize value. We might think we have a great team and we're smarter than other people in the market because we have all this physical flow: 'hey, we're in these markets, we know more than other people, let's use that specialist knowledge to get in and out of trading positions'.

It's hard to ask the same person to do both speculative and risk management trading. How would you remunerate that person? Usually, speculative traders want some kind of profit share where they eat what they kill, but on the other side you are being paid for keeping the shareholders out of the penalty box.

Much as I like to think I can succeed at both styles of trading, I do think it requires different personalities or at least different motivations. It would just feel very incoherent to work through a bunch of topics in risk management for the different product sets we have, and then to walk out of that meeting and say, 'OK, let's start punching'.

There's also a very different philosophical underpinning to the different approaches. Most hedge trades that corporates undertake are more on a 'buy and hold' model.

We might hedge our corn supply, and then roll the hedge to every new supply agreement because our hedging is always related fairly directly to physical flow. But for most speculative traders if you don't exit positions within an hour then you're not a real trader.

Natural hedges

On the risk management side, I've become a big fan of natural hedges for the simple reason that I can only execute a financial hedge a maximum of 12 months into the future because that's where the futures liquidity typically resides.

But my shareholders don't just want 12 months of protection because they aren't planning to sell their assets any time soon. They would prefer five or ten years of protection and the only way to manage that duration is through natural hedges.

When I came to Greenfield, our debt was all in Canadian dollars, but our revenue was split between Canadian and U.S. dollars, as well as Euros. Sometimes we had windfall gains and sometimes we had windfall losses because of the mismatch between the cashflow statement and the balance sheet.

Arguably, the best thing I did to protect Greenfield's shareholders was to denominate our debt in the currencies of our cash flows. We took on some U.S. debt, some Euro debt, some Canadian debt so our cashflows matched our debt service.

That's kind of a perpetual hedge that would be anathema to someone with a pure punting mindset. A born speculative trader would never come to that solution because their mentality would be 'no, this is great because it provides more trading opportunities, I can trade the FX and international interest rates as well as commodities'.

Brokers and exchanges love that 'trade, trade, trade' mindset because it generates more fees, but as a shareholder, you would say 'let's put six to 12 months of financial hedges in place, but let's also try to structure our business geographically in places that make sense with corporate debt that makes sense to sustain our growth'.

Risk management would ideally put those natural hedges in place, and then constantly retune them at the prompt end because the risks in any environmental market are not static.

Chapter 16

Launching Brazilian biofuel credits

Plinio Nastari is the president of Datagro Ltda., Brazil´s leading consulting company on agricultural and bioenergy markets. Plinio has a master's and a doctorate in agricultural economics from Iowa State University, and taught as a professor of economics at the Fundação Getúlio Vargas in São Paulo from 1984 to 1999. He founded Datagro in 1984 and has since built it into a major consultancy with over 200 staff and with clients in more than 50 countries. Plinio has served as a member of Brazil's National Energy Commission, the Commission for the Re-examination of the Energy Matrix and the Interministerial Council on Sugar and Alcohol.

You could call me maybe the world's most reluctant trader. I only ever did one trade in my 40-year career in the bioenergy markets, and I have absolutely no plans to do another one.

But that one trade from a very reluctant trader opened the door for a new market that has already helped to decarbonize over 100 million tonnes of transport fuels.

I am an agricultural economist by training and inclination. It was in fact pure frustration that briefly turned me into a commodity trader, although I am very pleased with the result.

The story began in 2016 when I was invited onto the National Energy Policy Council, which is one of the three ministerial councils of the Brazilian government.

The council is composed of 11 ministers and one member of civil society, elected or appointed from a three-candidate list and chosen by the president. The mandate is for an initial two years, and I stayed for a second term, which is the maximum.

I found serving on the council to be a big burden to be frank because there were 11 government ministers on one side, and on the other side, just me representing the broader country. I was always trying to check whether the ministers were making the right decisions, and I felt the heavy weight on my shoulders of representing broader Brazilian society.

DOI: 10.4324/9781003359739-20

But we managed to do a lot of interesting things during this period and to make a lot of significant changes to the energy sector.

We were able to privatize part of state-owned energy firm Petrobras' refinery network; we modernized the whole gas sector; we invested in the electricity distribution system, which was a shambles and we set a schedule for increasing the mandate of biodiesel blending in Brazil.

Introducing RenovaBio

These were all real achievements but the policy where I was most heavily involved was the 2017 introduction of the Brazilian National Biofuel Policy (RenovaBio).

RenovaBio recognizes the strategic role of biofuels in the Brazilian energy matrix as well as their role in reducing greenhouse gas emissions from the fuel sector.

The goal of RenovaBio is to reduce the carbon intensity of the Brazilian transportation matrix by expanding the use of biofuels and creating a carbon credit market to offset emissions of greenhouse gases by fossil fuels, thereby contributing towards Brazil's Nationally Determined Contributions (NDCs) under the 2015 Paris Agreement.

Under the scheme, the Brazilian government establishes ten-year national decarbonization targets each year, which are converted into mandatory individual targets for fuel distributors. Fuel distributors that cannot meet their target have to buy decarbonization credits, known as CBIOs, from biofuel producers who have voluntarily certified their production and received CBIOs.

One CBIO is equivalent to one avoided tonne of CO2, so the most efficient producers of low-carbon biofuels generate more CBIOs per unit of production. Biofuels must also be produced in accordance with Brazilian environmental legislation and cannot come from deforested areas.

I came up with the idea of RenovaBio because the problem in the Brazilian biofuels industry has always been the lack of a long-term target that gives players in the industry and outside the industry a sense of where we are heading so that they could direct investments accordingly.

That lack of clarity was crazy to me because biofuels in Brazil is a really big deal indeed.

Target acquired

By the early 2020s, ethanol represented anywhere between 40 and 48% of Brazil's gasoline demand. No other country is anywhere close to that. Then in diesel, we are already substituting 12% and are in line to go to 15%. We are also starting a very ambitious plan to produce biogas, biomethane and biokerosene, also known as sustainable aviation fuel (SAF).

But before RenovaBio, no one in Brazil had any idea where all of this would end. Nobody had a reference point. My idea was, well, why don't we use the Paris Agreement as a reference to create decarbonization targets for energy transport in all areas: land, sea and air.

We could then use this decarbonization target to establish a system – a voluntary not a mandatory system – of certification that would allow us to measure the efficiency of each producer in terms of their carbon intensity, measured in grammes of CO2 per megajoule.

These certified producers would then generate decarbonization credits that they could sell. Fuel distributors selling fossil fuels would be obliged to buy offset credits to offset the polluting sales of fossil fuels.

From the conception of the idea until the signing up the law was just 11 months, so it was remarkably quick for such a major undertaking.

The secret to the rapid progress was that I ran all of the related industries through the proposal, and I asked them to send letters of support to the minister of mines and energy. He received 54 supportive letters from different sectors and when the proposal was sent to Congress, there was very little opposition because all of the related sectors already knew what was going on.

RenovaBio was approved in the lower house by 299 in favour and only nine against and was approved in the Senate by unanimous acclamation.

Initial discussions began in January 2017 and on 26 December, RenovaBio was signed into law. To make the CBIO system work, we had to also get a presidential decree creating the concept of environmental assets.

In Brazil, a law next needs to be regulated or detailed as regulation. The first decree regulating the law was signed by the president at my firm Datagro's conference in March 2018. Usually in Brazil, the president can only sign decrees at the palace, but he obtained the authorization to sign at our conference.

During the signing ceremony, the president asked me to sign the decree as well so I'm happy to say I have a copy at home of the decree signed by the president, by the minister of mines and energy, and by myself.

We spent the next two years working through the regulatory details and approving the surveyor companies that would carry out the certifications, then on 27 April 2020 the trading of CBIOs was finally authorized.

Trading reluctance

You can imagine how excited I was to see trading begin. And so you can imagine how disappointed I was when nothing actually happened.

There was no trade after the launch in the last few days of April, so we thought maybe the new month would see some activity, but then nothing happened in May either.

By the middle of June, I was getting very worried. I spoke to my two sons and said we have to do something. After all this work and everything that was done, nobody's trading CBIOs.

Eventually, I said, 'well, we can participate'. We wanted the market to get going and we were getting really anxious that nobody was kicking it off, so we decided to do it ourselves.

The legislation allowed for non-obligated parties to trade CBIOs. Anybody can buy decarbonization credits – investors, speculators, private individuals or companies – not just the fuel companies.

That's exactly what we did. We decided to offset the carbon emissions from our Datagro conferences in 2020, which was equivalent to around 100 CBIOs.

I called the trading company Sucden, who were an authorized intermediary and I asked them to go to the market and buy me 100 CBIOs. They traded on our behalf with Santander Bank, who was acting as an intermediary for Adecoagro.

We bought our CBIOs for 50 reais per tonne of CO2, which at the time was equivalent to around $10.

As I said, I was a very reluctant trader, but the market needed to see a trade go through.

Sure enough, after that things started to move. That first trade opened the doors and since then we have had traded and certified CBIOs equivalent to more than 100 million tonnes of CO2.

I never traded again; I just made that one purchase, and the rest is history. We publicized the deal all over the newspapers; we made a press release and gave the credit to Sucden, to Santander, to Adecoagro. We made a big noise about the deal.

I cannot say for sure that trade is what made the market happen but, after that first one, trading started to develop because people saw that it was possible.

Green future

I decided to dedicate my career to agricultural economics when I was still an undergraduate and for my doctorate, I developed an econometric model to simulate the behaviour of the sugar and ethanol industry in Brazil.

That's how I started my involvement with biofuels and sugar. When I returned to Brazil after my studies in the U.S., I struggled to find a job and that's when – basically, from the lack of any alternative – I launched Datagro as a consulting company.

Over the years, Datagro became successful and today we have over 200 employees working in eight offices, with clients in more than 50 countries. My only regret is that there is never enough time for all the things I want to do. I think 24 hours is too little and I wish that the day had more.

I have watched the ethanol industry in Brazil for more than 40 years now, and I have seen it almost die four or five times for different reasons. But I think now there is no reason for it to slip backwards: Brazilian biofuels have become very competitive, and they are also supported by strong legislation, like the blending mandate and rules that reward the use of sustainably produced biofuels.

RenovaBio has also helped to promote efficient use of sugarcane. One tonne of cane in energy terms can be equivalent to 1.2 barrels of oil, but traditionally the industry in Brazil used this energy inefficiently. RenovaBio incentivized greater efficiency and the use of all parts of energy cane.

We can see the results: we have already seen producers diversify from sugar to ethanol, then to bio-electricity, now to biogas and biomethane.

We're heading now towards 2G – second-generation ethanol – as well as the conversion of ethanol into SAF, the use of ethanol in sea transport, and the capture of biogenic CO2 to produce synthetic fuels like e-methanol. We are even seeing the growth of pelletized bagasse, which is being sent to Europe as a coal substitute.

All of this diversification was accelerated by RenovaBio because those producers that have become more efficient in energy and environmental terms are able to sell more CBIOs. They are incentivized to raise standards because a cubic metre of ethanol from Mill A is no longer worth the same as a cubic metre of ethanol from Mill B.

De-carbonizing progress

What is also encouraging is that CBIO prices are being set by the market rather than by the pen of a bureaucrat. Any efficiencies captured by the industry are transferred into price terms and that means that consumers are able to capture efficiencies as well.

By 2035, which is the longest dated target that I have seen, RenovaBio will have led to the decarbonization of 740 million tonnes of CO2, which is huge, equivalent to the annual emissions of France.

I remember being invited to a conference in Berlin in 2019. Brazil had already approved RenovaBio but the trading of CBIOs hadn't begun yet. Well, the German authorities opened the conference by saying they had established a ten-year target of reducing carbon emissions from transport by 9.2 million tonnes.

When it was my turn to speak, I explained that in the first year of RenovaBio, Brazil was planning to offset 14.5 million tonnes and in ten years we were planning to offset more than 700 million. Of course, everybody looked at me and said it wasn't possible.

I told the audience the rules were approved, and so I was very confident. Sure enough, between 2020 and 2023 Brazil has already offset 100 million tonnes. In the first 11 years of its existence, the leading electric car company

Tesla decarbonized 3.7 million tonnes. But Brazil already did more than 100 million and we're heading towards 740 million, all of which are certified!

Perhaps we can draw a lesson from my brief career as a trader, which is that if you want to see change, sometimes you have to make that change happen yourself.

Environmental markets need encouragement to develop. These markets aren't usually born fully developed and with great liquidity. Active trading is the best way of generating price signals, so firms or individuals need to take the initiative to get trading moving because the long-term benefits are incalculable.

Part IV

Trading biodiesel and feedstocks

Biodiesel is a renewable fuel produced mainly from vegetable oils, animal fats and waste oils such as used cooking oil (UCO).

Its environmental benefits include reducing lifecycle greenhouse gas emissions compared to petroleum diesel, decreasing reliance on fossil fuels, and aiding waste management through the repurposing of discarded oils.

The market for biodiesel has expanded globally as decarbonization targets and blending mandates have driven demand. Other related bio-products have also emerged, such as renewable diesel and sustainable aviation fuel (SAF).

Used cooking oil, palm oil, soy oil and animal fats are among the most common feedstocks of biodiesel and the other related products. Europe and the United States are the biggest import regions, while Asia and South America dominate the supply side.

Feedstock supply chains in those regions are closely tied to local agriculture and to waste collection systems, such as the one Dhimas Arif Wibowo developed for Indonesian UCO.

Once aggregated, these feedstocks are then traded internationally by market participants such as Neville Atterbury, Gaetano Lucisano and Filippo Basevi, who describe the complex international trading landscape for biofuels.

Traders highlight the critical role of logistics and the need for a detailed knowledge of both supplier and customer, given the complexity of this highly fragmented and rapidly evolving market.

DOI: 10.4324/9781003359739-21

Chapter 17

Biofuels

From arbitrage to assets

After graduating from the University of Cape Town, Neville Atterbury joined commodity trading house Masefield Group as a research analyst in 2009. He was subsequently appointed Masefield's assistant trader for European biofuels, based in Hamburg, Germany. Masefield's biofuel business was acquired by Ambrian Capital Plc and named Ambrian Energy, where Neville served as a biofuel trader and from 2014 as trading director. In 2018, he joined Rosneft Deutschland in Berlin as senior biofuel trader as part of Rosneft's team build-up and start of their own marketing activities in Germany. After teaching a few people at Rosneft to spell biofuels and highlighting the sector's profitability to them, he was promoted to head of a new renewables business unit in 2021. Neville returned to Hamburg, joining Ambrian Energy, which merged with its sister company HGM Energy in July 2023, initially serving as director and eventually as one of the managing directors. In 2025 he took on a new challenge, building an international commodity business, Ameron Energies, together with former colleagues and with the support of the Vollkammer family, owners of Ambrian Energy.

The early days of the biofuels market were a different kind of animal.

My classic trade happened in 2011 when I picked up the phone to one counterpart at an oil major and bought some biodiesel. I hung up and then two minutes later phoned another trader at a different oil major and sold them the same material for €75 per tonne more, back to back, in northern Europe.

And a few weeks later, I did the same thing again! All because of the perceived value of a piece of paper – an official sustainability certificate – a 'new' development in the world of biofuels.

That exact experience was obviously not likely to be repeated often. Trades that are both very simple and very profitable do not happen too often in the life of commodity traders.

After all, it was a different era back then. The biofuels market was still new and so fragmented that a lot of traders did not understand value across mandates or borders, and neither did the legislators.

DOI: 10.4324/9781003359739-22

Whenever new markets emerge, the margins usually start out very high for the first participants, but they typically get eroded relatively quickly as the information flow improves and as other traders enter the market.

That was definitely what happened with the biofuels market, and continues to do so around whatever is 'new'. And it feels like every year has been packed with a different kind of 'new' in the biofuels space.

Evolutionary process

Broadly though, like with all commodity markets, the biofuels market – and every sub-segment that developed, and keeps developing – has experienced phases of evolution.

The first is a high-margin and more opaque phase. In the case of biofuels, this was exacerbated by incentives to speed up adoption in an attempt to arrest climate change.

The second phase is one of maturity: as the market attracts more participants, it formalizes through mechanisms such as sustainability certification, liquidity improves and futures markets begin to develop.

The third phase is when the focus shifts from stand-alone trading to asset ownership and from processed biofuels to feedstocks origination.

One could argue that every different type of feedstock and biofuel have gone through or are going through similar patterns, although at varying speeds.

First, let's cover some dry stuff: the foundation of biofuels was laid by a 2003 EU Directive, mirrored by a similar U.S. Directive in 2004 shortly followed up by the U.S. Renewable Fuel Standard mandate starting from 2006.

Traded volumes exponentially increased in the run up to the April 2009 EU Renewable Energy Directive (RED) and amendments to the EU Fuel Quality Directive (FQD).

The legislative developments meant that the U.S. and EU markets progressively started to look for biofuels from all over the world that would help firms meet the new targets. This enabled producers and traders to bank enormous margins.

In short, poorly thought through legislation resulted in biodiesel facilities mushrooming in low-cost production areas like Argentina and Southeast Asia.

During that period, everyone was simply focussed on getting volumes of biodiesel into the final diesel blend. Firms just needed to get the 7% biodiesel into the blend, and they were prepared to pay up to make sure they could comply.

Blender's credit

A lot of traders took biodiesel from Argentina and Southeast Asia to the U.S., where they would drop a tiny volume of U.S. diesel into the tanks in order to qualify for the U.S. 'blender's credit', which was a tax credit from the U.S.

government that was supposed to promote the blending of biodiesel into the U.S. diesel pool.

But once the collection of the $1/gallon blenders credit had been triggered, a lot of firms would ship the same product across to Europe. This was an incredibly profitable trade. When the product first loaded, the material was 100% biodiesel or 'B100', but then after the minor blending in the U.S., it became 99% biodiesel or 'B99'.

Traders made substantial money on the difference between the purchase price of B100 in Argentina or Asia and the final sales price of B99 in Europe, more than allowing for the costs of shipping to the U.S. and subsequently on to Europe.

Allegedly one trader even bought himself a yacht with his bonus from this B99 trade, and named his yacht 'Splash and Dash' because that's kind of what happened: *splash* your biodiesel on arrival in the U.S., collecting the tax credit and *dash* off to the EU where most of the biodiesel demand was.

The B99 arbitrage trade was wide open for years, but eventually, the Europeans put an end to it by adding an anti-dumping duty on U.S. products, and eventually the U.S. finally converted its biofuels incentive scheme from a blender's credit to an eligible only producer's credit.

Paying for paper

The end of the B99 trade was followed by an era of increased maturity in the biofuels market and a shift in focus onto the actual emissions savings achieved by the products.

Biofuel futures markets started to emerge, and liquidity finally grew so that traders could hedge their exposure as well as trading the derivatives. You could manage price risk much better, which benefitted traders, but at the same time those crazy margins disappeared.

The golden days of high trading margins on vanilla trades were over and that also resulted in a decline in pure arbitrage trading, or at least unless you cheated!

Let me explain: the biofuels market in Europe was the pioneer of sustainability proofs or certificates, leading the way in being able to show where the product came from and how *green* it was in terms of its emissions make up.

These certificates developed over time, to where today you can see the volume of emissions from cultivation, transportation, processing, shipping, etc., and even have a correction factor for indirect land use change.

These foundational concepts in biofuels are only now being rolled out to other commodities in the EU, like coffee and cocoa.

In the early days, each company made up its own few sentences to fill in under the new contract clause, *the sustainability clause*, to indicate compliance with, for example, child labour laws, protecting bird life and orangutang habitats. This simple clause then developed into several pages over the years as multitudes of lawyers across the globe occupied themselves with refining it.

Nowadays, a firm technically just needs to state that its product is certified according to this or that standard that developed as legislation required, which should give buyers enough certainty of the product's credibility, although that does not exactly stop the lawyers from lawyering.

In Europe, this process is dominated by the German-based International Sustainability and Carbon Certificate (ISCC) scheme, of which Ambrian Energy was a founding member.

This is what enabled us to early on understand the value of these sustainability certificates, providing the background for my classic trade.

Although, before these certificates were digital and in an auditable ledger, they were just PDFs and anyone with a printer could fabricate them – and, boy, did they!

Asset pursuit

In that ten-year period from around 2005 to 2015, which I would call the emergence phase for biofuels, you could run a trading business without owning assets and you could make good money.

In my view, that is no longer possible on a sustainable basis going forward.

That's why you see big traders buying and investing in physical biofuel businesses along the chain. Many are moving from an asset-light business model to an asset-based model. In the U.K., Greenergy was a good example of this, owning significant biodiesel production, which greatly supported the wholesale fuel supply business. They were recently themselves acquired by the trading house Trafigura who was in pursuit of assets.

Ultimately, you need a critical mass of assets that you can build a *sustainable* trading business around; you need to fulfil some function in the market (other than printing documents).

Trading margins on vanilla trades, even for good strategies, are thin and there's only so many companies that have the spare cash to try and pursue those opportunities.

Capital allocation has become more of a topic for this industry too, because in the old days a trading firm could put down 2% capital and borrow the other 98% from a bank with relatively relaxed conditions. That won't happen today.

The bank will ask a trader to put down a lot more equity to fund the trade or strategy. Interest rates to fund trading activities are also no longer in the era of ZIRP (zero interest rate policy), which makes for it being a completely different game in terms of the economics of taking on trading positions. And then in diligent companies there is the company internal minimum rate of return to compete with.

Another way in which the pursuit of assets shows up is the way in which biofuel producers invested in ensuring their product's emissions savings are better than their competitors.

The Swedish ethanol producer Lantmännen grasped this early on and built a carbon dioxide (CO_2) capturing unit alongside their ethanol plant.

The captured CO_2 was liquefied and sold locally instead of being imported, and the ethanol sold from that facility commands a healthy premium, which resulted in an investment payback period of only a few years.

Other ethanol plants capture the CO_2 and provide it to nearby greenhouses with much the same effect.

Investments were initially slow to go into the production of another 'new' product, hydrotreated vegetable oil (HVO).

HVO is a clean-burning, diesel-like fuel produced by hydrotreating virgin and waste organic oils and fats, allowing it to directly replace fossil diesel in existing engines. While more expensive to produce than conventional biodiesel, it yields a high-quality, paraffinic diesel with superior performance.

Finnish refiner Neste initially sold HVO at a discount to diesel to incentivize people to try it. Even then, they had to be saved by a massive Finish government bailout, following very effective lobbying. But the tide eventually turned, and on average Neste enjoyed more than a decade of profit margins in excess of €500 per metric tonne.

Several others have since caught on, and many a refinery has converted their facilities to enable co-processing of bio feedstocks, to tap into the same margins.

This is resulting in overcapacity of HVO and co-processing units, and we have recently started to see several investment projects of this nature being cancelled. This is partly also due to the lack of viable feedstocks, which highlights the shift and focus to bio feedstocks, where the supply is increasingly scarce and expensive.

Go to waste

If you wanted to operate as a stand-alone physical trader today, the better trading margins are in waste and advanced feedstocks like used cooking oil (UCO) or cashew nut shell liquid, rather than in processed biofuels.

Margins in feedstocks are still very healthy indeed, but the trade-off is that you are dealing in much smaller volumes.

In the B99 days, a typical trade might be for 20,000 tonnes, while in the mid-2010s, you could be trading 5,000 tonnes and could still make that work. In feedstocks, you might be loading containers of used cooking oil out of Asia at no more than 25 tonnes each. This creates an incentive to bulk the waste, and increasingly larger feedstock clips are being shipped.

The margins are good, but it's a lot of work aggregating small volumes. There are guys making good money doing the hard work of collecting the difficult material from all around the world, then blending and filtering it before selling it to biofuel producers or crude oil refineries that blend it into their processes creating a co-processed diesel with a bio share already in it.

These refiners and larger trading houses typically prefer deals involving significant volumes, even if that implies smaller margins. There are definitely trading opportunities in feedstocks though, just as in the early days of biofuels.

The value is also moving from trading the bulk biofuel more to the niche feedstocks in part because current legislation is written to promote the use of genuine waste feedstocks.

That is making some of the niche feedstocks sought after and giving them a higher value because ultimately firms that are pushing into renewable diesel or sustainable aviation fuel (SAF) need to find more of these waste streams, especially since they are increasingly not allowed to rely on fuels that could also be considered food.

Renewed focus

I've been working in the biofuels markets from Germany for more than 17 years now and it's interesting to see how the government mandates have evolved over that time.

When I first started out, it was the big scramble just to find enough volumes of biofuels to meet the requirements for blending.

Today, several markets have evolved and it's not so much about simply meeting the blend target, it is more about how much CO2 is actually saved by what you put into the blend.

The drive to waste and advanced feedstocks is underpinned by a shift from volumetric blending to actual emissions savings targets: for example, rapeseed/canola oil biodiesel use results in a 60% emissions reduction relative to fossil diesel, compared with a 90% reduction for biodiesel made from used cooking oil.

Technically, you are 50% closer to achieving your target with used cooking oil biodiesel. This has resulted in a change for restaurants: from having to pay up to discard their used cooking oil to now being paid handsomely.

That increased focus on actual greenhouse gas intensity has moved the industry forward.

Firms can no longer just meet biodiesel quotas with palm oil or rapeseed/canola oil. Now they need to go and look for genuine waste products, like used cooking oil, that saves a lot more carbon versus raw materials like palm, soy or rapeseed/canola.

In effect, value has migrated upstream from processing and blending towards origination, aggregation and control of scarce waste streams.

Expect change

It's this constant evolution that makes the biofuels market so fascinating. We have been through a few transitions already and you wouldn't bet against further transition.

In one sense, the biofuels market is like all new commodity markets, which go through a phase of opacity and higher trading margins, to greater transparency and lower margins.

But in another sense, the biofuels market is uniquely different for participants because, besides solving supply and demand issues and managing price risk, you also need to respond to evolving government policy and often extreme intervention.

The implications of these different and ever-changing blending mandates and incentives have provided opportunities and challenges over the last couple of decades. Biofuels as an intersection between the agricultural and fossil fuel industries requires traders to stay on the forefront of this evolving market, whether it be in the area of sustainability, lobbying or anticipating changes to national mandates. That alertness creates the conditions for sustained success.

Eventually all biofuel markets are very likely to return to their roots as an agricultural policy tool, rather than being primarily driven by climate policy, which they are today. This will usher in yet another 'new' era.

One should not forget that biofuel mandates started in Europe as an indirect tax on consumers, enabling Brussels to hide from its budget the enormous subsidies traditionally given to farmers. The combatting of climate change narrative was incidental. The recent Swedish slashing of mandates should serve as a stark reminder of the market's origins.

Chapter 18

Finding the value of used cooking oil

Dhimas Arif Wibowo completed his police training in 2013, and in 2014 he started work as a police officer in Samarinda, the capital city of the Indonesian Province of East Kalimantan. Late in 2015, he began to collect used cooking oil (UCO) and in 2018 he founded his first company, PT Green Energi Utama, in Samarinda, East Kalimantan. In 2020, Mr. Dhimas expanded his company's operations to Malang, East Java. Over time, PT Green Energi Utama has become a significant player in the collection, storage, distribution and export of UCO for eventual processing into biodiesel.

I started out in the biofuels business originally because I was looking for a way to supplement my earnings as a policeman.

I collected used cooking oil (UCO) in jerrycans from private houses, restaurants and hotels in the evenings after work was finished.

I would store the UCO in the small house that I was renting. Then, when I had enough collected, I would sell whatever I had to local traders in order to make some extra money.

That was hard and physical work. Even now that I have had some success in this business, I can tell you that I still remember just how much a full jerrycan of UCO weighs.

At the time, of course, I didn't really know what UCO was used for. I just knew that it had a value and that collecting it would make me some extra money on top of my police officer's salary.

With time, I started to learn about how the UCO business works: how UCO can be processed and blended with diesel to improve the petroleum fuel's environmental profile. I also learnt that the real money in the UCO business is in selling to the export market.

After I finished my period of active duty in the police, I moved back to my home province. I started to really focus on my fledgling UCO business.

After a couple of years, I was still collecting material and selling to other firms, but I had managed to expand my operations and to take on staff to help me increase my activity.

DOI: 10.4324/9781003359739-23

I was able to grow the business from collecting around 500 litres of UCO per month in 2017 to around 20 metric tonnes per month.

Wedding bells

I married Mrs Puput Deni Iswara, my wife, in 2018, and together we founded our first company, PT Green Energi Utama.

I was still on the books of the police force, so Puput became the chief executive of our firm. In Indonesia, government employees are not supposed to be listed as executives of private companies.

When we started our firm, my dream was that one day we could become an independent UCO exporter.

We immediately began the work to get ourselves certified by the International Sustainability & Carbon Certification, which confirms that waste products are truly sustainable, traceable, climate-friendly and do not contribute to deforestation.

We also applied for all of the licenses we would need from the Indonesian government, and then we started talking to potential buyers from Europe and elsewhere.

The first deal

We met with a lot of buyers, but they all told us at first that we were just not big enough for them to do business with.

We had collected enough UCO to fill one shipping container, which is equivalent to 20 metric tonnes. Most of the buyers told us that they wouldn't accept just one container, and that they would only buy between 100 or 200 metric tonnes.

We asked them to give us a chance. Eventually, we found a buyer who told us, 'OK, we can take your single container, but we need you to increase your capacity and your quantity step by step'.

Of course, at that point we had zero experience of the export business, so we didn't know what was normal.

For instance, the most common business model in Indonesia is for a seller to ask for advance payment before delivering any goods. Advance payments are really common here and so we also asked our buyer to pay in advance.

Our buyer told us very firmly, 'Look, we don't really know your company and this is our first deal with you. Everyone has heard of us, but nobody has heard of you, so there's no way we can give you payment in advance'.

Now bear in mind that this one container was like our life. We had paid for all of the UCO in advance, and we were really stretched financially.

I looked at my wife and she looked at me, and we were just both hoping that our buyer would prove to be credible and trustworthy because we really needed that money.

We did get paid in the end, but the bank we were using to process the payment was quite slow as well. It took an additional week before the money finally reached our account.

What a relief.

We had been so worried about whether or not we would get paid for the container. That was a very nervous period waiting for the money to arrive.

Integrated supply

That first trade meant everything to us. It proved that we could compete in the export market and that we could succeed.

Once the payment for that first container finally arrived, we turned to each other and said, 'This export business seems to work, let's keep going'.

We started to increase our quantity. First, we expanded from one to two containers. We extended our operations into East Java in 2020, and from then on, we were able to supply up to ten containers per week.

It has been our good fortune to grow very quickly. From East Java, we moved into Central Java. We then opened up a hub in Balikpapan in Borneo, and we expanded our operations in other parts of the country.

We have developed quite a different business model compared to other exporters in Indonesia. Most Indonesian firms are pure traders: they buy from a supplier or multiple suppliers, and they look to sell to a foreign end-user or to another trader.

At least 90% of Indonesian exporters don't get their UCO directly from the point of origin – the restaurants, hotels and private houses – they rely on a network of third-party collectors.

Some of those suppliers are even individuals with 18–25 litre jerry cans, which is how I started out myself.

There are thousands of these suppliers in Indonesia. A small supplier can usually bring somewhere between one and five tonnes of UCO to your warehouse at a time, while a bigger supplier might be able to supply around 100–200 metric tonnes per month.

Our firm has a different business model. We decided to be fully integrated, so we collect our own supply: we employ our own drivers to pick up the UCO directly from the point of origin.

We operate a call centre, where our customer service agents take calls from restaurants and so on, who let us know once they have enough UCO. We then put together a schedule and we dispatch our drivers to collect the material.

We are obviously competing with all of the other potential collectors. Any given restaurant knows that there are a number of potential buyers who could come by and do a pick up any day of the week.

We have to work very hard to keep our suppliers at the point of origin loyal to us. We even started a loyalty card programme and then we also started offering to exchange UCO for other basic goods like rice or dairy products to make us more attractive to them.

Our approach is all about making the people at the point of origin feel comfortable with us. The big challenge for any UCO trader is to stabilize and guarantee supply.

We do whatever we can to get suppliers to sign longer-term contracts and to keep them loyal to us through special treatment, but ultimately, we know that it all comes down to price and payment terms.

Typically, at the point of origin, most are looking for 'cash and carry' – you pay them the cash and you can carry out the UCO. Some will accept an advance payment of maybe 30% or 50% before we pick up the material. But then, if another firm is paying more, even if it is just 100 rupiah (one U.S. cent) then some will not supply us, even if we have already made an advance payment.

We are dealing with more than 3,000 restaurants across Indonesia in 2024, and it's an intensive business to manage. There's a lot of drama in primary sourcing.

I have worked with some of these restaurants for nearly ten years, and others for less than a year. There are always new points of supply emerging.

If one restaurant closes, another swiftly opens. In Indonesia, many people, especially in the big cities, want to take it easy in the kitchen, so they tend to eat out a lot.

Fully connected

The barrier to entry in this industry is quite low if you only collect UCO, but not everyone can survive the challenges of managing logistics.

Indonesia has plenty of low-carbon feedstock, but you have to be comfortable potentially operating across 17,000 islands and dealing with various ethnic groups, languages and cultures.

I didn't set out to be an entrepreneur, and neither my wife nor myself had any significant business experience when we founded our firm.

I think it was our good fortune to start out as the smallest of small suppliers. Because we started from the ground up, we really truly understand how the UCO supply chain works.

We are the first exporter in Indonesia to operate a truly integrated system. Most exporters are working through other firms, whereas we oversee the UCO from the moment of pick up until the export cargo leaves the port.

We operate our own trucks, warehouses and even our own weighing bridge. With us, everything is connected.

Our integrated approach is great for margins, but it also means we have great traceability and transparency. On any given day or for any given cargo, we can track precisely where our UCO came from.

Next steps

As I said, our breakthrough trade was selling an export cargo to Europe, and Europe has consistently been the main destination for our UCO. More recently, we have started selling more to the U.S. and to Asian countries, like Japan, South Korea, Malaysia and Singapore.

Our export destinations are growing, but usually our Asian buyers are just processing our UCO into UCO methyl ester (UCOME) – a very pure biofuel – and then exporting the UCOME to Europe themselves.

It seems clear that the next step for us should be to produce UCOME ourselves in Indonesia. That might take some time, though, because the regulatory environment is not yet clear here and so the rules around processing UCO into UCOME are something of a grey zone.

There is still great upside for this business as long as we keep the same focus we have had up till now.

My family was not well-off and our circumstances were difficult, but I am a bit of a dreamer and I had a dream of creating a sustainable business that, ultimately, I can pass on to my children.

The philosophy behind this business is pretty simple. It's clear that not everyone is born with the same opportunities. The main thing that matters is that you show spirit and ambition.

If you start a business, you have to throw yourself into it with all of your feelings and all of your heart. Being an entrepreneur will cost your time and it will cost your sleep. You will sacrifice yourself and your energy.

I don't focus on the challenges; I focus on how we can achieve our goals and targets. I always tell my employees to think about what they can do for the company rather than what the company can do for them.

That's because if you put your heart into your work and you do your best for the company, then your reward will definitely come.

Chapter 19

Trading biofuel arbitrages

Gaetano Lucisano

After graduating from Italy's Politecnico di Torino with a master's degree in electrical engineering in 2006, Gaetano Lucisano initially worked as a project engineer. In 2008, he joined Italian energy giant ENI's refining and marketing division, initially as an oil supplier based in Rome, and then as a system trader and then a biodiesel trader, with both roles based in London. Gaetano left ENI in 2015 to join Petroineos Trading in London, where he set up the firm's biodiesel trading activities and was book leader for biodiesel. In 2023, Gaetano moved to Abu Dhabi to join ADNOC Global Trading as the firm's senior biofuels and feedstocks trader. Then in 2026, he was appointed as head of biofuels at Spanish energy firm Moeve, based in Madrid.

Biofuels is a unique commodity market. It's obviously much smaller than a classic commodity like crude oil, but at the same time, it is much more complex. It is precisely that complexity that makes biofuels so interesting to trade.

There are so many aspects that are changing every day and that you have to watch: as well as the usual supply/demand and transport economics that are typical of any commodity market, biofuels traders also need to be on top of changes in legislation, political sentiment and technical specifications.

Products like diesel or gasoline seem very vanilla by comparison. In those markets, you look at whether you can ship material to other regions economically or not, and you look at physical stock levels, and that's about it.

In contrast, in biofuels, there are so many different products and so many parameters to trade around. You have ethanol, biodiesel, renewable diesel, biomethane, sustainable aviation fuel (SAF), bio-tickets and the various feedstocks and blendstocks.

These are all different markets but they all interact with each other so a trader like myself really needs to stay up to date on everything, even the areas that aren't directly related to what I might be working on that particular day.

DOI: 10.4324/9781003359739-24

That complexity is the beauty of biofuels. It's really different from trading a classic fossil fuel: every single importing and exporting country has its own rules and every single product has its own peculiarities. You really need to understand the details and the specifics in order to make money.

Arb economics

One of the key discussions for biofuels traders on any given day is whether or not the 'arb' is open or closed. By that, we mean whether or not it is possible to arbitrage – to ship material profitably – between one region and another.

If the 'arb is open', then the price difference between two regions is greater than the cost of loading, transporting and delivering biofuels or feedstocks from one region to another. But if the 'arb is closed', then the price difference between regions is too narrow to cover transportation.

The importance of the arb makes understanding and managing freight and logistics costs are absolutely crucial tools for a biofuels trader. My trading style is to optimize constantly and I optimize the freight component just as much as I optimize my commodity trading.

If I have a strong command of logistics and I can transport my shipments more economically than other traders, then that can make the difference between the arb being open or closed for me.

Other traders might look at the economics and think that the arb is closed, but when I look holistically at the overall value of a cargo, then sometimes I can see a way to open the arb.

Biofuels is not like crude oil where you load the commodity in one port and then discharge it in a second port and that's the end of the trade. Instead, I'm always thinking about trading different parcels from different locations together on a single larger vessel.

My strategy is not to look at the economics of individual parcels in isolation. Instead, I try to look at the entire picture and to aggregate volumes. I try not to think about whether or not the arb is open or closed for an individual parcel, but whether or not a trade will work overall.

If I can place multiple different parcels together in the different tanks of the ship, then that allows me to charter a larger vessel, which brings my overall shipping costs down and helps me bring material profitably from Asia to Europe.

Shipping is still the key when it comes to biofuels trading so the first step when I am putting a trade together is to charter a vessel. Typically, we look at a 40,000–45,000 tonne ship because that larger size gives me the best economics.

Then I need to work on filling that vessel as economically as possible with material that I can place in a different region at a profit.

I can end up with as many as ten different types of biofuels onboard, all in segregated tanks. Some are my cargoes and others belong to third parties because, if I have a space to fill, I will always try to find other potential users. After all, making sure the ship is full brings down the overall shipping cost for my individual parcels.

Shopping run

Recently, I had a very successful trade, where I booked a larger vessel and we ended up calling at 12 different ports: we loaded at seven and discharged at five. That level of shipping complexity would be hard for most traditional commodity traders to imagine.

I had SAF, biodiesel and various feedstocks onboard. We started by loading 5,000 tonnes in one port in China, another 5,000 tonnes at a different port in China, then we went down to Taiwan for 7,000 tonnes, then across to Malaysia and Indonesia for another 5,000 tonnes each. I also picked up some 5,000 tonnes parcels along the way for a third party, and so on.

After we finished filling the vessel in north and southeast Asia, it sailed to Europe. We discharged part of the parcel in the Mediterranean and then the rest in northern Europe in Rotterdam and Amsterdam. The whole voyage took somewhere between 45 and 60 days.

I first developed this 'whole cargo' trading strategy when I was at Petroineos and I have developed it further now at ADNOC Trading. Essentially, it's a way of turning shipping into an integrated part of my trading activity.

The concept is to develop the flows like building blocks. No single parcel makes a difference in value, it's all about the value that you can generate from combining different parcels. Some traders look at 5,000 or 10,000 tonne parcels in isolation, but I look at them as part of the overall calculation within a ship of 40,000–45,000 tonnes.

I look at the ship and its storage plan: I might see that there are 15 or 20 tanks, so I start planning: 'I can put 2,000 tonnes in biodiesel in this tank, and then…' The goal is to maximize each product to fill the ship entirely.

I often rent out any remaining space to the oil majors or to European refiners. They tend to focus on moving small parcels, which works well for me, because helping them out by finding spare tanks for them brings down the cost of my freight. The optimization benefits the whole trade.

I aim to load different mixes of products based on demand at the time. Within the ship, they are all fully segregated parcels so we avoid any cross-contamination.

The plan is to always keep building on the original strategy and optimizing as much as possible. For example, I can discharge in the Mediterranean and then fill the same tanks up again with different material that I can take to northern Europe. That's what I would call secondary optimization and, again, it all adds value.

Mastering logistics

It's difficult to fill a vessel in Asia with just one type of biofuel or with material from just a single supplier. That means you need lots and lots of counterparties with different supply and demand profiles.

The complex nature of this strategy means that I need to be on top of my suppliers and receivers all the time to make sure that we avoid delays.

Sometimes a delay in one port can compromise the loading at the next one. I always need to be on top of the operational logistics, making sure that my suppliers are aware of the schedule and that we can build some flexibility into the various loading dates.

Sometimes I might have to give a discount or pay a premium so that I don't lose the trade through misaligned schedules.

I spend a lot of time talking to agents to make sure that we have the latest and the most precise information, for example, about which berth we will be assigned and so on.

If a trade like this is going to work the way I have planned, then I need to be always watching the operations, and that is something I have learnt from some difficult experiences.

You can have the best trade in the world on paper but if you start paying extra fees because the vessel is late to load or discharge, then you will lose money. You need to have everyone aligned to make sure that every aspect is smooth.

Operations are important in trading every physical commodity but even more so in biofuels. A really good operations team can give you an extra edge. For example, you might spot that it is cheaper to load ship-to-ship from a barge to the main vessel, rather than docking the vessel at the terminal.

Those kinds of tweaks reduce the cost across the whole supply chain. You might save $20,000 here and $30,000 there, and that makes shipping and logistics a source of value alongside the commodity trading itself.

Smooth handling of complex operations is frequently the difference between opening and closing the arb.

Experience tells

This is not the kind of trading strategy that you would be able to put together on your first day in the biofuel market.

You need to have a strong network and decent experience. Once you have been in the industry for a while, you start to understand who does what and which suppliers can be more flexible, which are more restrictive, which ports are more congested, which ones are easier.

You need to have this overview clear in your head in order to understand if you can pull the trade off or not.

You build that knowledge over time with experience. Sometimes we have to rearrange our plans because we might need to call at a port that is super congested and which might delay the vessel for ten days and ruin the whole trade.

This style of physical trading also requires patience: you need to build the trade over time. I might find an attractive 5,000 tonne parcel and then I start putting building blocks around that to improve the overall economics.

It's August now, and I just did my first trade now for 10,000 tonnes of material for loading in November. Right now, I don't have anything else lined up because it can take more than a month to fill in the whole picture. But I know that by the time November rolls around, I will have all the building blocks in place to have a full ship.

Growing liquidity

Liquidity on biodiesel has picked up each year throughout the 2020s. In 2015 or even maybe 2020, I don't think you would be able to do what I am doing today.

The market has been growing, and there are more biofuel flows out of Asia. This market used to be very Euro-centric, with occasional cargoes coming from South America and Indonesia, but now it is much more diversified and there are many more producers across North and Southeast Asia.

The growth in suppliers and locations provides many more opportunities to optimize, which wouldn't have been possible a few years ago.

When I joined the biofuel market, it was in very early stages of development. There was no market yet for SAF, for hydrotreated vegetable oil (HVO) or for renewable diesel. There was just trading in biodiesel and some feedstocks, and even those were often traded in containers and flexibags, whereas now you can load 40,000 tonnes of feedstock out of China alone.

The market has been evolving and with this evolution, new opportunities emerge. In the language of trading, as some arbs permanently shut, others open.

One thing that hasn't changed is that the market is always very volatile. That makes risk management very important, and we are lucky that over the past ten years or so, new futures contracts have emerged.

That has been very helpful. Everything in biofuels trades on a flat-price basis, like $1,000 per tonne etc., rather than on a floating index price, as in some other commodities.

That flat-price exposure means you need to hedge. You need to have something to protect the risk of prices collapsing or shooting up, depending on which way you are trading.

When I buy usually biodiesel, I always hedge with derivatives to reduce my price risk. But at the same time, I am confident that my economics are so strong that I should still make money when others are closer to breakeven.

Biodiesel in the blood

I started my career in the refining side of the business and I was involved in the conversion of ENI's Venice refinery into a bio-refinery.

That experience provided me with a ground-level understanding of biofuels, and so when I was in London trading diesel for ENI, the firm asked me to build out a biofuels desk from scratch.

I am a very curious person by nature so I asked a lot of questions and I developed my knowledge. I read a bit, but you can't read too much about biofuels, you just need to learn by doing, and that's how I gained experience.

Curiosity is an important attribute for any trader, but it is especially helpful in the biofuels market. If you are not a curious person then I can't see how you could do my job. Every day you need to learn as much as possible. You can't just stop at the first gate; you always have to try to understand the 'why' behind it.

Beyond curiosity, a biofuels trader also needs to have social skills. This is not a market where you trade on a screen and you never know who your counterparties are.

You have to deal with people directly and in person: this market would not suit someone who wants to sit in the office and trade uniform cargoes of diesel every day.

When you are trading diesel, it's also usually trading house to trading house. But this is totally different, you have to interact with different cultures and styles. A Chinese producer is totally different from a Spanish producer, for example.

Biofuel trading is very much done at a personal level and is based on relationships. A trader needs to build bridges so that he or she can do long-term business rather than just opportunistic trades.

In my line of work, I meet a lot of entrepreneurs because the biofuels industry was built by small companies. And when you are doing business with smaller firms, sometimes as a trader you might need to give away a little bit of money because you know that you need to develop the relationship.

If you don't fight for every last cent, then you know that hopefully that supplier will come back to you. It's all about understanding people. Sometimes you accept a lower profit today for a longer-term benefit.

In this market, it doesn't always pay to be greedy and try to make a quick buck like a normal trader. That approach doesn't work in biofuels; long term is the way to go.

Compare that with the usual trading that happens over the phone for gasoline or diesel. All of those counterparties are big trading firms and so you always try to maximize value, no matter what.

Looking forward

The intellectual challenge and the relationship side are two of the reasons why I really like biofuels. As a trader, you have to do your own business development: you are always looking for new opportunities and new suppliers because it's not a mature market.

You are trading but you are also exploring other different ways of making a profit, such as through origination or through operations.

Clearly, there are ups and downs, but the market has got to a point where the growth is there and it looks like it is here to stay.

Of course, the prospects vary from product to product. Maybe biodiesel doesn't have as much growth ahead compared with the others, but overall biofuels are still the most obvious way to decarbonize transport.

The rate of adoption might slow because of geopolitics or a weak global economy, but it remains clear that, if the world wants to decarbonize, then biofuels are the cheapest way.

I believe that low-carbon fuels are the future. I am bullish about the prospects for this market over the next 10–20 years. Maybe in the future there will be more biofuel traders than pure diesel traders.

Chapter 20

Finding value in feedstocks

Filippo Basevi joined his family's firm Victoria in 1993 in Genoa, Italy. He served as head of soft commodities before moving in 2009 to become head of the biofuels and waste-based feedstocks desk. Between 2009 and 2013, Filippo was also chief commercial officer of the Dutch trading company PFP Nederland BV, which traded biofuels and biomass from Rotterdam. He left Victoria in 2016 to move to the United States where he founded Mattico International in Florida to procure, originate and trade in biofuels and their feedstocks. Between 2020 and 2022, Mattico partnered with Iberia Bioenergy America Corp., where Filippo served as managing partner. Mattico is currently expanding into new areas like sustainable fuels for the aviation and marine industries.

It was 1992 and I was in the middle of my time at university when my mother called me. My father had suffered a serious health issue, and so she told me, 'you need to go to the office now and take your dad's place'.

Of course, I left my business and economics college and, at maybe 21 years of age, I started out in the markets. I joined our family commodities firm, which my grandfather had founded in 1954 in Genoa, Italy to trade and broker raw materials.

Luckily, my grandfather was still around to teach me about the basics of the international trade and about commodity payment terms, logistics, how letters of credit worked, and so on. I was very young so you can imagine what a steep learning curve it was.

Two years later, my father had partially recovered, and he came back to the office. My first thought was 'great, now I can go back and finish college' but by then I was already too involved in the business so I thought I would delay my studies a little bit longer.

Here I am now, more than a few decades later, and I never did finish college. But I would say I learnt a lot more by starting work so early than I ever could have learnt in the classroom. You have to learn fast when you are on the ground, otherwise the competition will leave you behind.

DOI: 10.4324/9781003359739-25

This career is not for everyone, but, given my family background, commodities were already in my blood. When I was just a child, I remember my grandfather telling me stories about commodities, and even then, I was fascinated by this world.

I spent the next 25 years working in Genoa in various capacities, ending as head of the biofuels and feedstock desk, before in 2016 I moved with my family to Miami, Florida to develop a new biofuels and feedstocks business. My firm Mattico has a special focus on the U.S. market but I don't neglect the client portfolio that I built up over many years in Europe.

Sourcing supply

My core business is the origination, procurement and the sale of biofuels and of the waste-based feedstocks that are used to produce renewable diesel, biodiesel and sustainable aviation and marine fuel.

Since I stepped into this business in 1993, I have worked with most of the major biodiesel and renewable diesel plants in Europe and the U.S. I have dealt with pretty much every form of biodiesel, including used cooking oil methyl ester (UCOME), palm oil mill effluent methyl ester (POMEME), soap stock methyl ester (SSME), soybean methyl ester (SME) and tallow methyl ester (TME). I've also handled dry bulk cargo material for the biomass and biogas industry as well as glycerine for different industrial applications.

I must have done hundreds of deals during my career, but the best trade that I ever made was spotting the growth of the biofuels market and positioning our firm to take advantage.

When I started working with vegetable oils, around 2000, biofuels were very rare. There were just a few U.S. and European plants and a few pilot plants in Asia.

All the vegetable oils that I was moving in those days were for food consumption, like selling crude palm oil cargoes to Nutella producer Ferrero, for example.

When the biodiesel market started to get going, my experience moving crude palm oil cargoes gave me a natural opportunity.

I expanded the business to place crude palm oil for biodiesel production and electricity generation. At that time, there were co-generation power plants in Europe that would burn palm oil for power generation.

It was 2005 when I introduced Italy's largest green energy producer to one of the largest palm oil collectors and shippers in Malaysia. I put together a deal whereby the Italian group would take 20,000 tonnes of crude palm oil every month to produce power at their plant in the north of Italy.

That deal was a sort of milestone for me because, at the moment, the industrial palm oil market for energy production was quite new and there were just a few buyers in the world who were able to commit to such a large volume every month.

I was probably the only person who could have put that deal together because I had the contacts in Asia as well as a strong reputation in Italy, in part because my family's firm was well known and trusted. That relationship lasted for a few years and it worked out very well.

Trade in crude palm oil was successful for a while, but the issue of sustainability and deforestation soon became apparent and the product was all but banned in many countries.

I needed to reorient the business, and this time I focused on the biodiesel markets – I brought the first palm methyl ester (PME) cargo into Genoa port in the Mediterranean – and, in particular, on the so-called waste products, like UCO, animal fats and acid oils.

This turned out to be an inspired move: there is currently a great demand for bio-feedstocks from Europe and the United States and, despite the recent tariffs, the market is only going in one direction.

The U.S. market is growing so fast because the processing plants are huge in terms of their consumption of feedstocks. The majority of existing U.S. fossil fuel plants will eventually be converted into renewable facilities so demand will increase substantially.

Obviously, not all of these plants have completed the transition, but as more and more start showing up in the market, we can expect to see substantial demand.

Managing country risk

The U.S. clearly represents a giant opportunity, but I had another reminder recently that you have to be nimble in this market, which is so dependent on political will.

In early 2025, I was putting together substantial deals between South American tallow collectors and U.S. importers. I had been moving a lot of feedstock from South to North America, and the trades had all worked well.

But then in July 2025, U.S. President Donald Trump announced tariffs of 50% on Brazilian imports, with the measures officially taking effect in August 2025.

Of course, with a 50% surcharge, Brazilian material was no longer going to be attractive in the U.S. That flow stopped from one day to the next, so I had to stop and say to myself, 'OK, let's figure out how to navigate this' because it wasn't clear what was going to happen to that business.

My counterparts in Brazil were expecting to sell to the U.S., but because of the additional tariffs that was out of the window. I had to quickly figure out where I could re-route the material. The obvious opportunities for me were other countries like Canada or Europe.

I made some calls and got deals done. Then, even better, I found clients in Europe who were looking for a shipment of Canadian renewable diesel. Now, I could do two trades: Brazil to Canada with the raw material and then Canada to Europe with the finished product.

What started out from being a big problem to me – the U.S. situation – turned into a significant opportunity.

It's a question of having the right mentality and seeing trading opportunities in the midst of what might at first appear to be a crisis.

Being prepared to handle different flows and different materials at the drop of a hat is part of the nature of this business. The biofuel markets are so politically driven that there are often changes in regulations, tariffs and duties, specifications and so on.

You always have to know how to adjust, and you have to have a wide enough network of contacts that you can make some calls and find alternative deals.

Market development

Most of my deals are 'spot', which is to say for single cargoes, rather than for multiple cargoes over a longer term. I think perhaps because the market is so unstable a lot of people on both sides prefer to wait and see what will happen next, rather than locking in deals too far ahead.

I am seeing an upturn in interest in longer term deals, though, and I think this reflects the growing importance of big oil companies in the market.

Traders are happy to go to the market at the last minute and look for a spot parcel that is preferably distressed and preferably cheap.

Oil companies don't tend to operate like that. They need to plan ahead because their main job is to produce fuels. Trading fuels or raw materials and buying at the best price may generate additional profit, but their first duty is to maintain the fuel supply. They cannot risk facing a shortage of products or raw materials.

When we set a long-term agreement, we try to fix the volume, quality, terms and conditions, but not the price. Instead, we link the price to an index, such as biofuel prices published by Argus Media, or agree to negotiate a fixed price each time before shipment.

The greatest opportunities are likely to be in sustainable aviation fuels (SAF) and decarbonized marine fuels.

SAF is becoming increasingly attractive as more airlines are conducting experiments. The market for renewable marine fuels will also be huge. It just won't be as simple as everyone thinks.

Many people are under the impression that ship engines are very robust and can burn anything, any kind of waste product from anywhere, unlike the very sensitive jet engines that power airplanes.

As many companies are now discovering, this is not the case. Shipping companies apply very strict parameters in terms of sulphur, phosphorus and metals.

The challenge is to find environmentally friendly ingredients that can be successfully blended with on-board oil, allowing ships to run partly on renewable fuel.

Looking forward

Shifting from vegetable oils to biofuels and feedstocks was absolutely the correct strategy, as recent years have proved. Making energy products from waste feedstocks is great for the environment and has also proved to be a very good business.

The new focus on SAF and renewable marine fuel, as well as the growing use of renewables in land transport, means that this will be a huge market.

My job is already non-stop, and over the next few years it is only going to get more intense.

These markets are not for everyone because you have no free time, no real holidays. There's no Christmas and New Year for me. Every time I wake up in the morning, whether it's 5 a.m. or 7 a.m., the first thing I do after my eyes can focus is to check my email.

When I was first dating my wife, I warned her that, 'if you see me checking emails in the middle of the night or when we are travelling or at the beach, don't worry because that's part of my life'.

I have customers and suppliers all over the world in every time zone and with totally different holidays so I can never stop. There's always something going on: either an opportunity or an issue that needs a solution.

I love to travel and to meet people in person and to get to know their organizations. If you know how to manage meetings, even informal meetings, and how to behave properly around other people, then you will find it's a winning combination.

The key is to make the trip, present yourself properly, be well dressed and have good manners. That seems normal and obvious to me, but it is not so common nowadays. A lot of people fail to display the appropriate professionalism and humility and so it's hard for them to succeed in this market.

Some European people, perhaps for historical reasons, seem to think that they are impressive just because they come from Europe. But business doesn't work like that. Times have changed, and if anything, it should be Asians coming to Europe full of confidence.

Just having the right personal characteristics puts you already a step ahead in business. Whether I am in Europe, Asia or South America, I try to have the same approach: my counterparts can rely on me 100%.

Sometimes when I am working with big corporations, I might be chasing a person for a decision and then I get a message that they might be delayed in answering because they are travelling.

I just think 'wow, what does that even mean?' I am always travelling myself, but that's what technology is for. When I travel, I make sure I have my phone with me, and I check my emails every day and night.

Perhaps it is these attitudes that separate people who want to build their business and are responsible for their own profits and losses from those who just want to show up and get paid.

I myself know where I stand: I love this business, but it's not just my job, it's my life.

Part V

Trading voluntary carbon schemes

The voluntary carbon market developed out of a desire by private companies and organizations to offset their greenhouse gas emissions in the absence of, or in addition to, any regulatory requirements.

Unlike compliance markets, which are created by governments and require specific entities to hold or surrender emission allowances, voluntary carbon markets operate outside of government control. Quality standards for voluntary carbon are set by individual registries, by broad industry consensus or by global initiatives such as the airline carbon offset scheme designed by the International Civil Aviation Organization (ICAO).

Occasional scandals in the sector have led to a growing interest in greater oversight, with Egypt's mixed regulatory regime seen as a potential model by some (Chapter 22).

Voluntary carbon offsets are generated by different types of projects, such as reforestation, renewable energy, cookstove provision or methane capture.

Unlike the mandatory carbon market, there is no single price for voluntary carbon offsets. Prices can vary dramatically according to the supply and demand for different types of projects at any given time, creating both risks and opportunities for traders.

Linkages are sometimes permitted between the voluntary and mandatory markets. In these cases, voluntary carbon credits can be used to offset some compliance requirements or carbon taxes.

These linkages generate firm demand for voluntary offsets as well as providing a price floor, but traders also need to be cautious because the rules can change and any such linkages may be swiftly terminated.

DOI: 10.4324/9781003359739-26

Chapter 21

Trading market structure

A Swiss national, Alfred Evans holds a doctorate in law from Columbia University, a diploma in Russian from Tver State University and a master's degree in international finance in mathematics from the University of Amsterdam. He started his career with the U.S. EPA, then with Clifford Chance, joined agricultural trader Cargill in 1996 in their structured trade finance division, before moving to GE Power Systems in 2000. In 2003, he joined agricultural trader Bunge, where he held a series of senior positions and worked in Geneva, Moscow and London. Alfred is currently the CEO of Carbon X Tons, a start-up putting the global carbon market on blockchain a firm he co-founded in 2023. Alfred lectured at the University of Geneva on valuing ecosystem services in natural resource trading.

The most exciting trades for me are when you can profitably demonstrate your understanding of market design at a granular level.

The fun part for me when I was trading carbon was immersing myself in the theory of the emissions markets and then being able to turn that knowledge into actual, rewarding trades.

Maybe I'm more risk averse than the average trader, but I'm not interested in just flipping a coin and hoping that I am short Brent crude oil when the market crashes. My competitive advantage as a trader was always that I was prepared to go deep and really try to figure out the fundamental drivers of the market that translated into trading opportunities.

I began thinking like a lawyer and considering the theoretical and legal underpinnings of the market and then I looked to translate that knowledge into the real world.

As a result, there were times when I spotted an opportunity that wouldn't have made sense to a pure opportunistic trader, but which made complete sense if you focussed on how carbon markets are designed.

We always treated carbon as a commodity. But I quickly realized that carbon is an unusual commodity, in that the markets create demand, rather than responding to consumer buying. As a result, market design and market

DOI: 10.4324/9781003359739-27

structure has a disproportionate effect on prices and trading strategies in carbon, much more than it does in any other commodity.

My best trading ideas came from nothing more than taking a lawyerly view of market structure and from my understanding of the way that different elements of the carbon market can interact with each other.

Fever pitch

I kind of fell into the carbon markets by accident. I was working at the agricultural trader Bunge in 2006 when they acquired a stake in a carbon development business in Brazil. At the time, I was looking to move back to Geneva from running Bunge's operations in Russia and so my bosses said to me, 'hey, we have this new business over here. Please take a look at it'.

Throughout my career, I've always been 'Mr Figure This Out For Us'. I was the guy that got handed the new projects, especially when they are both new and complicated. Probably the only thing that connects the disparate experiences that I've had in my career is that people have turned to me when they need someone who can find solutions in novel situations and then execute.

Bunge had some idea about starting an investment fund that could finance carbon offset projects. I went out on a roadshow to see investors, but the concept of a carbon development fund soon evolved instead into us launching a pure carbon trading fund.

We went to the U.S. and did a roadshow there to some asset managers who knew commodities and carbon. We thought we would try out our schtick first in the U.S. and then, once we had our pitch down pat, we could take it to Europe where there were mature carbon markets and where we had a better chance of actually raising some money.

But of course, we ended up raising four times more money in the U.S. than we had targeted for the whole fund before we even got back to Europe. Carbon markets were hot in 2006 and we had an incredible story.

Our pitch to investors was that Bunge are going to co-invest with you and we are going to give you the best risk-adjusted returns because, as a large commodity company, we can arbitrage between pure trading and physical project credits.

For most firms, it was incredibly hard to price or develop projects that deliver carbon credits because there's so much project risk, quality risk and credit risk involved. But those are all elements that Bunge understood well because we had agriculture and energy operations all over the world, which gave us access to a supply chain of potential carbon credits that other people didn't have.

After all, if you want to develop carbon credits from a palm oil plantation in Colombia, do you want to work with a bunch of bankers sitting in Paris or do you want your partner to be the company that buys all of the palm oil in the project?

We raised more money than expected, and I ended up as the chief investment officer of probably the largest carbon trading fund at the time. And I'm happy to say that unlike many of the other early carbon funds we actually made money for our investors.

Project focus

One of our core investment beliefs was that the lowest cost way to access carbon was through project credits or offsets. These are projects where somebody somewhere did something to avoid carbon that would have ended up in the atmosphere under a business-as-usual scenario.

Let's say you capture the methane from a landfill in India and you are given carbon credits as a result that you can sell to somebody in another market who at the time maybe finds that it is more economic to buy credits rather than to reduce their own emissions.

At an economic model level, project credits make sense because they drive environmental financing to where emission reductions are cheapest. From an environmental point of view, it doesn't matter where the emissions reductions happen, it's just important that you have overall reductions. Achieving reductions where it is cheapest to do so is a key feature of efficient markets.

The other type of carbon market is a permit market, like the European Union's Emissions Trading Scheme (EU ETS), where the permits are issued by governments.

These markets exist in every major economy (including the United States) and put a price on more than 30% of global emissions. In those markets, a country or region has taken its carbon budget and assigned it to certain sectors of the economy. When you buy credits in a permit market, you are taking a tonne of carbon out of the market that would otherwise get used up.

From its launch in 2005, the ETS became the most important permit market. And as part of the Kyoto Protocol, the European Union said that if their companies couldn't access enough permits from the permit market, then they would be allowed to use offset credits derived from the project market, which was overseen by the United Nations (U.N.) through its clean development mechanism (CDM).

That decision created an interlinking mechanism between the two market types: European permits and U.N.-accredited projects.

Given that link, carbon in those two markets should be fungible from a pure trading perspective, right? Permits and credits should have been trading at the same price because that interlinking mechanism makes them functionally the same thing.

But when we looked at the market in 2006 and 2007, there was a huge difference in prices between European carbon and the project credits that were theoretically eligible for the European market. This anomaly didn't seem to bother a lot of traders. That was partly because most traders were focussed on one side of the market or the other.

The people who were developing CDM projects were focussed more on the investment side and how to develop projects and create credits rather than really trading them. Meanwhile, the folk in the permit market were generally at big power companies. These were huge, regulated entities that were enjoying huge windfall gains from the free emissions credits they had been given by their governments, and so they were just enjoying the boost to their bottom line rather than watching the CDM.

Magic moments

When we looked across the two markets from a trading and commodity point of view, we asked ourselves what is the true swap value between these two assets, given that the credits being created under the U.N. protocol are theoretically eligible for the EU market?

Our insight was that the only reason the two assets weren't trading at the same price was bureaucracy. The European permits were issued in registries controlled by the European Union and the project credits were issued by the U.N. and were held in U.N. registries.

The magic moment when prices would converge would come only when the European registries and the U.N. registries were linked together, allowing firms to actually move project credits to their EU account and then use them for compliance purposes.

Our response was to put on a huge position where we went long project credits because they were 10 euros cheaper and we went short European allowances.

The bet we were taking was a huge relative value trade. We were betting that the bureaucrats – under pressure from utilities who wanted to use their project credits for compliance in the EU – would eventually get their act together and link the registries in time before the compliance periods.

We felt we had a solid understanding both of how the regulatory processes worked and the technology of how the registries operated. Our fundamental belief was that the E.U. was not going to let regulated entities get caught in a squeeze where they were unable to use the credits they had bought under the U.N. CDM.

With the view that the anomaly was going to get fixed, we knew that the moment it was fixed, the two markets would move toward price convergence. At that point, the two certificates would become the same product, and the 10 euro price spread would collapse to almost nothing.

The magic moment for project credits would be the time when they would become eligible to be used in a regulated market.

As that moment edged closer, the market responded. The price relationship of credits and permits shifted every time there was an official update or one of the registries announced that it had done some beta testing or so on.

We had put on a huge position early on and we sat on it for two years. The price convergence developed step by step and slowly, but by March 2009 the price spread between the two markets had moved from 10 euros to virtually zero. At that point, we cashed in both legs of the trade and made a lot of money for our investors.

Do your homework

I guarantee you that if there were 100 people trading carbon in Europe at that point, then maybe two of us had actually read the Kyoto Protocol and the implementation documentation and the EU ETS legislation, and were following the committee drafts of the amendments that actually determined how the market operated.

My background as an environmental and commodities lawyer was one reason that we had a trading advantage. We knew how the market worked behind the scenes whereas other people just saw the daily moves and were looking at connections to other commodities like coal and power.

We had all sat on big commodity trading floors and we thought of carbon as a commodity, another input in industrial supply chains. That's why we looked for the kind of trades a typical commodity trader would consider, like relative value trades or time swaps.

Our relative value trade between the European permits and the CDM project credits paid off enormously.

Our investors wanted to see a fund that gave them a better risk-adjusted return on the price of carbon. We ended up outperforming the market by about 70% but we tried to stay under the radar as much as possible, deploying bespoke carbon finance structures using trading finance.

Our goal was to have nobody know what we were doing and to avoid as much noise around the fund as possible. Any market reputation we enjoyed was around the fact that because of the Bunge industrial footprint we were able to develop quality projects in places where other people had difficulty operating.

I don't think that any of our relative value trades got a lot of attention in the market at the time. You couldn't just look at a screen and see what we were doing, and we obviously had no interest in telling anybody how we were trading.

Traders look forward to taking a risk and having it work out. But at a broader level, this trade gave me a lot of intellectual satisfaction. The theoretical knowledge I had acquired about what an economist's model of an environmental market might look like was suddenly translated into an exciting market.

Market design is so crucial for environmental markets. You need to think of them as commodities but at the same time you need some additional skills and technical awareness of market structure that impact price movements. Just moving somebody from the coal desk to the carbon desk isn't as likely a path to success compared with our approach of building deep market knowledge.

Carbon 2.0

In the end, so many project credits were delivered into the European ETS that prices fell sharply, while questions also emerged over the quality of some of the CDM projects. From 2013 onwards, the European Union stopped allowing CDM permits to be delivered into the ETS.

Prices for carbon crashed, and the markets went into temporary hibernation. This really marked the end of the first phase of carbon trading. For a few years, no one wanted to talk about carbon projects. You could not get a job if you mentioned carbon and we scrupulously scrubbed all references to carbon from our resumes.

It probably took until 2020 before people started wanting to talk about carbon again. I started getting approached by people who knew I knew carbon, but my first reaction was 'I don't want to talk about carbon because I want to work!'

For a lot of those folk, carbon markets 2.0 were a shiny new thing, but some of us had already been at it for 20 years and so we slowly got pulled back in. The one fact that has emerged after decades of these environmental markets is that, out of all climate policies attempted, the only thing that actually brings down emissions is putting a price on carbon.

I guess that is the nature of new markets everywhere. It might be gas markets in the late 1980s and early 1990s or Russian equities or crypto or whatever, but if you look at any new asset class, they follow the same trajectory: prices driven by nothing related to the real world, then a massive crash and then a period where they discover genuine price fundamentals rather than hype.

If you look at a ten-year time series for virtually any new market, you always see a euphoric rise, a major crash and finally a reaction to real fundamental drivers.

Carbon has had a hiatus where nobody wanted to talk about it and the markets were bad, but in the meantime the markets were discovering their true fundamentals. In the background the regulated emissions trading regimes became embedded in corporate planning and spread across the world with active markets in China, Korea, the EU, U.K., Canada and a number of U.S. states.

The market is fundamentally different in that very few project credits are eligible for use in regulated emission trading systems. Instead, the price signal driving emission reduction projects only comes from voluntary buying for net-zero offsetting targets. This fragmentation between different kinds of carbon credits repeatedly thwarts policymakers' shared goals of scaling carbon markets.

And so, here I am again, back working in the carbon markets, or maybe now we are in carbon markets, version 2.0.

Chapter 22

Trading onshore Africa

Omar El Nemr studied mechanical engineering at Italy's Politecnico di Torino before returning to his native Egypt, where he joined investment management group ENARA at its headquarters in Cairo in 2020. Omar initially served as a business development officer focussing on green hydrogen, smart meters, PV module manufacturing and energy storage, before being appointed ENARA's lead carbon project developer in 2022. Between late 2022 and early 2023, Omar served as head of project development for Libra Carbon, Egypt's first emissions reduction financing platform, a joint venture between ENARA, the Egyptian Stock Exchange and the Agricultural Bank of Egypt. In 2023, Omar joined carbon project developer Value Network Ventures (VNV) as Middle East and North Africa lead for project management and structuring.

Because I'm Egyptian myself, I used to think I must be biased to think that Egypt was the best jurisdiction for voluntary carbon trading.

After all, it seemed too unlikely that I was actually lucky enough to be working in the right place at the right time. Was Egypt really as progressive as I imagined, or was I just feeling patriotic?

But I finally realized that I'm actually not biased. I started to have conversations with people in similar roles around the world, and it's very clear that the voluntary carbon markets in other jurisdictions aren't as sophisticated.

The Egyptian regulator has been truly ahead of the game in terms of supporting market development and providing direct oversight of carbon projects. Their work has led to an impressive level of sophistication here.

A lot of that regulatory and market development work was done in the run up to the COP-27 climate conference, which was held in 2022 on the Red Sea coast of Egypt in Sharm el-Sheikh.

Hosting COP-27 was a game changer for the environmental movement within Egypt; the timing was fantastic and the conference left a great legacy.

DOI: 10.4324/9781003359739-28

I don't want to imagine what might have happened if Tunisia or Algeria had hosted COP-27 instead of Egypt. The preparations for COP really pushed the Egyptian authorities to think hard about carbon markets.

One of the breakthrough moments was the announcement at COP-27 by the Financial Regulatory Authority (FRA) of Egypt that they would launch a carbon market – the first regulated market in Africa and the region.

I was fortunate enough to benefit from that positive environment when we were looking to get the first onshore African carbon deal done.

Development studies

I had studied mechanical engineering but I was always interested in finance, in energy and in the nexus between the two so I thought renewable energy would be the ideal place for me.

I started work looking at developing renewable power production and power purchase agreements in Egypt. Then I was tasked with looking into alternative modes of finance for our projects and carbon popped up.

My boss at the time warned me not to waste my time. He argued that 'carbon is dead; carbon died in 2012'. But I thought there was maybe something still there to explore, so I wrote a case study looking at how selling carbon offsets could support the development of renewable energy in Egypt.

At the same time, we started to hear that the Egyptian Exchange (EGX) was also looking into carbon markets in the run up to COP-27, so the signals were positive.

We went to chat to the EGX in 2021, and that was my first meeting with H.E. Dr Mohammed Farid Saleh, who was EGX executive chairman at the time.

We quickly realized that the potential for carbon markets in Egypt was a lot bigger than purely supporting renewable energy. In particular, we saw a big opportunity in agriculture.

We were wrestling with the question of how to enable access to the international voluntary carbon markets to actors in the Egyptian economy and specifically smallholder farmers.

There wasn't an obvious answer. There were no Egyptian carbon project developers, and most international developers wanted to be paid in US dollars into foreign accounts, which was tricky due to economic hardships at the time.

As a first step, we created Libra Carbon, which was Egypt's first carbon project development company. Libra Carbon was owned by investment firm Libra Capital, a subsidiary of renewable power firm ENARA Group.

Everything seemed to be aligned: we had a local developer, a local trading platform in the making, and strong political support. But then came the slowdown: more than a year passed and nothing happened. No projects were developed and no credits were issued.

Regulatory oversight

During that year, I had moved to start work at Indian carbon project developer VNV. I had originally met VNV's co-founder Sandeep Roy Choudhury in Sharm el-Sheikh at COP-27 when we were looking for some advice from a developer who was strong on the agricultural side.

VNV registered a few of our projects on the FRA's first regulated VCM, which was hosted on the EGX trading platform, but there was no interest. It felt for a while like some of the positive momentum that COP-27 had generated was slipping away.

The key in turning the situation around was Dr Farid's move from the EGX to become chairman of the FRA.

Dr Farid brought a new energy back to the discussions. At the FRA, he started writing the rules and regulations that were missing in Egypt. His team wrote the rules for domestic carbon trading, for listing local projects, and so on.

Dr Farid realized that there are often question marks about voluntary carbon projects, so he worked within his sandbox to fix those issues.

Dr Farid would often say that regulators aren't climate scientists so they can't opine on the methodologies that underpin carbon projects, but regulators can certainly ensure there's no negligence, fraud or misconduct in the market.

As the regulator of the non-banking financial sector, the FRA can ensure that it has sufficient oversight over carbon projects and can check where the money is going.

If we say that 70% of proceeds go to the community, then the FRA will ensure that happens. Within their remit, the FRA is doing what it can to build confidence in the market.

This is not something that other regulators have been confident enough to take on. I have heard people call Egypt a 'regulated voluntary market' because of the strong level of regulatory oversight here. Maybe Egypt is the first regulated voluntary market in the world.

Carbon as an asset

Eventually, the rules were all written, and, even better, there was a prime ministerial decree making carbon a financial instrument. That decree put carbon on the main stage, and made it just like equities or bonds.

VNV were engaged from very early on so we were the first to finish the new certification process and get our projects properly accredited within Egypt. Once that happened, we hit the phones and went on a roadshow to promote the work we were doing and to market the credits.

Eventually, we got a range of buyers interested and that's how the first trade happened.

The deal was for 4,000 credits in total and we sold at $18 per ton of carbon, so there were no price concessions to get the deal done.

There wasn't much drama to the trade itself, which took place on 13 August 2024. The trade was just two firms clicking on the EGX screen, so we decided to have a little ceremony instead to mark the moment. We wanted something with the cameras rolling to show that something momentous had happened.

The party ended up turning into a very big deal. The FRA organized a grand ceremony with six ministers in attendance: the minister of investment, trade and supply, environment, economic development, agriculture and parliamentary affairs. We took photos and it was big news in Egypt at the time.

The publicity around the first trade took carbon beyond the perception that it was purely something that the ministry of the environment cared about.

We told everyone that this was the birth of a new asset class. The first carbon trade was like the first equities trade in Egypt, or the first commodities trade. It made the market legitimate; it formalized the market in a way that garnered interest from a cross-section of different Egyptian authorities.

Wider implications

That first trade was only 4,000 credits, but it sent a sign that we were open for business and it opened the door in terms of public recognition.

Carbon has now become slightly mainstream in Egypt; everyone knows about carbon. Two years before, no one would have known anything about carbon, now everyone knows something. Awareness has increased dramatically in Egypt.

Because of the work of the FRA to promote the carbon market, if you go and talk to any Egyptian investment bank or any insurance carbon, then they all know what a carbon credit is.

That's not the case in the wider region. Financial firms in Tunisia or Algeria probably don't know what carbon is or they don't care, whereas in Egypt most financial institutions now know about carbon and how it works.

As a result, it's a great time to be a carbon developer in Egypt and the region. I don't want to jinx it but the financial sector has a lot of interest and they are asking how can they support market development. They know their regulator is onboard with it so they see it as an opportunity.

I'm getting calls all the time from investment banks and from lenders. In general, the early 2020s have been a tough time for voluntary carbon globally, but in Egypt things are going quite well.

Perhaps it would have been a different story if I were a foreign developer, who was just flying in, wanting to develop a project and then get their carbon and their dollars out.

VNV actually set up shop here. We formed a company in Egypt and because I'm Egyptian, it's a different game. It's not what some people call 'carbon colonialism', where we throw in our fishing rod and reel money and carbon back out.

Although the regulated market allows for trading in several currencies, VNV is happy to trade in Egyptian Pounds, and we are happy to keep that money in Egypt to develop more projects here and to stimulate the domestic market.

Africa rising

Our trade on the FRA's VCM was the first regulated carbon trade to take place in Africa.

Obviously, millions of carbon credits have been generated in Africa and sold internationally by foreign developers to foreign buyers, but this was the first time a carbon trade had taken place on an African venue.

There has not traditionally been much domestic interest in carbon trading in Africa. Africa represents only 3% of global emissions and so most Africans don't see why they should pay for environmental projects.

At the end of the day Africans don't want to pay because they don't feel like it's their mess to clean up. Why would I pay to decarbonize when I didn't experience 100 years of industrial growth?

The African subsidiaries of multinationals are also not interested. They will typically tell you 'that's not my problem, go and talk to headquarters' or 'carbon is a global issue, go talk to the global team because I don't need any more work'.

That's why it was such a big deal to get a deal done within Africa. After all, the ultimate goal for Egypt and for Africa in general is to use carbon projects to attract foreign direct investment.

The clear advantage that Egypt now has is that the FRA rules provide investment security. When you can show that these products are vetted by a sovereign, by a national regulator, that's a lot better than no regulatory oversight.

Greed is good

Egypt has had some economic challenges, so we needed to move the perception domestically away from carbon as a luxury, as the cherry on the cake, towards carbon as a way to attract foreign direct investment. Once we achieved that, well, that's when the scales started to tip a little bit.

In my view, we have to change the narrative from carbon credits being purely about sustainability and get people comfortable with credits as a standard financial instrument.

I want carbon to stop being 'a cute thing you do for the climate'. It should instead be a way to attract climate finance. The market doesn't only have to be just for people that care about the planet, you can make a financial killing as well.

We are talking about an impact investment tool. The conversation has to be about carbon projects and trading as a business, rather than just another form of aid. Projects are a way to drive foreign investment into a country like ours with a struggling agriculture sector and are a way to increase international cooperation towards climate action.

My investors don't need to become climate experts. I've been telling them to treat this as any conventional asset class when cashflows are securitized with an offtake from a reputable corporate.

The investors don't necessarily need to know that I'm going to use their money to plant 5 million trees in Upper Egypt. What they need to understand instead are the typical financial parameters like the timescale, the reliability, their rate of return on capital invested.

The way to mobilize finance at scale is to bring financial institutions to the table and figure out a structure that lets them win.

Since that first trade, there has been an upshift of carbon activity in Egypt and I think it will pick up even further when we hear that first successful story of carbon investment.

I'm waiting for the first transaction that makes a serious amount of money for an Egyptian financial institution. Once the word gets out that there's real money to be made investing in carbon, we are going to see the market move to the next level.

At the end of the day, everyone wants to see some upside from the voluntary carbon markets, and that's equally true whether it's bankers in Cairo or smallholder farmers in rural Egypt.

Chapter 23

Re-aligning CORSIA spreads

Simon Crooks holds a master's degree in applied and computational mathematics and a doctorate in physics from the University of Oxford, where he also worked as a post-doctoral researcher. Simon left academia in 2006 to join financial trader Man AHL as a senior quantitative analyst. He moved in 2011 to Graham Capital Management, where he moved from senior research manager to portfolio manager. After leaving Graham in 2013, Simon became co-chief investment officer of investor Quantitative Strategic Investments as well as serving as a partner in carbon trader Fortinbras Asset Management; he continues to hold both roles, as well as serving as a partner in carbon markets specialist firm Vuelta Carbon.

I have always believed in going direct to the horse's mouth when it comes to understanding market fundamentals.

Doing your research is particularly important in environmental markets. It doesn't matter what other people are saying, what matters is the official documentation. Read the rules!

This isn't the oil market, where there are sometimes shady deals going on. Most environmental markets are typically transparent and clean, with clear regulations in place.

Yes, there is always uncertainty about what will happen next in terms of political will, but when there are existing rules in place, the key to success is to look at them and to actually read them.

Traders can sometimes be lazy and can gravitate towards the consensus view of the market. It's easy to fall into a bias towards what is perceived to be the standard approach.

I come from a mathematics background, and I can tell you that anyone who understands statistics knows to steer well clear of the consensus.

You can put a group of world experts together in a room and ask them for their opinion. But if the one guy who actually knows the facts is outside the room, then you shouldn't believe the consensus. It's your job as a trader to look for every possible angle. You need to do your own research and seek out that guy with the answers who might be outside the room.

DOI: 10.4324/9781003359739-29

If I were to give any advice to a young trader, it would be to understand your market as deeply as possible, and to focus hard on information that you know to be actually true.

You can make real money by doing your research, as we proved when we started trading voluntary carbon futures in 2021.

Let's dance

The financial crisis of 2008–9 nearly killed off the environmental markets. Climate action became a nice-to-have item for governments. The die-hards kept going but there was no real voice. Volumes in the markets dropped to virtually nothing.

Then around 2018, the market started to revive. The rhetoric around climate change from governments started getting a bit punchier, so we changed our trading focus from interest rates to environmental markets.

Our first focus was the compliance markets. We took an initial position in the EU Emissions Trading Scheme (ETS) when permits were trading down at around €5 and we held on to that position all the way through the subsequent massive bull run.

That trade made us money, but we realized that our longer-term approach to trading had to change. The EU started saying, for example, that they didn't want the ETS to trade above €100. Politics was always going to trump fundamentals in the compliance markets, so we switched to shorter-term trading in the ETS.

We also started to turn our focus to the voluntary carbon market. The more we looked at it, the more we thought it was a promising time to get involved.

We saw giant investments going into exchange platforms, into trading infrastructure and into every aspect of the voluntary carbon ecosystem, but the trading volumes were still poor.

We didn't see many other trading groups out there. It was like it was all set up for a party but there was nobody dancing. That told me that we should get our dancing shoes on.

We went to sign up with all the various voluntary carbon platforms, brokers and exchanges and they bit our hands off.

We started quoting bids and offers across all of them. The liquidity wasn't good enough for automated market making, but we could still apply the logic and approach that we had developed for interest rate trading.

From the CORSIA's mouth

The most important framework for trading voluntary carbon was the Carbon Offsetting and Reduction Scheme for International Aviation (CORSIA).

CORSIA was adopted in 2016 and became the first global scheme to focus on improving the environmental performance of a specific sector, in this case the global aviation industry.

CORSIA provided rules and a framework for airlines to buy and sell carbon offsets from projects around the world. The positive benefits of these projects were intended to offset the environmental impact of air travel.

Other sectors beyond the aviation industry also adopted the CORSIA standards as a useful framework so the scheme became the key reference point for the voluntary carbon market.

Because I always want to get to the horse's mouth, we spent a lot of time really working to understand CORSIA. Before we started trading, we studied all of the official documentation: what the processes were, what was the scheme's direction of travel, etc.

CORSIA was not straightforward. There was a pilot phase where participation was voluntary, and which was designed to last from 2021 to 2023. Then there was a first phase between 2024 and 2026, and a second phase from 2027 to 2035. All the different phases had different requirements.

We identified one element of CORSIA that was not well understood by the broader market: offsets from the scheme's pilot stage could still be submitted into phase one for up to three years.

Some people assumed that the futures contract expiring during phase one would only reference phase one credits, whereas in reality the contract was always going to continue to reference credits from the pilot phase.

The CME Group exchange had launched a futures market based on the CORSIA scheme in March 2021 and so we were able to express our view on the future direction of voluntary carbon and to trade prices all down the curve.

One of the things that struck us about the futures market was that the spread between December 2023 prices and December 2024 prices for CORSIA-eligible certificates was massively negatively offered on the screen.

That didn't make much sense to us.

Valuing a year

We realized that a lot of people must be thinking that the offset certificates for December 2023 wouldn't be eligible for delivery into the first phase of CORSIA because the offsets had been produced during CORSIA's test phase.

Firms were worried that they wouldn't be able to do anything with the December 2023 certificates, so the certificates would have limited value. Traders were trying to sell 2023 and to buy 2024 at all costs.

We were confident that we had interpreted the rules correctly and that the 2023 certificates would still be eligible for the next three years, but we still went to see CBL, who operated the trading platform for certificates.

We asked CBL what their plan was for the switchover from the CORSIA pilot phase to phase one. They confirmed that they would accept anything that was eligible under the CORSIA guidelines.

We were doubly confident then because we had actually gone to the horse's mouth for confirmation, and so we knew we had the best current information.

We went back to the office, and we put in a very low bid on that inter-year spread. We offered to buy the December 2023–December 2024 spread at –$0.36, so valuing 2023 at 36 cents lower than 2024.

People were hitting our bids left, right and centre. We were getting filled bang, bang, bang.

If I'd have had enough finance to run bigger positions, I would have just traded that spread until I was a billionaire because a few weeks later the exchanges confirmed that December 2023 was still going to be eligible for delivery into the first phase.

Very soon after that, the spread between the two years that we had bought at –$0.36 rose to zero or parity: everyone realized that the certificates for the two years were basically worth exactly the same.

We had known that all along, but a lot of people didn't go to the horse's mouth to get their information. They had made assumptions based on data that wasn't there.

The bad trades are usually the ones that stick with you, but this is one that I remember for all of the right reasons.

Academic discipline

I didn't start out wanting to be a trader. In fact, my introduction to environmental issues actually came from my academic research.

I was just finishing up my master's in mathematics at Oxford, and I was thinking about joining the army as a helicopter pilot, when a friend said his boss in the atmospheric physics department was looking for someone to look at solar changes and the effect on climate.

The university ended up offering me a place on the doctorate programme and some extra funding, so I moved across from mathematics to climate science.

I loved being in a world where people that weren't necessarily experts were interested in what I was working on. Mathematics at doctoral level is so niche that it's hard to explain to anyone outside the immediate field without their eyes glazing over but climate research was fascinating.

I was working closely with Professor Myles Allen, who is the smartest person I've ever met and who was one of the leading climate change scientists. Myles was great for me because he was so busy that he would often send me along to events in his stead.

I got to work on papers with Myles and to sit with politicians and other academic experts. I even ended up as a contributing author to the Intergovernmental Panel on Climate Change's (IPCC) fourth Assessment Report.

My academic career was flying, but money was always a worry. I come from a working-class background; I had good parents, but I didn't have any financial backing. I certainly didn't have a massive trust fund waiting for me so I felt I couldn't carry on much longer in a career that was earning me just £20,000 per year.

My girlfriend, now my wife, was also working at Oxford as a biochemical researcher, but she didn't want to be an academic anymore either. She went to take a job with the government in London and she suggested that I move down to London as well.

I was looking around and I saw an advertisement aimed at academics wanting to move into finance. I went to do an interview at one firm, but I didn't get the right feel from it. The second firm I tried was Man AHL, which had a totally different atmosphere and was really welcoming.

My interview was just a proper good chat, and I ended up having a friendly argument with the interviewer about mathematical concepts. Man AHL offered me a job on a six-man team that was running an investment portfolio of $15 billion. I never looked back.

My scientific background doesn't automatically make me a better trader than the next person, but it does mean that I bring some academic rigour to the market in terms of doing my own research and going straight to the horse's mouth.

It might sound arrogant, but it does also open doors in the environmental markets when you can say that you've been a trader for nigh on 20 years, but you are also an actual climate scientist.

My background might not get me sat at the top table straight away, but it certainly means that most people are going to give me the time of day.

Opportunity knocks

In one sense, the challenge has changed from putting together winning trading strategies to finding the best way of financing trades.

There are a lot of trading opportunities out there, but there is always a shortage of investment in our industry. When a big deal comes in, you don't want to be scrabbling around for finance because no trader wants to let opportunities go begging.

Not so long ago, we saw someone looking to sell 2020 voluntary carbon certificates and to buy 2021 certificates. If I had had the financial firepower available that day, I could have taken that trade, sold the 2020s at a profit on another platform, and bought 2021s cheaply from another source.

In that one trade, I would have made $1,000,000 with a few clicks of a button. That's the deal that got away.

The trading opportunities are very large as more and more firms start to look at voluntary carbon, but investors still view it as a niche market so finding funding is not always easy.

Demand for voluntary carbon certificates is growing, but it is not always informed demand.

Often corporate firms are happy if they can buy the offset certificates they need within their general corporate budgets, without worrying too much about the exact price.

You might look at a company website where a firm is massively promoting its focus on sustainability, but when you drill down you find that in a corporation of 1,000 people, they have one 20-something year old who is in charge of carbon and sustainability.

It's absolutely mad. Someone who used to be the intern might be managing a giant budget to buy additional carbon offsets so that the firm can hit its net-zero pledges.

There can be a lack of specialist knowledge outside of the small niche of firms that truly understand the voluntary carbon markets.

And, given that the knowledge discrepancy is still so high, it's not surprising that there are a lot of sharks in this space. I've seen people selling credits for $18 that they bought for $2.

That's not our style. As traders, we don't want to rip people off because that's not the right thing to do, nor is it a good long-term strategy.

Our role, as pure financial traders, is to iron out price discrepancies and hopefully make a profit along the way.

The voluntary carbon markets are still not efficient, so you still often see price discrepancies open up between platforms, brokers and exchanges, between different types of voluntary carbon projects, or between different time periods, as happened in our December 2023–December 2024 spread trade.

Our job is to bring those various price spreads back into line and to make sure that prices are where they ought to be. That way the market can see where true value lies.

Voluntary carbon used to be a backwater. Now, since the Paris Agreement, carbon offsets have come into the spotlight and are one of the key tools in the fight against climate change. The planet needs these markets to become more efficient.

Chapter 24

Trading carbon-compensated crude oil

Juan Carlos Santacruz Martínez studied finance and business management at the Escuela Colombiana de Ingeniería in Bogotá, Colombia. Juan Carlos started his career in 2009 as a market analyst at Colombia's national oil company Ecopetrol. He moved to the trading and business development team in 2014 and is currently employed as the senior trader in Ecopetrol US Trading LLC in Houston, Texas, leading the marketing of Colombian crudes in the U.S. markets, the supply of North American crudes for the company's refineries and trading optimization initiatives. In 2021 and 2022, he led the development and establishment of Ecopetrol's carbon trading desk and acted as lead trader of carbon-compensated crude oil. Juan Carlos was also responsible for the consolidation and coverage of the firm's carbon credit requirements. As well as his trading activities, he also served as an internal advisor for the carbon compensation roadmap of other commodities, such as natural gas, as well as other processes in the company's value chain. In 2024, Juan Carlos moved to Houston, where he works as a senior trader for Ecopetrol U.S. Trading LLC.

It probably seems strange that someone with a background in crude oil trading has ended up so focussed on the environmental side of things, developing a carbon-compensated crude oil strategy, and buying and selling voluntary carbon certificates.

After all, it sometimes seems strange to me as well.

Some people might think that my background in oil is a drawback in the environmental markets, given that the green movement is keen to reduce sharply the use of crude oil and of other hydrocarbons.

But I see my background as an advantage: it's great when environmental initiatives come from a team that normally trades not-so-green products like heavy crude oil. That means that our firm Ecopetrol is serious: if a trading team like ours is committed to these projects, then it means there is a genuine market and a genuine economic rationale behind the initiative.

Beyond the company's decarbonization strategy that strives to reduce carbon emissions through a number of initiatives, our trading team treats carbon like any other new commodity opportunity. It's a product that has its

DOI: 10.4324/9781003359739-30

own dynamics in terms of prices and the supply-demand balance, and there's a lot of risk and opportunity, partly because the voluntary markets are at the first stages of development and clear rules and criteria are not well established yet.

Our trading team is used to looking at WTI, Brent and other grades in the oil futures market where there are a lot of transactions almost every minute of the day, and the price is very clear to everyone. In contrast, environmental markets are still progressing towards standardization, and I think it will still take a long time before they get there.

Our initial focus has been voluntary carbon offsets, which is not an easy market to understand. It's been very useful to have experience in trading different commodities, like crude oil and refined products.

Over the years, our team has developed a clear approach to valuing commercial opportunities in different commodities and that's what we bring to the table in the environmental markets.

The crude oil team has been leading our carbon trading initiatives because at the end of the day our firm wants to apply the same rigour and the same trading techniques to these newer markets that we have developed while trading oil, which is still the biggest commodity market of all.

Measured impact

A few years ago, the management of Ecopetrol made a commitment to develop an energy transition strategy and to reduce our company's environmental footprint.

Since that date, the firm has been working to reduce the company's carbon output by improving its industrial processes, by using renewable power where possible, and by developing hydrogen projects among a number of other environmental protective initiatives.

But beyond the industrial side, our team started to think about what that drive towards greater sustainability might mean for our supply and trading business, where we trade substantial volumes of Colombian and international crude oil.

The first step for any commodity trader is to understand his or her natural position in the market: are you a 'long' (a seller) or a 'short' (a buyer) and how large is your position; how much do you need to buy or sell?

As a major producer of crude oil, Ecopetrol has substantial associated carbon emissions so if we wanted to offset those emissions, we would naturally be short carbon offset certificates. But we first needed to truly understand the carbon footprint of our crude oil.

We kicked off an initiative to measure the carbon footprint of our flagship grade, Castilla Blend, which is a heavy crude oil grade.

We hired external organizations that specialize in the measurement of carbon emissions. They began to carry out an analysis of our carbon impact all along the value chain, step by step, from the production field and then onto the pipeline that brings the oil all the way to the Coveñas terminal on the Atlantic Coast, from where we export our crude oil.

It was a very long process because there was a tremendous amount of information that international specialist companies required in order to measure the emissions and audit them, but finally in September 2021 we were able to quantify the carbon intensity of Castilla Blend.

Seeking compensation

We learnt that Castilla Blend's environmental impact, after applying all of the emission reduction initiatives that the company has in place, was equivalent to 32 kilograms of carbon dioxide (CO2) per barrel, which is a medium level of carbon intensity relative to other comparable crudes.

As traders, we now properly understood the size of our position: when we sell a cargo of 1 million barrels of crude oil, our exposure to emissions will be 32,000 tonnes of CO2.

To offset the emissions of a standard crude oil cargo, we would need to turn to the voluntary carbon market to buy 32,000 carbon credits, as each credit or certificate represents a ton of carbon that has been reduced, avoided or sequestered by a specially designed project.

Now that we truly understood our position and our exposure, my boss Juan Carlos Fonnegra and I started to think about what we could do with this information.

We became convinced that we could develop a market for 'carbon-compensated' crude oil, where we would supply both the physical oil and the appropriate number of offsetting certificates as a single package. This would allow us to offer a commodity with a lower carbon footprint to our end-user clients.

The concept of carbon-compensated crude oil ticked a lot of boxes for us. It would fit with Ecopetrol's corporate sustainability goals; it would be an added-value service for our customers; it might help to future-proof demand for crude oil from more environmentally conscious countries, and it also offered us additional trading opportunities.

We started to test the water in 2021 with our traditional buyers and we quickly learnt that many of the buyers were not ready. Ecopetrol mostly trades with refineries in the U.S. Gulf and in 2021, they didn't have a clear strategy around sustainability.

Carbon-compensated crude oil is obviously going to be more expensive than a typical crude oil cargo, and so it was a difficult pitch to U.S. buyers that they should pay more for their oil supply when they didn't themselves have a sustainability strategy in place.

Love me tender

Finally, in December 2021 we had the inspiration that rather than trying to convince individual buyers to do a test trade with us, we could simply hold a tender for a carbon-compensated cargo of Castilla Blend that would be open to all of our counterparties.

The concept was that a tender would allow us to see which of our buyers would have the greatest interest. We also wanted to test the market to see what kind of price levels people were prepared to pay for the environmental component.

We typically work closely with around 20 clients and around half of them participated in the tender, which was ultimately won by the Chinese state-owned oil firm, PetroChina.

Some of the premium PetroChina paid might have been the result of their interest in refining that specific grade of oil, while some would relate to their interest in the carbon compensation side.

It was probably a mix of the two, but PetroChina has since opened a carbon trading desk in Houston so maybe this first trade was a pilot for them.

After we awarded the tender, we hired an experienced inspection company to certify the carbon content of the cargo and to certify the offset certificates that we paired with it. Then we delivered the documentation as a single package to the buyer.

Delivering value

That first cargo with PetroChina raised interest levels in carbon-compensated crude oil, while at the same time more firms, particularly in Europe and Asia, had begun to develop their own long-term sustainability strategies and so were more interested in working with us.

After that initial trade, we were able to sell an additional four cargoes of carbon-compensated crude oil in 2022 and to expand our pool of counterparties to include firms like Repsol, Reliance, P66 and Citgo.

The reality of course is that the further development of this market will depend on a couple of factors: one that we can control and the other that we can't.

The part that is beyond our control is the global economy. When firms are doing well and are profitable, then they are more prepared to look at environmental initiatives.

The invasion of Ukraine in 2022, for example, initially led to much higher commodity prices, which put a lot of economic pressure on some countries. Their priority naturally became simply to ensure they could get hold of the commodities they needed, rather than considering the benefits of buying a raw material with a lower carbon intensity footprint.

The other threat to market development is one that we can absolutely control, which is ensuring the highest possible standards for the carbon credits we supply as an offset to our crude oil. Buyers of our carbon-compensated crude oil have to be confident that the deal has actively benefitted the environment.

Every decision about carbon credits comes down to a balance between the cost of the certificates versus the perceived quality of the underlying carbon project. In terms of the cost, you see a wide variety of carbon credits in the market trading at different levels: from renewable energy to waste management, reforestation, some with co-benefits to the community.

The decision about which carbon credits to use was an absolutely crucial one in terms of our corporate sustainability strategy.

Most of the operations of Ecopetrol take place here in Colombia. As one of the main focusses of our energy transition strategy is to do as much as possible to benefit the communities in the regions where we operate, we obviously looked to Colombia as the main focus for our purchases of credits.

We discussed our approach with our chief executive Felipe Bayón because Colombian credits were a little more expensive than other alternatives. We ultimately decided to pay a higher cost to select the best-quality carbon credits that we could find in Colombia.

Our initial focus was renewable energy, then from 2022, we only purchased credits that were to do with reforestation and that were no more than five years old, were accredited by the Verra carbon registry, and had co-benefits for local communities in Colombia.

Trading carbon

As well as buying credits to match our sales of carbon-compensated crude oil, I was also increasingly buying credits to offset Ecopetrol's corporate emissions.

We have been on a journey to make our processes more efficient or to substitute power generation in the fields or refineries for something environmentally friendly like wind or solar, but even so we could not reduce our emissions sufficiently through our own efforts. It was clearly necessary to be active in the carbon credit market to cover our requirements.

We saw that there was a very fast-growing and dynamic market for international carbon credits. Even in Colombia, the market was very dynamic. The country has a carbon tax, but the government allows the purchase of carbon credits to be offset against any liabilities under the carbon tax, which has strongly stimulated market development.

More and more companies are joining the carbon market and there were some very interesting opportunities, not only to cover our operations, but to also do some trading and optimization activities.

We have ended up looking at the voluntary carbon markets in a very similar style to the way we optimize around the crude oil slate for our refinery. If we buy a cargo of WTI crude oil and then we have an opportunity to replace that cargo with a cheaper crude oil or a better-quality grade, then we sell the WTI cargo and we buy another crude.

Ecopetrol is always short in terms of carbon credits. We can cover those requirements by simply buying carbon credits, but we can also optimize. We can sell out of positions that we have taken in the past and can maybe substitute the credits we hold with others that are still acceptable for us in terms of quality but where substitution makes some economic sense.

In the future, we will aim to make this optimization a regular source of profits, although our main focus in the short term will still be the carbon compensation of our crude oil and offsetting those corporate operations where we are not able to eliminate all emissions.

In the slightly longer term, we will maybe move to a greater focus on trading rather than procurement because hopefully our internal requirements will fall as we are continually working to shrink our carbon footprint.

These improvements will also hopefully drive down the carbon intensity of Castilla Blend to below 32 kilograms of carbon per barrel, which will ultimately mean we need to buy fewer certificates to pair with our carbon-compensated crude oil.

Back to school

It's been a very steep learning curve for an oil guy like myself to get up to speed on the environmental markets.

I have spent almost 14 years working on the petroleum trading side within Ecopetrol. It's a big shift to move from a very standardized market and a relatively transparent industry to look at an area that is completely new and remains very opaque.

Yes, carbon is a commodity, but it is a commodity that has very different dynamics and where the markets are changing and developing all the time.

What is reassuring is that every company, not just us, is learning on the job. We are all trying to understand how the carbon complex works; we are all trying to predict how regulations could develop. The trading rules could change any time and we can't afford to be surprised.

One of the most attractive elements for me is that now that we have done some learning and experiments ourselves, we can help to support other companies on their journey. It has been very encouraging to see that some of them at least are responding positively.

We have already come a long way from that first tender for carbon-compensated crude oil. It has been fascinating to be part of this new market dynamic, even though we understand that it will take years for compensating the carbon intensity of every crude oil cargo to become the global standard rather than the exception.

Chapter 25

Trading cross-border Chinese emissions

Jeff Huang holds a master's degree from Beijing's China Foreign Affairs University. He spent ten years working in the exchange, derivatives and fintech space, before joining the Chicago Climate Exchange (CCX), where he served as vice president between 2005 and 2010 when CCX was acquired by the Intercontinental Exchange (ICE), after which he joined ICE as managing director for Greater China. While at CCX, Jeff helped to develop the Tianjin Climate Exchange with CNPC/PetroChina. He left ICE in 2016 and the following year he founded AEX Holdings in Hong Kong as an advisory and market development service. Simultaneously, Jeff was appointed chief advisor to the Chongqing Petroleum and Gas Exchange. Jeff also assisted in the founding of AsiaREC in Hong Kong, the only independent non-profit in Asia that tracks renewable energy attributes. Jeff now is an independent director at Adama Ltd., listed on the Shenzhen Stock Exchange. Jeff is a regular speaker and columnist on China's energy and environmental markets and has served as a consultant for the China Securities Regulatory Commission (CSRC).

China operates the largest mandatory carbon market on the planet, the Emissions Trading System (ETS), which currently covers 8 billion tonnes of carbon dioxide emissions, according to an official government report.

China also hosts a giant voluntary carbon market, the China Certified Emission Reduction (CCER) programme, which allows companies to trade carbon reduction credits that are derived from six sectors, including reforestation, solar power, offshore wind and mangrove vegetation creation.

The CCER scheme has had a somewhat chequered history. It was launched in 2012, but was suspended in 2017 when responsibility for its administration was transferred from the National Development and Reform Commission (NDRC) to the Ministry of Ecology and Environment (MEE).

DOI: 10.4324/9781003359739-31

As early as August 2021, right in the middle of the COVID-19 lockdown, there were rumours that the MEE had plans to restart the CCER soon.

The timing seemed auspicious because I had started operating a company in Hong Kong called AEX Holdings. I wanted to develop a business around the high-quality, high-integrity end of the CCER market.

Before the original CCER scheme was suspended, there had been some concerns around the quality of some of the projects submitted or the quality of the data associated with them. I wanted to show that there were some great projects within the CCER market that could stand comparison with any international projects.

The obvious global standard for us to match was the Carbon Offsetting and Reduction Scheme for International Aviation (CORSIA) scheme that was developed by the United Nations' International Civil Aviation Organization (ICAO).

The CORSIA guidelines are very well designed and, as a result, they appeal to a lot of potential global buyers of carbon offsets, not just airlines.

In my view, ICAO is also a real watchdog: they will be very careful, very mindful of the reputation of their scheme and that helps to generate market confidence.

Sourcing quality CCERs

My concept was and remains: if we harmonize standards and harmonize trading, then we can bring best practice into the CCER market in China and help the market grow strongly.

At present, only a small portion of the CCER market is eligible for CORSIA, but I wanted to get a trade on the books for a CORSIA-eligible CCER project to encourage other developers on the mainland to raise their aspirations, and to show potential buyers outside mainland China that CCERs can meet the highest global standards.

I started looking up and down for CCER-eligible projects that would meet or exceed the CORSIA standards.

By good fortune, at that point in 2021, I was invited to speak at a roundtable in Beijing by the Elion Group, which operates a number of environmental projects. Elion Group plants trees in the desert in inner Mongolia and has invested more than a billion renminbi in solar power.

The chairman of Elion Group was at the roundtable and I sat down with him and his team and explained CORSIA to them and the value of meeting international standards.

I explained what a forward physically delivered trade might look like and I asked them whether they would be prepared to step up and try a trade.

Nobody else in China seemed keen to step up because everybody was waiting for the government to formally restart the CCER scheme, even though years had passed since it had been suspended.

I was very fortunate to meet Elion Group. They were forward-thinking guys and they are listed on the stock market so they were comfortable both with transparency and with trying new things.

Ultimately, they said 'yes' to me so I had the seller locked in.

Now I needed to find a buyer.

Making the deal

I did the same kind of tour around Hong Kong explaining the market to people who asked me, 'what the heck is a CCER?' Nobody seemed to have heard of it.

I got a lot of questions: 'why do I need to buy CCERs? What is the voluntary carbon market? What if I buy some offsets from China but then get hit with an accusation of greenwashing?'

Eventually, I found a Hong Kong law firm and a prominent individual (former deputy head of the Hong Kong EPA) who were willing to step up and buy some offsets.

The deal finally happened in August 2021. The transaction size was relatively small, for 10,000 tonnes of CCERs from an Elion Group solar power project in the Kubuqi Desert, but it was highly symbolic because it was the first cross-border transaction involving CCERs with forward physical delivery.

The fact that CCERs traded cross-border sent a powerful message: first, it showed that there was real international demand for Chinese projects that are strong enough to meet the most rigorous global standards.

It also showed that Hong Kong could potentially act as a bridge or a trading hub, linking the mainland with the international markets. This already happens in the equity markets, where we have the Stock Connect scheme that links the Hong Kong Exchange with stock markets on the mainland.

Is it so far-fetched to imagine a Carbon Connect scheme that links the CCER and other potential Chinese carbon markets with the international carbon markets? The Hong Kong authorities certainly believe it's possible, and I was keen to get a deal done to show the way.

Because the CCER scheme was still suspended in 2021, we set a forward delivery date to give both the buyer and seller a little bit more cushion to deliver under the relaunched scheme.

The deal was done, and money was changing hands, but – lo and behold – the restart didn't happen in 2021, it didn't even happen in 2022, it only happened in January 2024.

We had built some time lag into the trade, but we never expected that the official restart of the CCER scheme would be so late.

In March 2025, after an eight-year hiatus, MEE issued close to 10 million tonnes of new CCERs, which now trade on the spot Beijing Green Exchange. In the same month, the MEE deputy minister made public remarks about connecting CCER and global offset standards.

Bringing harmony

Because this was the first cross-border CCER trade, it received a lot of publicity in the newspapers. People seemed to like the fact that we were focussing on the high-quality space and were trying to drive up Chinese standards and data transparency to reach international levels.

Honestly, I would not have done that deal if we couldn't emphasize how some part of the CCER market is perfectly able to comply with international standards.

A lot of people don't seem to appreciate how crucial transparency is: around the project, the data, the trading and the settlement of the deal. If we are ever going to harmonize the Chinese and European schemes then we have to push hard on transparency.

The idea was to open the door and to show the powers-that-be in Beijing that there are serious buyers for CCERs in Hong Kong and elsewhere, if you are willing to push for high standards and open the door for trading on regulated exchanges.

A liquid, well-regulated market for CCERs in China would allow international buyers of physical offsets as well as trading firms to gain access to the onshore market, driving up both standards and enabling robust CCER pricing.

There are for sure a lot of investors out there that would love to be able to trade a potentially huge asset class, like the Chinese carbon market.

The pre-2017 CCER market never really took off, in part because international buyers couldn't access it and, secondly, because there were some concerns around data quality and around the independence of the registry, which is directly operated by the government.

The trade we did – international standard and via Hong Kong – showed a potential path forward for the market. The next steps might be to build out a forward price curve and then maybe to get something like a regulated swap execution facility set up in Hong Kong to allow risk management.

Giant potential

It's difficult to overstate the potential of carbon as an asset class in China. The scale of both the ETS and the CCER markets is huge, even beyond the scale of the European ETS.

Right now, Chinese compliance firms can use CCERs to meet up to 5% of their requirements under the Chinese ETS. That means there could be demand of up to 250 million tonnes of CCERs per year, just from ETS users in the compliance market. That number will reach 400 million tonnes per year by 2026, 5% of 8 billion tonnes of emissions allowances.

At that point, it will be hard for the CCER market to satisfy the demand from the compliance market, let alone any additional demand from voluntary purchasers. The compliance people will potentially just hoover up all the issuance.

The interest within China will only grow in the wake of the EU's introduction of its Carbon Border Adjustment Mechanism (CBAM), which came into force in 2026.

CBAM applies a charge relating to the carbon emitted during the production of imports into Europe of carbon-intensive goods, such as aluminium, cement, iron and steel.

The concept behind CBAM is to create a level playing field in terms of carbon, and to prevent industrial processes from just relocating to areas outside Europe with lower environmental standards.

Chinese exporters will have to show they are covered by an equivalent carbon regime in order to limit the number of expensive European CBAM certificates that they need to buy.

Given that Chinese allowances currently trade at the local equivalent of less than €10, compared with European carbon prices of around €65 per tonne, there is a lot of scope for the Chinese allowance prices to increase. It's hard to imagine that the Chinese government will be comfortable with that price spread being captured by the European Union.

If the authorities in China somehow make the cap tighter, and raise the carbon price onshore to something like €55, then the spread to the European carbon market will be much smaller.

The question for the authorities is 'do you want money to stay in China or do you want the money to go into European coffers?' CBAM forces that kind of calculation.

Of course, down the line it will be very interesting to trade the spread between the Chinese ETS allowances, the European ETS allowances and the CCERs, in a truly internationalized setting.

Civil society

I was happy to start the debate by getting the first cross-border deal done.

I maybe have some unique advantages when it comes to carbon market development because of my background, going back as far as the Chicago Climate Exchange.

I can be a little bit boastful about that because I have the scars on my back from working for all of these big financial firms in China and for both international and local exchanges. When it comes to getting a market started, most people don't have the network and Rolodex that I have.

The Chinese market has huge potential, but one of the factors holding it back is the lack of an independent carbon registry in Asia. In the U.S., there are a few, with Verra the most prominent, and there is the Gold Standard in Europe, but we don't have anything comparable in Asia.

To misquote Abraham Lincoln, we need a registry in Asia for Asians by Asians. I want to see Asian counterparties on both sides of the trade and I want them to be happy to do business using an Asian registry that is comparable to any international registry in terms of standards, oversight and transparency.

The experience of waiting seven years for the CCER registry to reopen was not positive in terms of market confidence so hopefully we can see some change here. So many of the projects registered on Verra and the Gold Standard registries come from Asia, but both have little board representation of Asian people.

At the end of 2024, the Hong Kong Finance Service Development Council published a white paper on internationalizing China's carbon markets. Among the recommendations it made: setting up a Verra-like NGO in Hong Kong and exploring CCER forwards trading regulated by the Hong Kong Securities and Futures Commission (SFC).

We should borrow the Western model, their application of the rule of law, and broad participation from members of a vibrant civil society, but we should develop something ourselves in this region.

At the end of the day, though, we can try to change things as individuals but we don't have any actual power because that belongs to the government.

What we can do, however – and what I did with this trade – is to show clearly the advantages of meeting higher standards and keeping the Chinese markets aligned to the rest of the world. Then we hope that someone is taking notice.

Chapter 26

Offsetting in the Japanese market

Keisuke Kimura studied at Waseda University and Waseda Business School in Japan, where he focussed on carbon accounting and entrepreneurship. He also undertook further studies at Harvard Business School and at the University of Oxford. Keisuke joined the Automotive and Mobility Group of Mitsubishi Corporation in 2008. He held increasingly senior positions in Japan, Brazil, Mexico and the United Kingdom, before returning to Tokyo in 2020 as a manager in Mitsubishi's business development team, focussed on carbon credits and electric vehicles. In 2023, Keisuke left Mitsubishi to co-found ExRoad Co Ltd, where he serves as chief executive. ExRoad facilitates carbon trading and its social implementation in the Japanese market.

My interest in carbon markets dates back to my bachelor's degree at Waseda University when I first studied political science and economic structures like the European Emissions Trading System (ETS).

From then on, I was always very enthusiastic about carbon markets. But when I joined Mitsubishi Corporation in 2008, I was assigned to the firm's automotive business and so I put that interest on hold.

Then, while I was living in the U.K., my company gave me the chance to study at Harvard on a leadership programme for half a year. During the programme, I had a chance to consider deeply what I really wanted to do.

I decided that I wanted to be involved in the environmental sector. I went back to Mitsubishi and looked at creating a carbon credit business, where we would lease cars and offset their emissions with carbon credits, among other initiatives.

Afterwards, I enrolled at Waseda Business School, where I studied global management and entrepreneurship under Professor Masao Hirano, and wrote a master's thesis entitled 'Conditions for Creating a Decacorn from Japan'.

Eventually, I realized that I wanted to be an entrepreneur, to create a business. I decided to go independent and so I left Mitsubishi and co-founded ExRoad.

DOI: 10.4324/9781003359739-32

I had just had a child and that had made me reflect deeply that I wanted to create a better world for him. In 2050, my son will be around 30 years old. That doesn't seem so far away, but we already know that the planet then could be hotter and more difficult than it is today.

I wanted to be part of the solution to make sure my son's life isn't overshadowed by climate crisis, so I decided to follow my passion for the environment and to establish a company.

Going it alone

It might seem crazy to some people to leave a good job at a very large and well-respected company like Mitsubishi Corporation in order to develop an environmental start-up.

A lot of people still have the idea that they will work for the same company throughout their career. But actually, there is a growing trend for younger Japanese people to establish their own companies. The government supports this trend because they want to increase the number of start-ups.

The availability of venture capital is also increasing. It's a good time to be independent and to establish a company in Japan.

As a start-up, our aim is to use carbon credits to empower climate action. We want to increase the number of carbon credit transactions that take place in Japan.

Japanese companies are normally very honest, and they have very high integrity, so most are already working to decrease their emissions as much as possible. Firms are making good progress but sometimes it takes time to overhaul operations and facilities.

But we are in a climate crisis, so we don't have so much time to act. We need to do everything we can to accelerate companies' climate actions.

In addition to reducing their own emissions, Japanese companies need to support others to reduce emissions or to remove carbon dioxide from the atmosphere.

The Japanese carbon market is really immature today and firms still need education. Many Japanese companies are still struggling to decide how they should act because the rules are not so clear and also there are some risks to reputation in terms of accusations of greenwashing.

Nonetheless, some forward-thinking Japanese firms, especially in the energy field, are already starting to purchase and utilize branded carbon credits from the global market.

The number of transactions and the trading volume is growing steadily from a few millions of tonnes of purchases in 2022, and this will only increase. But there are some pain points in the operation for most potential buyers.

One of them is that communication is in English and complex.

For Japanese people, talking with foreign partners in English to find the best carbon credit is not so easy and getting information in English takes time and is costly, especially when there are so many different potential brokers, traders and suppliers to communicate with.

ExRoad supports Japanese companies, firstly by supporting their communication in procurement using our digital solution. We can discuss with foreign partners on their behalf.

This kind of hand-holding support might seem very primitive, but making the process easier will definitely help Japanese companies trade carbon credits appropriately, increasing the number of carbon credit transactions in Japan.

Credits as branding

Peer pressure really works in Japan.

If a big company offers products with environmental offsets, then its competitors will do the same.

We have already seen the big Japanese gas providers like Tokyo Gas and Osaka Gas supply carbon-neutral LNG. Now even smaller players like drink vendors are getting in on the act by offering offset products.

The potential for the offset market here is very large.

Firms consider offsetting their products as part of their marketing proposition. They are obviously very concerned about greenwashing, so they want to follow the highest standards, but they definitely want to increase the value of their brand by adding carbon credits to their products.

ExRoad's breakthrough deal was when we arranged the carbon offsets for the Japan Mobility Show, which took place in November 2023, and which used to be called the Tokyo Motor Show.

The Japan Mobility Show is a very big event and we worked with the organizers to buy carbon certificates to offset the emissions related to holding the show.

It was a really good opportunity that we really appreciated.

Obviously, I came from the automobile industry and my co-founder Keigo Kitahara previously worked in one of the big public relations companies and so he had a strong relationship with the sponsors of the event.

We measure and offset the Mobility Show's emissions with a mix of high-quality carbon credits. We bought some from Japanese brokers. We also deal with more than 20 international players, so we received offers from them and bought credits over the counter.

Even though the organizers of the Mobility Show didn't have a strong preference about the type of credits that we used as offsets, we believe that the key is to use carbon offsetting to create a positive narrative.

As we have marketing experience, we can provide some advice about maximizing the value of the credits by choosing relevant credits that help to tell a story.

For example, we proposed to the Mobility Show organizers that we buy Japanese carbon credits that had been generated by electric vehicles.

In another case, we bought offsets on behalf of an industrial manufacturer that had recently started a business in India. We proposed that they purchase carbon credits generated in India because they can then refer to that investment, not only in Japan but also in India.

We don't treat carbon credits exclusively as financial commodities; we treat them also as having a marketing value.

This added value increases the value of the carbon credit.

Yes, we recognize that carbon credits are a largely fungible environmental commodity, but we also believe that specific credits can be worth more to certain customers because they fit their corporate narrative.

If using electric vehicle credits increases the brand value of the Mobility Show, for example, then those specific credits are much more valuable to the organizers than to other potential buyers.

We can potentially sell certain credits to certain firms at a higher price than others might pay.

Offsetting events is now a hot topic here in Japan, and we are also offsetting some golf events as well. This kind of activity is increasing and becoming popular; Japanese people are starting to know about carbon offsets and to expect events like soccer matches and consumer products to be offset.

The market is very immature, but it is growing.

For firms, establishing a strong environmental narrative can increase their corporate and brand value as well as contributing to Japan's Nationally Determined Contribution (NDC) under the international Paris Agreement of 2015. We are trying to cultivate that market here in Japan, and to help companies think about how they can use compliance and voluntary carbon credits in their marketing.

Greening Japan

The Japanese government launched a carbon pricing and trading scheme in 2023 as a trial, the GX Emissions Trading System (GX-ETS), which covers more than 600 big enterprises.

The scheme works on a cap and trade design similar to the European ETS. The main difference to the European scheme is that Japanese companies can also use domestic and international credits as well as official allowances to offset their emissions.

The compliance market will grow from now on, thanks to the GX-ETS, but we can expect some difficulties on the supply side.

There is quite a limited supply of domestic Japanese credits, or J-Credits, and also a shortage of additional international credits produced under JCM (Joint Crediting Mechanism) consistent with Article 6 of the Paris Agreement.

The supply of Japanese credits is obviously not going to be enough as more and more companies need to purchase domestic credits to achieve their target.

The price of credits is likely to rise under this scenario, but even then, domestic supply is not likely to be enough. It's possible that the government will decide to open the door to foreign credits. ExRoad is part of the working group discussing whether certain voluntary credits from abroad could be approved for inclusion in the GX-ETS.

It is clear that the Japanese market for carbon credits will increase. There are big opportunities to develop carbon projects locally and internationally, while the need for brokers and advisors who can help businesses navigate the new rules and can help source scarce adequate credits will also grow.

I am particularly bullish about the prospects for industrial removal carbon credits. Japan is an industrial country, and so the government wants to maintain our traditional strength in the industrial field.

The government is pushing companies hard to develop new technologies like carbon capture and storage so in my opinion this sector will grow very fast.

Opportunity knocks

I presented at the Asia Climate Summit in October 2023, where I met a lot of foreign players, suppliers and developers. They were all interested in the Japanese market, but they found the Japanese market really complex.

The language is different; the business practices are different. International firms are looking for someone to support them to develop an environmental business here in Japan. We want to be the gateway for those companies.

At the same time, we know that the domestic compliance market will grow and that there is still a very good opportunity for the voluntary sector.

Activity levels are already increasing as entities like the Mobility Show's organizers come to understand the value for their brand of engaging with environmental issues.

The official framework and the future direction of the rules are still relatively vague and unclear, though, so some big enterprises still cannot decide whether or not they should get involved. That provides an opportunity for a start-up like ours to take the lead.

We will do our best to develop our business and to achieve our purpose, which is to accelerate climate action in Japan through carbon credits.

Part VI

Trading biomass

Biomass refers to organic matter such as wood, straw, agricultural residues or processed waste that can be burned directly or converted into energy.

The main environmental advantage of biomass is that its production is renewable, with carbon emissions from combustion often offset by the regrowth of source materials.

In well-managed systems, sustainably produced wood pellets or agricultural by-products replace fossil fuels and help meet decarbonization targets. Ensuring that the supply of biomass is genuinely sustainable is crucial to maintaining the industry's environmental credentials.

In Europe, the use of biomass for power generation is steadily increasing, supported by policies such as the European Union's Renewable Energy Directive and by national incentives that encourage substituting coal and gas with biomass.

Biomass is also growing in significance in North America, particularly in regions with abundant forestry resources.

The biomass market, particularly for wood pellets, is generally stable in terms of pricing, although it experiences infrequent but sharp price spikes driven by supply shocks, infrastructure constraints, or sudden swings in demand.

Successful trading often hinges on physical logistics, inventory management and the ability to respond to unpredictable events, with storage capacity conferring a strategic advantage.

DOI: 10.4324/9781003359739-33

Chapter 27

Trading the bark spread

Remco Frenken obtained a master's degree in electrical engineering from Delft University of Technology in the Netherlands in 1993. His first job was as a research engineer and project leader for KEMA Consulting. Remco joined Dutch utility Essent in 1998, where he served as head of power trading and as origination manager for Germany and central and eastern Europe. In 2009, Essent was taken over by German utility RWE and he became senior vice president for global green commodities, origination and mid-market. Remco was appointed managing partner of energy advisors UMS group in 2012, before later moving to Priogen Energy in 2018 as head of business development and origination. Since 2019, he has run GLEAM Consultancy & Management, which provides advisory services to the global electricity sector.

I am an engineer by education, so I always love to combine technical know-how with commercial insights. That's what gets me excited and that's the theme that has run throughout my career.

I'm not a pure speculative trader: for sure, there are much better gamblers out there than me, while other traders may have bigger appetites for risk.

I do have one superpower, though. I was always the guy who could take a trading strategy and then figure out how to apply it to physical assets, like power stations, so that we could get the best out of them without endangering their performance.

I started work in the engineering side of the electricity industry, but I was always interested in the commercial side so when the Dutch power market opened up to private-sector competition in the late 1990s, I realized that would be my sweet spot.

I was hired by a power producer that later became Essent. It was a great time to join the firm because Essent had decided they wanted to fully embrace the markets and trading.

DOI: 10.4324/9781003359739-34

Flexible plants

I joined the trading team under an American boss with a big pedigree, who was brought in to create a trading culture and who was probably paid more than the chief executive of the time.

The desk was a mix of trading and technical backgrounds. I started to specialize in working with the managers of our power plants to make sure that we were taking full advantage of any optionality in the asset.

In trading terms, a power plant is essentially a giant option. The skill is to monetize that option by smart operations and smart trading.

That might sound like a pretty trivial observation nowadays, but back in the early 2000s, we had a real edge because not everyone had made that conceptual leap as quickly as Essent.

We embarked on a journey to make our power plants more flexible. That mission happened to coincide with growing environmental awareness in Europe, which led to new government subsidies and requirements that changed utilities' economics altogether.

The Dutch government had started to offer pretty generous subsidies to encourage utilities to make more use of biomass in power generation because its environmental profile is better than that of coal.

Biomass is organic matter that can be burnt to generate power, usually in the form of a hard dry pellet. The material is usually either renewable, like wood, straw or energy crops, or else would normally be wasted, like sawdust.

Essent wanted to start burning more biomass in our coal plants but there was a problem: we quickly realized that pellets only have two-thirds of the heating value of coal. If you simply swap out tonnes of coal for the same quantity of biomass, then suddenly your 600 megawatt (MW) plant can only produce 400 MW of electricity, which is not what anyone wants.

You need a lot more tonnes of biomass than of coal to produce the same amount of power and you can't physically get all of that additional material into the boiler.

We clearly had to sit down with the plant managers to think about fuel flexibility and about how best to make biomass work from both an engineering and a trading point of view.

Mills and boon

Before environmental factors entered the market, we used to just think about how to maximize the profit from making electricity out of coal. We call the relationship between the price of coal and the price of electricity, the 'dark spread'.

Generators were always geared towards maximizing the dark spread, but introduction of subsidies for biomass along with the 2005 introduction of the

European Emissions Trading System (ETS) changed the rules of the game entirely.

As we turned our focus to the profit from producing electricity from biomass, we came up with the concept of the 'bark spread' as a complement to the traditional dark spread.

Our goal was to maximize the bark spread by finding the optimal frontier between the loss of efficiency from co-firing with biomass and the positive financial benefit of avoided ETS costs and government environmental subsidies.

Among a whole host of factors, we had to take into account the Dutch biomass subsidies, the output and efficiency gap between coal and pellets, and the cost of any emissions certificates we might need to buy if we used significant volumes of coal.

We ended up building an extremely complicated trading model that effectively had four legs: coal, pellets, carbon emissions and electricity. Just to make it more challenging for long-term planning, all of these four legs shifted in value hour by hour.

In its simplest form, if the dark spread for a 600 MW plant was pretty poor, say something like €1 per MWh, we might want to burn biomass instead and run the plant at just 400 MW output in order to reduce our carbon footprint while being (more than) compensated by subsidy payments.

On the other hand, if customer demand was high – for example, during the evening peak in the winter – and as a result the dark spread became exceptionally good, then we might want to run the plant full out, using coal to hit 600 MW, irrespective of the carbon price or subsidies.

Essent ended up pioneering some of these formulas and models because other people weren't quite there yet.

Biomass complexities

The unique nature of biomass added to the difficulty of figuring out the most efficient model.

Our firm had decades of experience in managing coal, but biomass was a very different animal, both in terms of physical handling and in terms of market structure.

For example, you can use derivatives to hedge the price of coal as well as the price of electricity and of emissions certificates, but there were not, and still are not, any financial markets that allow you to manage price risk for biomass.

Emissions certificates and electricity are basically datapoints in an electronic system, but pellets are a real-world physical challenge: when you pay for them, you've got them. Then you either have to use the material or else find someone that might want to buy it from you.

Even biomass storage is more complicated than for coal, not that coal is straightforward either. Pellets have to be stored indoors, for example, or else they rot. That is expensive, and you also need to put sensors all around the material to make sure it never overheats. Similar to coal, even with careful storage, the pellets still degrade a little bit all of the time.

The market structure was also different to what we were used to. Coal is much more flexible because if you don't want a delivery, you can easily sell the cargo and divert the shipment because there are so many other potential coal buyers out there. In contrast, there are fewer biomass buyers, and they all have different requirements.

These are all key insights that we learnt the hard way.

We quickly realized that, if we were serious about biomass, we would need to set up a physical biomass trading desk. Without biomass futures, you can't hedge your price risk, so the next best thing is to be able to manage your physical flow.

We realized that sometimes we would need to sell our pellets, or else we would need to call the pelletizer that we were buying from to say, 'hey, don't deliver the material to us just now'. That's not something they like to hear but everything can be possible with additional payments.

Challenging model

The impact of co-firing with biomass on power plants is another thorny issue that we needed to understand better.

If you run on biomass, your minimum load – the lowest capacity at which you run the power plant – needs to increase a little bit because the plant needs stability.

You always need a little buffer in your process when you are running a power plant and you need even more of a buffer with biomass, which is a more complex fuel. You can't risk that one mill trips and then the whole plant trips.

You have to increase the minimum load, which can cost some money because sometimes at night the price is so low that it's not that profitable to run the plant. That's where subsidies are crucial. There were times when we switched to running on increased minimum load at night because it was incentivized by the subsidies.

The bark spread also has to be calculated in real time because every single hour of the day and night has a different electricity price attached to it.

There's one other key constraint: you can't easily switch off a power station. It generally costs in the ballpark of €100,000 to restart a plant once it has been switched off. It also ages plants to switch them on and off. It's like constantly starting and stopping your car: each time, the wear and tear ages it a little bit.

The flexibility to run biomass is fantastic but it comes with a price. Flexibility generally means running plants in ways that they weren't designed for, so if you get it wrong, you can age the assets, your risk profile increases, and you are more likely to have operational problems.

A 600 MW power plant would ideally run at between 200 and 600 MW. If you go below 200 MW, you probably ought to switch it off. But if you switch it off, will it start up again tomorrow? It's the same as a car. When you switch your vehicle off in the depths of winter, you are always a little nervous about whether it will restart.

Whenever you look at optimization, you have to think about risks as well as potential profits. For example, with a coal station there's a one in ten chance that it won't start up when you want it to, and that immediately lands you with a €200,000 penalty from the system operator because you aren't operating as expected.

Perhaps you can understand why managing the bark spread was so complex.

Experience counts

Even with the best possible calculations, sometimes you have to overrule the trading model based on your experience. It might look like you are losing money but you're actually paying to reduce a risk of a bigger issue, like the plant not restarting.

We developed a trading model that tried to take everything into account, but then in day-to-day life, surprises happened. Actual life is never as simple as a formula. Those are the times when you have to have the discretion from senior management or risk managers to do the right thing.

That was all part of the culture at Essent at that time. We were challenging each other to do better and to make more money for the company, but we also understood that there was a price attached to certain risks. If you are taking those risks, you need some reward in exchange.

We were very fortunate that Essent was super supportive of developing trading because we are talking about tens of millions of investments. It's not that we could get the green light just by an email, but it wasn't that painful a process to get projects approved.

We had a good image within the company. The trading team was making so much money for the firm, that if we came with a plan, then there was a positive bias from management, which made our lives a lot easier.

Sourcing misstep

We had made a success of biomass co-firing, despite its enormous complexities, and we were keen to extend our use of bio-material by converting a fuel oil plant to run on palm oil.

Palm oil had a similar energy intensity to fuel oil, and it only cost us a few million to convert the three tanks we had to handle palm oil. We thought we were geniuses because now the plant could run on an additional fuel that gave us even more flexibility.

It felt like we were doing a great job. We were again earning big subsidies for not burning hydrocarbons. We already knew all the trading games from our time developing the bark spread, and now we had another additional fuel to play with.

We started buying a lot of palm oil. I think at one point we were one of the largest palm oil buyers in the world, even bigger than Unilever.

But then we started to hear from the environmentalists, 'hey, you guys are buying so much palm oil that they are chopping down rainforests in Indonesia'.

The first time you hear that, it's what Al Gore called an 'inconvenient truth'. The team had been proud of ourselves, but then we realized that maybe they were right.

Palm oil was a very different beast to wood pellets. We only bought pellets from sustainable producers so we knew that whenever we bought from Canada, the U.S., Estonia or wherever, there would be a new forest planted in its place.

I never doubted that we were doing something good with the pellets. They came from a forest that ultimately stayed a forest. It was harvested but replanted, and it meant that we burnt a lot less coal in our plants.

Palm oil is totally different. Producers chop down a rainforest and replace it with a monoculture plantation.

We only realized that with time. We felt good in the beginning but now I'm ashamed we bought so much palm oil. In hindsight, we did a stupid thing. That experience alerted me to always look at the whole value chain for bioenergy.

Future of coal power

Recently, I've been doing some advisory work with coal-fired generators in Canada trying to help them make their coal stations more flexible.

The plant manager generally starts by telling me, 'Remco, we always run as base load and we always run four of our five coal mills'.

The most important thing for that plant manager is that the power station is running nice and smoothly. But the new goal for a coal plant manager should be to increase flexibility.

Coal should not automatically provide base load power, in fact, the asset mission for a coal-fired power station should be to phase itself out, and, until then, to be as accommodating as possible to the growing volumes of wind and solar power.

That's easy for me to say because I'm not the coal plant manager, and there are many communities where people have worked all their lives at the coal station. But governments and companies need to put something on the table that will change the nature of the asset mission, just as the Dutch government did with the biomass subsidies and the EU did with the ETS.

No one's going to take more risk for free. Flexibility is complicated and it's expensive. Change costs money, but it can be achieved, and it's that mindset shift that will help us nail the energy transition.

Chapter 28

Biomass storage arbitrages

After holding various sales roles, Ronnie Kristensen joined Norwegian gas and fertilizer producer Norsk Hydro, now Yara, in 1996 as an area manager. He stayed for eight years before joining Norwegian oil producer Statoil, now Equinor, as a product manager. His intended responsibility was for natural gas, but he ended up in biomass. In 2009, the Statoil business was acquired by Finnish wood pellet producer Vapo A/S, and Ronnie moved across as market manager. After three years in the role, he negotiated the transfer of the business to Swedish forest product trading company Ekman & Co. Ronnie was named managing director of Ekman Denmark in 2012 and served as bioenergy division leader from 2019 onwards. In 2022, Ronnie joined CM Biomass as sales and procurement manager. Then in 2025, he was named sales director of Norway's Norbio ApS. A Danish national, Ronnie has served as a board member of the European Pellets Council, as the chairman of the Danish biofuel association and as the chairman of ProPellets Denmark.

The wood pellet business is notable for long periods of stability, where supply more or less matches demand and prices don't move much.

Generally, during those quieter periods, profits are quite stable and there's limited opportunity for trading, although there can be good business in monitoring the main markets and looking for arbitrage possibilities.

I certainly would not consider myself a hardcore trader in the sense of someone who is constantly on the phone buying and selling.

That kind of intense trading doesn't really exist in the biomass market. I see myself more as a businessman who buys and sells regularly and then trades when opportunities emerge.

Significant opportunities do sometimes emerge because this more-or-less peaceful market can be surprised by some really big moves.

The skill is to be on the right side of those big moves. But it's difficult because they don't happen frequently enough that you can bet on them.

When we talk through our strategy, for example, we talk a lot about how we can build up the business, but we can't talk about getting ready for the

DOI: 10.4324/9781003359739-35

next wild thing that might happen because we don't even know if anything will materialize.

It's not like you can build a business by just hoping for a crisis every fifth year.

When we talk about market positioning, it's more a question of trying to keep some optionality open and then hoping that you can find yourself in the right place at the right time.

From still to storm

I started in the biomass market in 2004. From that year, right through till the 2016–17 season, the seaborne delivered price of a tonne of wood pellets was always between €130 and 145, with lower specifications trading down around maybe €120 per tonne.

As you can imagine, price fluctuations were really limited. During that whole period, the price of pellets didn't move by more than €10 or €15 euros.

That range was roughly equivalent to our profit margin on a good day so you could trade a lot with very little risk because in the worst case, you wouldn't actually lose money, you'd just lose your margin.

The stability made us more willing to take positions and not just trade back-to-back. Most of our business at that time was a kind of agency model, where we would source supply from forestry firms and then immediately match the quantity with an industrial buyer, such as a utility.

Then in 2017–18, there was a surprise short-term shortage of pellets. Prices suddenly surged to €180 per tonne. Then later they even hit €200 because there was such a lack of short-term supply, even though people realized the mismatch was likely just to be for the 2017–18 season.

We were fortunately on the right side of the price move, and we made a lot of money on the product that we were holding as inventory.

We were very lucky that we were running quite high in terms of inventory at the time. Normally, we planned four plant turnarounds each year, although we sometimes only had three, so we had already built up around 50,000 tonnes in storage ahead of the plant being out.

Absolutely no one had predicted the price spike so we ended up having a good result all things considered, but I would say we only came out 'OK' and that we could have done even better.

There were a couple of reasons why we couldn't take full advantage.

Firstly, a lot of the bigger sales agreements we had in place were back-to-back, so the product was already committed.

Then, at the same time, we were reeling from the failure of our big supplier in Russia, the Vyborg Forestry Industrial Corporation Ltd., which filed for bankruptcy in July 2016.

We were selling roughly 500,000 tonnes of wood pellets in 2016, of which 300,000 tonnes came from Vyborg's Russian factory. It was very unfortunate for both them and us that they closed down production just before the market turned.

It hit us hard that we didn't have access to as much product during the price spike as we would have wanted. You can imagine that it's not easy to suddenly find a replacement supplier for 300,000 tonnes in a very tight market.

Luckily, between our inventory and some substitute suppliers, we were able to deliver what we had promised to our counterparts, and still take partial advantage of the surging spot prices.

Storage wars

As we saw in 2016–17, the bigger money in biomass trading comes from trading around product in storage.

Storage definitely gives you more opportunities to trade, but you have to be willing of course to take on much higher risks.

In other markets, you can hedge a storage position with derivatives, but there's nothing of the sort in biomass. People look at the price index that Argus Media publishes, but most deals are still done on a fixed-price basis and there are no risk management tools available.

Different firms will have different risk appetites when it comes to trading around storage capacity and looking for arbitrage opportunities. I experienced firsthand exactly how two different market strategies played out.

After the boom period of 2016–17, Ekman, my firm at the time, was selling 500,000 tonnes per year, while our rivals CM Biomass were selling 600,000 tonnes.

Whenever I went to conferences or events, everybody was talking about the two big trading companies that were competing with each other to dominate the market.

But beneath the surface success, Ekman was struggling. We had become over-reliant on a single Russian supplier, Vyborg, and we struggled to recover from their bankruptcy.

The market also changed a little bit and matured, which affected our agency business. Producers and end-users like the big power stations started to trade directly with each other in a way that they hadn't previously done. That meant there was a lot less room for a trading intermediary than there had been in the earlier days of the market.

In retrospect, we did all the wrong things, while our rivals CM Biomass did all the right things.

CM Biomass started investing in infrastructure and, in particular, in warehouses, which meant that they were really able to take advantage of any arbitrage possibilities that emerged. It was a classic asset-backed trading strategy.

Like us, they were buying a lot in Russia, but they were buying from multiple suppliers and then commingling products. That was probably the backbone of their success: ensuring a steady flow of reasonably priced material that they could then ship to the best paying markets.

Within a few years, CM Biomass had grown from 600,000 tonnes to 4 million tonnes, while Ekman had slipped from 500,000 tonnes to 200,000 tonnes.

Both companies had started with the same possibilities and had experienced the same market conditions, but they chose different paths.

We ended up selling the Ekman business to CM Biomass in 2022 and I moved across with the business as sales and procurement manager.

Return of the spike

CM's greater focus on asset-backed trading and greater storage capacity really paid off when the biomass market went through its next convulsion in 2022.

The Russian invasion of Ukraine in February 2022 led to a full-blown European energy crisis. There were concerns that Europe would not be able to cope without Russian natural gas: utilities were switching from gas to coal where they could, and they wanted to co-fire coal with wood pellets to reduce their emissions profile.

At the same time, private consumers were afraid that there would not be enough pellets for them to heat their houses.

And to add to the mix, there was also simultaneously a shortage of wood pellets.

The combination of factors drove demand for wood pellets sky high and made for an even more insane period than 2017–18.

After being relatively stable for five years, trading around the new higher range set in 2017–18, pellet prices went sky high, even reaching €600 per tonne.

Basically, panic had set in. Everybody was afraid and the market went crazy. Really crazy.

One of the Danish ministers even went on television urging people not to panic buy: 'you don't have to buy everything now'. But no one was listening.

In my view, there was never really a genuine crisis. There would have been enough pellets to match demand, if buyers had just been patient. But it absolutely wasn't possible for us to deliver a year's supply in just two months; the logistics just didn't work.

We actually had journalists taking photos of our warehouses and writing that we were deliberately holding back pellets in order to push up the price even further.

In reality, we had to process the material, get the pellets in bags, and then get them onto delivery trucks. It was not like we were telling anybody that we were sold out; we just had long waiting lists to fulfil. But the journalists still made out that we were scamming everyone.

Obviously, we benefitted from the greater focus on warehouses and storage that CM Biomass had brought. But even here, we didn't manage to maximize our advantage: the year before, prices had been slipping a bit so we had decided to reduce our inventory a little bit.

If we had known what was coming, we would obviously have kept more supply back.

This goes back to what I was saying: you can't build a long-term strategy around waiting around for unexpected events. After all, exactly the point of these events is that they are unpredictable.

Normally we say that in biomass, it's very hard to time the market, you generally just have to follow along. You sell whatever you can at market prices because even if you make a slight loss, you have to be active in the market, and to turn over your inventory and buy new product.

All you can do as a trader is to try to maximize the hand that you've been dealt. When all is said and done, it's too expensive to sit on too much material in storage, just on the off chance that something unexpected will happen.

Keep on trucking

If I think about my trading style, my main strength is that I am happy to colour outside the lines. I'm generally comfortable thinking outside the box and I'm flexible. I like to switch things up and, if they aren't working, then I'm fine to move in a different direction.

In a trading business, I think you have to be creative and open to change, particularly in a market like biomass, which tends to bite you whenever you get too comfortable.

Probably my other strength is my customer relations. It's still a people business after all, so it's crucial to build rapport and to understand your counterparts and their motivations.

Looking back, I learnt those people skills and to be flexible when I was a young man. My dad had a business delivering bread, baked goods like biscuits, crackers, cakes and crisps to shops from a fleet of around 15 trucks.

I worked for him for a while as a relief driver and it was a tough gig.

My dad didn't help me in any special way because he couldn't show the other guys that he applied different rules to his son. I can thank him for that now, but back then it was a bit rough.

Every morning at 5–6 a.m., you would start with a truck that was almost empty, then you filled it up with whatever you thought you might sell out of the 5,000 different bakery items that you could take. Then you would head out and visit up to 15 clients per day.

You would need to think about what the shops might have sold and then to make a lot of effort with the shopkeeper to push them to take your items. That was even harder as a substitute driver because I barely knew anything about the specific clients in advance.

Added to which, the pay was entirely based on sales commission, so you really had to learn fast. I would say that if you can thrive in a role like that, then you can be successful in almost any commercial role.

My experience on the trucks later got me a job with Norsk Hydro supplying propane. They gave me a company car, a basic salary and a commission structure, but I was starting from scratch in terms of developing a customer base.

My tactic was to park near where our competitors stored their propane bottles. Then I would drive around after their truck to see where they were delivering their bottles. Between that and cold-calling from the telephone book, I managed to build a market share of 30% over three years before I pivoted from the propane side to industrial gas, and later to biomass and wood pellets.

In my view, starting a commercial career in the real world is a good thing for anyone. It's a hard school but the lessons last a long time.

Chapter 29

Generating a win-win for biomass

Tom James began his career in commodities trading in 1989 with Prudential Bache in London. He went on to work for Mocatta Commercial and Crédit Lyonnais in London and Singapore, before in 1998 he founded SwapNet, the first electronic market for energy swaps. Between 2001 and 2008, Tom held various roles at Crédit Agricole, Bank of Tokyo Mitsubishi, Deloitte and Liquid Capital Group. In 2016, he launched the TradeFlow Funds, which invest in bulk commodity physical transactions and he co-founded TradeFlow Capital Management to manage these funds, where he acts as chief executive and chief investment officer. Tom holds a master's degree in energy risk management and a doctorate in commodities trading and risk management. He has taught at and been an executive research fellow at the Singapore Management University, held a chair professorship at India's UPES, and been an adjunct professor at South Korea's Ulsan National Institute of Science and Technology. He is the author of 12 books on commodities and risk management, and appears regularly in the media.

People tend to think of traders as sharks who live purely by eating their prey, but my trading philosophy has always been that there can be deals that are win-wins for all parties.

A trade where everyone benefits is a truly great trade. That kind of trading is repeatable, and it keeps relationships alive.

I had one of those genuine win-wins back in 2009. It was a trade where none of the counterparties were hard done by, and where for once all the pieces of the jigsaw puzzle fell into place easily and at the same time.

My starting point in trading, my basic strategy, is to start by throwing some ideas out there, just spitballing, and to stick everything on a whiteboard, however crazy it might seem. From there, I begin to drill down, to hone each idea and to look at every possible angle.

The aim is always to see if there's been an opportunity somewhere that has been overlooked. After that, it's a question of identifying all of the different pieces of the jigsaw puzzle and seeing if it's possible to bring them together to create some value arbitrage.

DOI: 10.4324/9781003359739-36

I had been doing some consulting work in the United Arab Emirates (U.A.E.) looking at ways to reduce their national carbon footprint. The government there was looking at what they could do in terms of alternative energy.

One of the thoughts was around the potential to use biomass to replace some of the coal that the U.A.E. was burning in its power plants. Biomass is an organic waste product, like wood or plant residue, manure or household waste. It does release carbon dioxide when it is burned, but considerably less than fossil fuels and the organic material is usually from a renewable source.

Palm waste

The launch of the European emissions market had given a significant impetus to the biomass market, as European electricity generators looked to replace coal with biomass in order not to use up all of their valuable emissions permits.

Quite a lot of Asia to Europe trade had developed, particularly in biomass like palm kernel expeller (PKE). PKE is a by-product of the extraction process for palm oil. It looks a little bit like dirt, but it can be burnt alongside coal, in a proportion of up to 20–25%, which represents a big saving on coal in terms of emissions.

Through my previous work for Malaysia's national oil company Petronas and their trading subsidiary MITCO, I had spent a lot of time in Malaysia and visited the palm plantations. I had already done a few trades where I imported PKE into the U.K. for co-firing.

I'd even brought some PKE in personally: I'd carried in a few 50-kilogram bags of the stuff so that it could be tested by U.K. laboratories and test-fired by a few U.K. generators, as any new fuel required licensing permission.

PKE was the material that first alerted me to the potential for biomass, but PKE was also in high demand from animal feed manufacturers. PKE contains elevated levels of crude protein and can be used as a supplement feed for livestock so there was competition for the raw material.

The competition made me turn my attention away from PKE and towards empty fruit bunches (EFB), which were a genuine waste product because absolutely nobody knew what to do with them.

EFB are the big solid woody bunches that are the part that is left behind in palm oil production once you've taken the palm shells out for processing. They look a lot like the part that stays on a banana tree once the bunches of bananas have been harvested.

EFB are tough to manage, and the problem is massive: there are millions of tonnes of them produced every year in Malaysia and Indonesia.

EFB have up to a 30% water content so you can't just burn them as biomass without spending a fortune to dry the bunches out artificially. At the same time, you can't just slice the EFB up and dump them on the ground in the plantation to rot down. The rotting bunches encourage fungus growth, attract pests and lead to soil acidification.

Disposing of EFB was basically a nightmare for plantation operators. Typically, most ended up just burning the stuff, but it would burn really horribly because it contained so much water, so it would end up smouldering away, which obviously didn't help with local environmental pollution in Malaysia and Indonesia.

Transforming waste

When I sat down with my white board to think about trading opportunities, my initial thesis was: there are lots of different types of waste, and lots of different countries that could use that waste as biomass, so is it possible to find a way to move the waste economically?

EFB was a true waste product, so I knew I could pick up significant volumes virtually for free. My only costs would be arranging collection of the material and then paying for trucks to transport it from the plantations to a nearby port.

The plantation operators would be grateful to give the material away. After all, by taking away their EFB, I would be helping them solve a significant waste disposal problem.

But, unless I could figure out how to get the EFB from a port to a consumer country at a reasonable price, then I would be stuck with tonnes of useless material.

In the case of EFB, there was also a second major question to be solved: how could I drive down the cost of drying out the EFB to make it usable by power stations? If I had to use a lot of input energy to dry the bunches out artificially, then I would not only be spending money but also reducing the environmental benefits of using biomass in the first place.

After some wrestling with the problem, the pieces of the jigsaw started to come together.

My first inspiration was to think about the crude oil that Malaysia and Indonesia imported regularly from the Middle East. In particular, I was thinking about how once the oil had been delivered to southeast Asia, the oil tankers that had brought it would be totally empty on their return, haul back, journey to the Gulf.

I thought that the tanker owners might accept a very low rate to bring EFB back with them stacked in some way on or in their empty tankers. That turned out to be the case, and I ended up basically just subsidizing the bunker fuel costs of the tanker on the return leg.

After all, the owners knew that they weren't going to have any other interest in using an empty crude oil tanker on its return journey: no one really exports oil to the Middle East.

Fitting pieces together

The deal with the tanker operators gave me virtually free shipping so I had solved my transport problem; now I knew that I could get the EFB to the port and from there to the Middle East at a relatively low cost.

I just needed to solve the second problem, which was how to dry out the material in an economic and environmentally friendly way. But in a sense, the fact that my cheap transport was to the Middle East was the answer to that issue. If there's one thing the Middle East is famous for, apart from oil, it is blazing hot deserts.

I had to get my timings right because people forget that at some times of the year, the desert can actually get quite humid, which would be no use for drying, but the rest of the time, the desert is very dry and hot. Laying out my EFB on the desert sands of the U.A.E. meant that I could dry them out practically for free.

After the fruit bunches were nice and toasty from their time in the desert, they could easily be sliced and diced and sold to the U.A.E. generators, which could burn the material, mixed with their normal coal input, just like any other wood fuel.

The virtually free waste material, transport and drying already made the trade profitable, but my philosophy is to keep looking at every possible angle in a trade to see if there are other opportunities.

The obvious additional upside was on the carbon certificate side. The trade would be reducing emissions in two locations by avoiding wasteful burning in the southeast Asian plantations, and by replacing coal burning in the U.A.E.

That meant that the deal could be certified as a voluntary emissions reduction (VER), according to accepted methodologies, and could therefore generate voluntary carbon offset certificates that I could sell in the over-the-counter market.

The other bonus that I discovered was that the U.A.E., Malaysia and Indonesia, as Muslim nations, had a lot of subsidies and trade credits in place designed to support and to increase trade between them.

Because I was increasing the volume of their country-to-country trade, I was able to bring the material into the U.A.E. without any duty payments.

Smiles all round

Adding together all of its different elements, the trade worked out quite profitably. It was a nice little trifecta: I benefitted, but then so did the ship operators, as well as the plantation owners in Southeast Asia and the power generator in the U.A.E.

The value was in taking advantage of so much waste. In their original form, the EFB were a pure waste product, while the tankers being empty on their backhaul to the Middle East was also a waste.

In my view, there's no such thing as a true waste product. There will always be a value to someone somewhere, it's just a question of solving or optimizing the logistics.

The majority of biomass that is used productively is still co-fired as an alternative to coal or is used by the packaging industry. Those usages tend to happen locally because most biomass is too low value to justify shipping costs, but this trade shows that there are sometimes international opportunities if you think creatively.

For me, the deal was a good illustration of how traders should try to think out of the box.

In any supply chain, there can be gaps. Can you optimize the freight somewhere, can you think of a slightly cheaper way of moving a product around? If you can, that will help everybody in the chain.

The deal also benefitted the environment significantly. We avoided uncontrolled burning by the plantations, and we displaced coal in the U.A.E. The tanker had to head back to the Middle East anyway, so bringing the EFB didn't add to its carbon footprint; even drying the EFB didn't use any additional energy because we benefitted from the desert sun.

Falling into line

There aren't that many times when all of the supply chain elements come together to the advantage of all of the parties involved.

Unfortunately, I wasn't able to repeat the trade too many times because the U.A.E. shifted focus from biomass towards nuclear energy and more solar power. The success of the trade, and its environmental credentials, relied a lot on the virtually free shipping and drying, so exporting EFB to another part of the world wasn't realistic.

Now, many years on, people are still finding ways to recycle or dispose of plantation waste, but I haven't seen anything out there that is much neater than the solution we developed: a freight arbitrage that generated emissions reductions in two different locations.

It's always satisfying as a trader when the pieces of the jigsaw puzzle all fall into place. That trade was one of those rare times when everything lined up and when everyone benefitted.

Part VII

Classic environmental finance trades

Environmental finance refers to the mobilization and deployment of capital to support projects and activities that deliver measurable environmental benefits, such as pollution reduction, carbon mitigation or biodiversity conservation.

The growth of environmental finance is closely linked to the development of environmental markets, such as trading in carbon, bio energy and renewable energy certificates. Without innovative financing deals, such as those covered in the following chapters, the environmental markets would not have reached anything like their current scale.

Environmental finance helps bridge gaps between project needs and investor appetite by designing products including securitized carbon portfolios, prepayment structures, and green bonds.

The environmental finance sector draws on traditional banking skills, such as credit structuring and risk management, but applies these to the specific uncertainties and timescales of environmental projects.

Further growth in environmental finance is considered essential for scaling investment to the levels needed to meet international climate and sustainability goals.

DOI: 10.4324/9781003359739-37

Chapter 30

Bringing securitization to carbon

Fenella Aouane started her career in commodities as a broker for Archer Daniel Midland (ADM) in London, before joining brokers REFCO in 1999 as director of energy. Fenella went on to manage the energy desk at Cargill Investor Services. She worked for Natixis from 2005 to 2008 as head of listed energy products, before joining Standard Bank in 2008 as director for energy and environmental markets. In 2015, Fenella joined the Global Green Growth Institute in Seoul, South Korea, where she served initially as a principal green finance specialist and more recently as managing director and head of carbon finance. Fenella has been a board member of the Climate Markets and Investment Association and an elected councillor for a London borough.

On my first day at Standard Bank, I was sent to a carbon conference in Cologne in Germany. I had a box of fresh business cards, and my instructions were to 'get out there and meet people'.

The bank needed to find potential buyers of carbon quickly because we had just reached agreement to market a large environmental portfolio – some three million certified emissions reduction (CER) certificates.

The CERs were going to be produced by a carbon project developer called Camco. At the time, Camco was one of the largest environmental project developers and they had projects all around the world that qualified to generate CERs under the terms of the U.N.'s clean development mechanism (CDM).

A lot of Camco's projects were in China, where they were developing renewable energy, as well as a large number of projects that improved the energy efficiency of industrial facilities like steel or cement plants, earning CER certificates by reducing the facilities' carbon emissions.

Camco would basically do all the heavy lifting for the projects: they would work with the facility to design the emissions reductions, implement the plan and register the scheme with the U.N. so that it would qualify for CERs.

As payment for their work, Camco had the right to keep a certain percentage of the CER credits issued by the U.N. They would then sell these CERs

DOI: 10.4324/9781003359739-38

in the market to banks or to energy or industrial firms that would either sell them on or would use them to offset their own carbon emissions.

Camco's business model worked really well generally, but it did mean that they had to manage their cashflows. After all, they weren't getting paid upfront for any of their development or implementation work. Before Camco received any cash, the projects had to be fully up and running and producing credits that they could sell in the secondary market.

Package delivery

What Camco essentially needed was what the financial industry calls 'securitization', which is when assets are pooled together and repackaged so that they can be transformed into interest-bearing securities, or lent against.

Camco was looking to generate some immediate cashflow from their portfolio of credits, so they put together a portfolio of ten of their projects. Their aim was to raise some immediate funds by selling some of their future production of CERs in advance.

It was early 2008, and it was before the financial crisis deterred innovation, so every bank under the sun was competing for the Camco business. Their chief financial officer Scott McGregor had a beauty parade of banks coming in to pitch them, and Standard Bank must have done a great job to get selected.

The bank started making regular payments to Camco, which generated the desired short-term cashflow. To cover our expenditure, it was imperative that we quickly find buyers for the credits that Camco was scheduled to issue over the next few years.

My boss Geoff Sinclair had suggested to Camco that the best way to market such a large portfolio was in the form of tranches. Splitting a portfolio into tranches was fairly common in some of the financial markets, like mortgages or credit default swaps, but this was the first time the model had been applied to the carbon market.

We split the portfolio into three tranches. The first tranche was the premium offering. It would contain the first CERs scheduled to be delivered. The probability of a successful delivery was obviously highest for the earliest delivery, so this tranche would attract the highest prices.

The second tranche contained the next wave of scheduled deliveries, and was larger than the first tranche. The third tranche was retained by Camco themselves.

The design was quite ingenious: it maximized the profitability of the soonest-to-deliver CERs, while the fact that Camco retained the third tranche gave buyers of the first and second tranches greater confidence in delivery.

Potential buyers knew that Camco had skin in the game and would only receive their own CERs once the first and second tranches had been successfully delivered.

Securing bids

My job from the first day I arrived at Standard Bank was to identify potential buyers for either the premium or the secondary tranche. I had to identify all of the players in the carbon market who might want to bid.

Once I had figured out a target list, I sent them out a teaser note about the concept of the deal. This was designed hopefully to intrigue the recipients enough that they would sign a non-disclosure agreement, after which we would provide all the details.

People were no doubt thinking that there was some very sophisticated distribution system in place to alert all the right people from the right organizations in a predetermined order. No chance! We were literally hunting for potential buyers and then manually entering their email addresses.

The initial invitation lists were actually limited by the number of email addresses you could add at one time into the bcc line in Outlook.

Outsiders often think that everything in the financial markets is highly organized and sophisticated when it's not. In fact, often really major deals, due to urgent timing or lack of systems are initially held together with tape and string.

Anyway, we managed to send the details out, and we got a good level of interest.

Our model was that potential buyers had to submit closed bids. We had a lot of interest, and ultimately the tranche system worked very well indeed.

Camco got some excellent bids. In many cases, the prices weren't far off the level where CERs that already existed were trading in the secondary market, reflecting good structuring as well as Camco's reputation as one of the most reliable project developers in the market at the time.

I remember feeling particularly satisfied when one of the power companies phoned up and was really annoyed that they hadn't been invited to bid. In fact, I'd rung the trader there and he had been rather snooty to me and waved me away as if I was some sort of fly.

Once we pointed that out, the trader's boss was furious because they had missed out on what ended up being a very popular deal. This was one that everyone wanted to be in on.

Once our buyers were in place, we had to negotiate the terms of an Emission Reductions Payment Agreement (ERPA), which at the time was something like 42 pages long. ERPAs were bespoke bilateral contracts for buying CERs, and we had to negotiate one with each of the buyers within a week because they needed to get their hedges in place, once the volumes had been assigned.

The buyers were mostly commodity traders, or power and energy companies. They received the delivery schedule from us, and then they would look at the CER forward market and hedge accordingly.

Crisis measures

We closed the deal in August 2008 and pretty soon afterwards the financial crisis hit. We had managed to place the trade just before everything went horribly wrong. We were lucky in our timing and fortunate in our buyers that had been selected. Only one firm ended up having to drop out during the negotiation phase of the deal.

Thankfully, Standard Bank wasn't that heavily hit because we were a South African bank rather than one of the American firms.

The securitization deal ran for three years, and every CER delivery happened. The money was paid out and the deliveries all happened: that alone would class it as a very successful deal. In retrospect, it was amazing that the whole deal was smooth all the way through such a major crisis.

Geoff had done an amazing job explaining all the details of the risks and convincing Standard Bank's risk management department to take the deal on because securitization for carbon had never been done before. There aren't many banks that would have been so brave.

Traditional financiers were very reluctant to lend money against CDM projects because they had always been viewed as outrageously risky.

We were lucky to work somewhere that was a little more open to the unusual. With the help of the deal structure, it worked out very well. It was a particularly nice trade because no one got ripped off; the deal worked out well for everybody involved.

The success of the deal meant that all the staff at the bank got paid. I did too. Previously in my career in the markets, I was almost resigned to the fact that I was probably always paid less than guys that were doing the same job as me. Did that make me somewhat miffed? Yes, of course it did.

There were instances where it felt that male managers (generally with chauvinistic tendencies) had a view that a male staff needed the money to support their family, whilst female staff pay was just 'pin money' on top of what their husband brought home.

There was always some level of sexism in dealing rooms at the time, it was 10–20 years before #MeToo went viral. Thankfully, Standard Bank was a lot better than most.

Saying that, my first job was dealing with the floor traders on the South African Stock Exchange. I can tell you that was not a place to be a retiring violet. In fact, that was pretty much the education from hell. At least, after that, I was never afraid of a dealing room or a trading floor.

I definitely think it's better nowadays, there are more robust rules in place and more transparency: either that, or institutional sexism and bias is better hidden.

Financing innovation

Our deal for Camco was the first securitization deal in the carbon markets, and it remains to this day virtually the only tranche portfolio deal. After that, there were certainly more portfolios that were securitized, and it got to the point where some single projects were securitized.

That deal opened the door, but we need a lot more securitization in the carbon markets so that project developers can get the money to make investments and to make quality projects happen. That still doesn't happen enough.

Now I work in green finance and often people in development think that the money will arrive somehow, without necessarily thinking about the financial side.

In a way, those days before the financial crisis was the heyday of the carbon market. The crisis and then the EU announcement that they were no longer going to accept CERs into the EU emissions trading scheme after 2012 pulled the rug out from under us.

All of our carbon business was in primary and secondary CERs, and as an African bank we held the largest portfolio of African CDM projects.

We limped on through until 2015 when Standard Bank finally said there's no money in CERs anymore and closed the desk down.

New horizons

I went over to GGGI in Seoul and worked in green investment services, similar to environmental project finance. Then in 2019 we began to realize that many governments just didn't understand enough about Article 6 of the Paris Agreement to participate in this new potential carbon market, which allows countries to once again trade international carbon credits with one another.

The GGGI business model is to support its member governments so we were in a fantastic position to step in and provide technical assistance, funded by donor countries we work with.

Thus, I returned to carbon and we started a carbon pricing department. We are helping potential seller country governments so that they can be ready to trade, giving them the tools to be able to figure out their strategy for Article 6 trading.

We launched a vehicle in late 2024 which means we are now also fund managing portfolios of international carbon credits on behalf of government buyers, so able to support some of the early transactions under Article 6. It's incredibly exciting to be involved right at the beginning of this resurgence of the market.

The international carbon markets are getting a second lease of life, with better (albeit more complex) rules, and many lessons learned. So many people from the old days are back in the markets that some conferences feel like a school reunion.

Even though some of us are now approaching veteran status, there's still infinite space for young people who are interested and passionate about the environment. There aren't many textbooks to read because we are still designing much of it as we move along.

We are creating bigger and better environmental markets as we go, so now is the perfect time to get involved.

Chapter 31

The Chinese barrier option

After studying environmental economics at university, Philip Hardwick embarked on a career in banking that saw him first work for Crédit Agricole, before moving in 2006 to JP Morgan. He served J.P. Morgan as an executive director for seven years, before moving to Barclays in 2013. After a year at Barclays, Phil founded a successful environmental consultancy business, Hardwick Climate Business Limited. HCBL sourced and advised on carbon reduction projects, biodiversity projects, climate finance and climate policy. Phil has also served as a member of the board of directors and as advisor to an Ecuadorian plastic waste removal company, biochar companies and many carbon market companies. He is currently chief executive of Everpath Limited, which is a subsidiary of BB Energy, where he is also head of environmental projects.

There's a cliché in the movies where someone shouts across a noisy trading floor to a trader who quickly clicks a button to put on a winning position and then spins around in his chair to give a big thumbs up.

People are left with the impression that that's what trading is, but that part – the final execution of the deal – is actually just the last 30 seconds of a trade that might have taken a year to prepare.

Those moments when you finally get the deal over the line are obviously quite fun, but I don't know that everyone appreciates the blood, sweat and tears that get you to that point.

In the environmental markets, it's not necessarily like a big deal happens every day: there are often weeks and months of hard work behind the scenes.

That was definitely the case for our Chinese barrier options trade. It was such a big transaction that it required a lot of preparation and due diligence, as well as a lot of creativity on the financing side.

DOI: 10.4324/9781003359739-39

Fuel switching

The project was first introduced to the bank by some very credible intermediaries who had a strong background in Anglo-Chinese business and diplomacy. Carbon project development was still fairly new when we first met with these gentlemen, and there were no blueprints for how to make trades happen. It was quite pioneering and that probably helped the creativity flow.

I had actually specialized in environmental economics, but when I graduated in 1997, like a lot of economists I went to work in a bank. Then, around 2008, when JP Morgan decided to invest in the environmental markets in a meaningful way, I was in the classic situation of being in the right place at the right time.

The project that these gentlemen presented to us was based in China and aimed to reduce emissions by moving away from the use of coal to make electricity in favour of less polluting natural gas. The project wouldn't fly today in the voluntary markets, but back then slowing Chinese coal consumption was, and still is, important in reducing emissions.

The project was a sizeable one and it would clearly qualify for emissions credits under the Clean Development Mechanism (CDM).

The CDM was part of the Kyoto Protocol environmental agreement, which was agreed in 1997 and came into force in 2005. The Kyoto Protocol enabled the establishment of flexible market mechanisms based on the trading of emissions permits. Markets and the power of prices became valuable tools for tackling environmental change.

A project that switched from coal to gas as a generation fuel in China qualified for the CDM, but the project developers were facing a significant problem. At the time they came to visit us, the economics of their project didn't stack up. The cost to switch from coal to gas needed a higher price for the additional CDM credits than the market currently offered.

The system was working, but the price just wasn't quite right. This is where the banks could add real value into the process. That's what you pay people to do in banks: to come up with innovative financing solutions.

The price is wrong

'Environmental finance' is a relatively new term but encompasses many traditional financial mechanisms. Carbon finance is so often really just project finance, i.e., finding ways to invest in often complex projects that address negative externalities, specifically reducing carbon.

Many people are eagerly awaiting a liquid tradeable CO2 market that will allow them to trade quickly and efficiently, never getting their hands or their risk profile too dirty. But the reality is that most carbon projects are fairly high-risk project finance investments, not for the faint of wallet and not for those that got all of their life experience from sitting financial theory exams.

The project developers in China were suffering from a perennial problem facing the sector: how can you develop a carbon reduction project when the price for the resulting carbon offset certificate and overall return from the project isn't guaranteed to cover your costs?

The world needs to develop useful technologies to reduce or remove carbon from the atmosphere, whether it is cleaner technology or reforestation. But the price that the environmental markets assign to those projects isn't always enough to get them off the ground. The question then becomes: what can you do when the price isn't right?

The concept that our team came up with was that the bank would offer the project developers a 'barrier option'.

A typical option gives the buyer the right, but not the obligation, to buy or sell a specific security at an agreed price, as long as he or she has paid the seller a premium, which is basically a kind of deposit.

In this case, the bank would act as the buyer, while the project developers would be the seller.

JP Morgan would pay a cash premium or deposit to the project developers. In exchange, we would receive the right to take over the operation of the project at a later date, if the price for carbon rose to such a point as to make the project economically viable.

We looked at the current market price for the environmental credits from the project and they were trading at around $8 per tonne of carbon avoided. If the market price were to reach $15 per tonne, then we would be comfortable that our option over the project was viable and valuable. At that point, we would take over the project, which we called 'knocking in'.

Our pitch to the developers was that, although they had done all of the initial work, they were going to go bust if they couldn't sell the project quickly. No one would pay them the $10 per tonne that they needed to break even, when current prices were so much lower.

Nobody would buy into that project at a higher than market price – that wasn't going to happen – but what the bank could do was to pay them some option premium that would tide them over and keep them in business.

The proposal worked for the developers because they could afford to wait out the period of low prices and could survive on the option premium alone.

In fact, they could do more than survive: I remember how the developers were dressed in the days before they were paid the option premium, and then I remember after we made the payment, one of the guys came into the office wearing a huge belt that looked like it had a giant gold dragon on it.

Knock knock

In a traditional option structure, the buyer acquires the right to buy a security in the future depending on the level of market prices at the time he or she exercises the option.

But in our barrier option structure, we didn't acquire the right to take over the project – to knock in – at the market price, but instead at a pre-determined level below the market price.

That's because all carbon projects come with project development risk, and you have to take that risk into account when you are pricing the option.

Let's say the developers sold us the option when market prices were $6 per tonne and the market price then rose to $15 per tonne, which was the level at which we had the right to take over the project, we still wouldn't actually pay the $15 market price, we would only pay $10 to knock in.

The difference between that market price of $15 and the knock in price of $10 was because, even once we had knocked in, the bank would still be looking at $4.50 of development costs and risks. At the end, we would aim to make a profit of around half a dollar per tonne.

At the point at which we were able to knock in, the project was still not fully developed; it was not a commoditized project. We would only be sure that we could successfully develop the project once the observable price reached $15 and we could go out and hedge at that level or else we could secure a long-term offtake buyer prepared to pay $15 per tonne.

We knew we could develop the project if we could buy at $10 and add in the other costs, but we were very aware that we had bought an option to knock into project development, which is very different to an option to knock into buying a fully formed commodity.

The person who pays the premium clearly gets to knock in at an advantageous rate. That's the *quid pro quo* of the transaction, which compensates the buyer for the risk that the market price never reaches a high enough level to justify the project.

On the flipside, the developer is sacrificing upside in exchange for security and for the opportunity to earn some premium to stay in business.

Raise the barrier

The Chinese barrier option was a much more real-world, practical option than just trading standard paper options.

For a start, the way we designed the trade actually enabled the project to happen. The money that we paid as an option premium kept the project developers alive while they waited for prices to rise. Without that payment, that coal-to-gas switch would never have happened.

In the end, we also made a lot of money out of that trade because it was such a large project and because the market ended up moving in the direction that we needed it to go.

The project got a lot of love internally, and, as you can imagine, as in any big organization the further up the food chain you were, the more credit there was! But for me as the operator of the project, it was primarily a really interesting piece of work.

It was a great trade for the bank, not just because it made money, but because it was the right kind of project at the right time.

The relationship between China and the West has changed a lot in recent years, but back then everyone was courting China. Tony Blair and various British governments had been wooing China for a long time and this kind of 'Sino-fever' was really pushing people to want to do transactions there.

The environmental side was also very much in vogue at the bank at the time, and so our project was considered a double winner.

There was a lot of senior love behind the idea internally. It's like the time recently when everyone wanted to do a blockchain transaction in some shape or form. We were the *plat du jour* during that time. There have been many other *plats* over the years. At that time, it was China but then it another year it might be Saudi Arabia or India. There will always be a next big thing and a new area where everybody will want to do business.

Some will make big transactions and succeed, and some will bet the farm and lose it. We were lucky that time to be one of the winners.

Mind the gap

This exact trade wouldn't be repeatable today for a few reasons.

The political environment between China and the West is just different now. Our transaction was done at a much more optimistic time in terms of international relations. People were much more forgiving of China's industrialization policy and much keener to go and do business in China.

It was also a time in the environmental markets where people were much more prepared to support coal-to-gas switching with carbon credits, whereas nowadays coal-to-gas switching is essentially taken for granted and treated not even as business-as-usual, as renewables would be the preferred technology.

It's working right when the quality of projects improves over the years. After all, those were the early days of the CDM and of the European emissions scheme.

The last reason why the trade would be trickier nowadays was that back then we had access to a deep and liquid paper options market, and we were fortunate to have really forward-thinking option traders at the bank, like my colleagues at the time.

There was a very active traded market in 2010–11, whereas today the liquidity for carbon options is a bit thin. The trade could still be done today but it would be a bit more challenging, and the risk management would have to be handled in a slightly different way.

For our trade, we knew that once I had signalled across the floor to Nigel Felgate and he had placed the options hedge and had given me the thumbs up – that classic trading cliché – we knew that we were in a strong position.

Lessons remain

Although it would be hard to replicate the exact nature of our Chinese barrier options trade, the drivers behind the trade are still the same today.

The need to find innovative ways to bridge time for any project until the price is right is as old as the sun. It's one of the oldest financial problems that there is.

In our case, the financial guys came up with a way of bridging a time gap. Applying barrier options to carbon project development theory was quite novel as well as good fun.

The market wouldn't deign to entertain a coal-to-gas project like this anymore and it's good that the market has moved on. But what hasn't moved on is the fact that you have plenty of project developers who are sat there wishing that the price of carbon was just a little bit higher.

We still see that all the time.

And even if carbon prices go up, the problem remains. At higher prices, customers will become ever more discerning and will demand better projects. That means better technology, and better technology will always be higher cost.

We will always be sat on the cusp of projects being viable or not because the environmental markets are always about generating ever-better projects. There's a really good role for financial institutions to play in all of this because without carbon finance those new generations of carbon avoidance or removal projects will not necessarily happen.

There's always going to be a battle against one of the fundamental aspects of markets, which is that buyers love low prices. In environmental and other pioneering markets, this is a bigger issue than in more mainstream established markets because new project technology is rarely cheap.

Chapter 32

Trading through pre-payments

Martin Berg graduated from the University of Bonn in Germany in 2001 before joining the Climate Change Unit of the Organization for Economic Co-operation and Development (OECD) in Paris. In 2005, he joined investment firm RNK Capital LLC as a carbon finance specialist after having completed a two-year graduate programme at Columbia University. In 2007, Martin moved on to join Merrill Lynch in 2007, where he worked as vice president leading the carbon credit origination and transactions of the Bank's commodity arm. In 2011, he joined the Treasury Department of the European Investment Bank (EIB) in Luxembourg and held various positions until appointed as Head of the Environmental Funds and Climate Finance Policy Unit. In 2020, Martin left the EIB to join the investment and advisory firm Pollination and helped to set up Climate Asset Management (CAM), a joint venture between HSBC Global Asset Management and Pollination. CAM is a specialist natural capital fund manager based in London, where Martin served as chief investment officer for CAM's Nature-Based Carbon Strategy until 2023 when he was appointed chief executive of the company, which has raised over $1 billion across two investment strategies.

My career in environmental finance started in the late 1990s. During my studies in Bonn, I had the opportunity to work as support staff for the U.N. Climate Change Convention conferences from 1998 onwards.

This sparked my interest in climate change and environmental market mechanisms, leading me to look for a career in the field.

My initial goal was always to work for the U.N. However, after completing my graduate degree in New York at Columbia University in 2005, I met a hedge fund manager who offered me an opportunity to work in carbon finance.

This was the time when the first emissions trading schemes and the flexible mechanisms of the Kyoto Protocol were launching, creating new and attractive environmental investment opportunities.

RNK Capital LLC, where I started working, was a small and less well-known player, which made it more difficult to compete with bigger players

DOI: 10.4324/9781003359739-40

such as utilities or larger financial firms that could easily secure offtake deals with large corporate sellers in places such as China.

RNK had to, therefore, find a niche offering to compete with these players as it had difficulties to find counterparties that were willing to enter into long-term purchase agreements of carbon credits.

Our solution was to innovate on the financing side.

RNK came up with a financing approach for prepayment deals where capital was invested upfront with carbon project developers to help projects get off the ground.

In exchange, RNK received a share of the resulting credits at nearly cost price. This structure was modelled on the concession agreements that are common in oil and gas exploration and production.

The approach was not only a way to enter into deals but also allowed to reduce the carbon price risk due to the lower purchase price. This was particularly important because carbon price exposure could not be easily hedged at that time.

Trash to treasure

RNK's first deals were for two landfill projects in Buenos Aires, Argentina, working with a reputable Canadian engineering firm that developed a solution to capture harmful methane emissions from landfill sites.

RNK paid the engineering firm on a turnkey basis, while local municipalities also received a share of the carbon credits generated by the project.

Financing was based on a breakeven price of roughly $3 per tonne for the carbon certificates generated by the landfill schemes under the Clean Development Mechanisms of the Kyoto Protocol. Despite not being able to hedge our position, RNK's risk protection was based on getting credits at a significant discount to prevailing market prices, which were trading between €10 and €15.

The spread between the breakeven and market prices allowed RNK to absorb most development risks and still have a very attractive investment opportunity.

This model was replicated for the landfill of the city of Belém in Brazil in 2006, where coincidentally COP30, the annual U.N. Climate Change Summit, was held in 2025.

We knew that it was unlikely that we would ever take delivery at exactly the $3 price that we were hoping for. But we knew that, even if the costs rose, we should have enough built-in margin to offset against any issues that emerged.

Although the projects faced delays and challenges, ultimately costing nearly twice as much as hoped, the market prices remained favourable in the €10–15 range, making the deals very successful.

Information flow

I believe that these financing structures are still one of the best ways to trade in markets where it is very difficult to hedge a long-term exposure, e.g. the voluntary carbon market.

In the absence of a clear benchmark price, minimizing the purchase price and embracing development risk is crucial. Early market margins can be significant, however, as the market matures, more sophisticated pricing and risk management techniques are required.

It was possible to achieve high margins in 2005 or 2006 when the environmental market was still immature. In the oil markets, there are live quotes almost every minute of the day, but back then those of us in the carbon market had to wait a week or so to read an article in *Point Carbon* magazine that would tell us whether the market was $1 up or $1 down.

When I first started out, there was no live data. You had to rely on market intelligence to know where the price was, and that made it really difficult, but also potentially more profitable.

As the market became more efficient, people struggled to achieve the same margins, and then they had to post collateral because it became a collateralized market where even the over-the-counter market required ISDA agreements, which made it difficult for smaller and less capitalized market players to succeed.

I recognized that more sophistication was required and moved to Merrill Lynch in 2007. At Merrill Lynch, I worked with a team to develop a model that used market data – especially delivery probabilities of projects based on type, geography and stage – to better forecast how much a project could actually realistically generate.

Using the common three-to-one ratio in trading, my team built a portfolio of transactions in different stages and hedged these out in the secondary market.

Commodity trading houses generally operate on this concept in markets where they have to go from physical to derivatives. However, few banks today are comfortable with emerging markets or providing structured credit to carbon project developers.

As information improved and the playing field became more even, you had to be much more aggressive to get deals done, so you needed good data and great analysis.

I remember the last deal I did at the bank in 2010. We were able to be the most aggressive bidder on a project because of the quality of our data.

We knew, for example, that for projects, like the one we were bidding on, there was typically only a 2% standard deviation between the estimates of how many credits the project would deliver and the historical record of actual deliveries. This allowed us to bid for a very aggressive price and bank on the delivery of the credits.

That kind of precision was a world away from my earlier experiences.

With landfill gas projects the standard deviation can be more like 30–40%, which means you can get your financial model drastically wrong.

Of course, in the early days you could build in enough spread to cover that variance. You were never quite sure what you would finally get, but the margins for those first projects were big enough to absorb any difference.

Carbon fund

I have been back in the carbon market since 2021. I currently run an asset management firm that looks to fill the financing gap in the voluntary carbon market.

The firm pools demand from corporate clients committed to net-zero and offers carbon credits at cost basis. Given that lack of pricing data, investors receive carbon credits per dollar invested rather than a guaranteed financial return.

The fund arranges secured offtake and simultaneous finance, building a portfolio of prepayments and payment on deliveries for voluntary carbon credits. This approach reduces market risk while still facing delivery risk and also reputational risk for supporting the wrong type of projects.

The firm has over 15 investors for this approach and has raised more than $500 million to invest in projects generating high-quality carbon credits.

Either the projects are already operating and we're just buying the stream of credits, or we are providing financing for projects through a pre-payment mechanism.

Initially, we were worried that this strategy would expose us to high carbon prices. But recent criticism of the voluntary carbon market has moved prices the other way. While this supported the investment thesis, the reputational risk remains and requires the team to focus on high-quality projects that eliminate these concerns.

These are the quirks of a voluntary market, where there's so much debate about which projects are good quality and which are not.

It feels like the market is trying to wean everyone off the low-quality projects. This is a process that will continue to run, until all sides can land on agreed standards and an agreed quality.

At that point, voluntary carbon will hopefully be a more typical market where the ultimate buyers will be reassured and will be happy to take quality projects onto their books.

We are still in a phase where lots of people don't really know whether to buy credits for $0.50 or for $50. Maybe they go one way, or another, or maybe they buy a few of each.

There's a lot of confusion out there, and it will take the market a few years to wash out some of the weaker projects.

You have to give new markets time to mature, and you have to expect some volatility. What encourages me now is that, although the pool of buyers is smaller, they are mostly quite well endowed and they are looking for quality.

These buyers are driving up standards and, once we see more certainty, I am confident the next tier of buyers will kick in.

In the meantime, though, mitigating price risk is the key to surviving and prospering in these volatile markets. Prepayment and other financing tools can be great tools to reduce that market risk.

Chapter 33

Developing forest bonds

Lasse Ringius studied at Roskilde University Centre and at the University of Copenhagen in his native Denmark. Between 1987 and 1992, Lasse undertook a doctorate in environmental regulation at the European University Institute in Italy, during which period he was also a visiting scholar at the Massachusetts Institute of Technology (MIT). After holding various professional positions in the environmental field, including with the United Nations, Lasse joined the World Bank in 2003 as a senior environmental specialist. In 2009, he was appointed senior carbon finance specialist at the International Finance Corporation (IFC). Lasse joined the Global Green Growth Institute (GGGI) in 2016, where he served as the first director of Green Investment Services, based at the institute's headquarters in Seoul, South Korea, and as country representative, based in Kathmandu, Nepal.

The reason I first got involved in the environmental markets was primarily because I was interested in exploring the interface between markets and governments.

I had observed that where you have strong markets, you tend to also have a big state. Government regulation appeared to facilitate the successful growth of markets.

I landed in the environment from the research side, rather than out of pure conviction. Of course, like any other stand-up Danish guy, I was concerned about the health of the planet, but it wasn't like I was always carrying a big green flag around.

Nonetheless, I ended up doing a doctorate in international environmental regulation. My professor had sent me off to look at environmental issues on the grounds that this was a new area to explore: governments and international organizations were clearly going to be key to driving market solutions.

After completing my studies and publishing a book based on my thesis results at MIT Press, I gravitated towards designing methodologies for carbon reduction projects and figuring out what tools and data would be needed to properly measure and monitor a project's impact.

DOI: 10.4324/9781003359739-41

A lot of work was going on in the late 1990s to build a credible and transparent system for tracking carbon reduction projects, which could then be independently audited and verified.

Much of the drive for that process came from the World Bank, which had received some initial funding from Norway, and which was doing trials of projects to see what worked and what didn't. There were others looking at the space at the same time, but the World Bank had a bit more firepower.

My experience advising the United Nations on methodologies was quite interesting to the World Bank, and they set me to work trying to figure out how to manage small-scale environmental projects like micro-hydropower, domestic solar, biogas, domestic appliances, bricks, cookstoves and so on.

The World Bank had a fund specifically dedicated to small projects and small community development projects. My job was to make sure that they had a robust methodology and that we could monitor their performance so that at the end we could claim the emissions offset by the project.

Commercial nous

I left the World Bank methodology team in 2004 to move across to the project development side. That was my first experience of the commercial side of carbon projects.

I remember being in a meeting with my then boss and making some lame remark like, 'I didn't realize you could make money out of carbon reductions'.

Looking back, my naivety makes me smile.

As project manager, I took more than ten projects from concept initiation to conclusion of a legally binding carbon offtake agreement. Following that, I became operations team lead overseeing a large team in charge of all World Bank carbon projects in developing countries. During my tenure, the deal team concluded 81 carbon off-take investments worth $540 million.

For real progress to happen, the public and the private sector need to work together from the beginning. We need to mobilize enormous amounts of capital in the service of the environment, and profit is a powerful motive for that investment.

The challenge of attracting finance became even greater shortly after I moved to the International Finance Corporation (IFC), the private sector arm of the Work Bank Group, in 2009 because carbon prices were tanking.

The IFC is a giant global development institution focussed exclusively on the private sector, and we had some ambitious plans, but the low carbon price was jeopardizing everything.

I started looking at different areas, and in particular at how to attract fresh investment into the carbon offset market.

I started exploring instruments that were outside the mainstream, which mainly set up carbon funds managing monies received from one or more investors that were investing in buying carbon off a portfolio of projects. A bilateral offtake agreement between a seller producing the carbon reductions and a buyer was the standard approach.

I was looking at forest conservation projects and at forest replanting and so forth. There were many good projects out there, but they needed more finance.

The traditional way that a carbon project developer would attract seed capital was with a relatively simple forward structure: the developer would lock in some or all of the potential future credits upfront in some form of an emissions reduction purchase agreement (ERPA) in order to access the funds to go ahead and get started on the project.

I wanted to see if we could go beyond these forward contracts and think about other possible funding instruments.

In particular, I started looking at the potential for environmental bonds.

The name's bond, forests bond

My first step was to do some serious study. I read a lot of papers and I talked to lots of different people. I learned about the different types of bonds, and I got excited about the potential role that bonds could play in carbon finance.

At its simplest, a bond is just a lending agreement for a defined period between a borrower and a lender. The borrower typically pays defined interest to the lender during the lifetime of the bond as well as repaying the bond principal, that is the original loan amount, at the end of the defined period.

There are trillions of dollars moving around the global financial system in the form of bonds, but some of my colleagues would ask 'why do we need bonds?'

My answer was that there were very few financial instruments in the carbon space at that point. You had over-the-counter carbon credits, which were typically hard for non-specialists to access and understand, and simple forward financing structures.

Where were the instruments for the bigger flows of money, for institutional investors and sovereign wealth funds? There was nothing out there that was designed to appeal to those kinds of investors.

I thought there should be a way that a fund could invest in an environmental project without anybody needing to be a carbon aficionado or some kind of carbon geek.

Portfolio managers that are managing huge sums of money don't always have time to do extensive research on a particular carbon project in Africa, etc. They might have 30 minutes to look at an investment opportunity – what is the credit rating, who is issuing the instrument, bond size, currency – and then they need to say either 'yes' or 'no'.

Of course, that's a simplification, but we needed to design a product that would work for those folks and that they could understand.

Offering a bond also gave the IFC the opportunity to go and visit major portfolio managers and fund managers who would otherwise not be exposed to the world of carbon.

We used our time with them to talk about climate change, the critical importance of forests from a climate perspective, and mitigation efforts, which was very valuable indeed.

The universe of banker-investors was receptive to the concept of an environmental bond from the get-go.

They liked the idea of a bond because they were dealing in bonds every day of their lives, but they also liked the idea that this was something different and a way for them to dip their toes into the nascent environmental markets.

Building a bond

The key to success was clearly going to be how we could package and sell the bond to make it as appealing as possible to potential investors.

Where we were creative was that we thought that there might be potential bondholders out there who for various reasons might be interested in getting carbon credits instead of a cash payment. Perhaps they would use the credits to offset their own carbon footprint, or perhaps they would want to play in the carbon market – by trading the credits – or maybe in a few cases they would buy the bond just to learn a bit more about the carbon market.

We thought there would definitely be companies that would see the value of such an instrument and would take a look at it.

We weren't looking for a huge commitment. We were never thinking about issuing a $1 billion bond or something of that size, but we thought maybe somewhere around $100 million might work.

The concept was that IFC would receive the initial capital from the bond holders. This would provide us with money to invest in IFC's overall portfolio of projects as is standard, while bond holders could choose to select carbon credits instead of the usual cash coupon.

Our plan was to work with a developer to produce carbon credits rather than going to the market to buy certificates.

Then, over the lifetime of the bond, which ended up being set at five years, IFC would make bond payments to the bond holders as agreed.

The novelty of this bond was that the holders had the option not to take the payments as cash but instead in the form of carbon credits.

We quickly realized that we would need someone to effectively 'backstop' the bond. We needed to find a firm that would be prepared to take the carbon credits produced by the carbon project in the event that the bond holders opted for cash rather than carbon payments.

I turned to my network to get a sense of which firms might be interested in kicking off something novel. I quickly discovered a potential opportunity with the mining giant BHP Billiton.

BHP were interested in doing something about deforestation, which they viewed as a serious problem, and saw a need for investment opportunities and instruments that could deepen the market for carbon from forests and attract a broader set of private-sector companies to help slow deforestation.

I was always very impressed with BHP. They realized that the mining business is clearly not green and that they had a big carbon footprint, but they wanted to understand what they could do to improve. BHP was willing to look into sequestration or preserving carbon. I always thought their staff was very knowledgeable, very responsible and very committed.

I presented the idea of a bond instrument to BHP, and they were interested because they understood that this was a way of getting carbon finance into the mainstream financial markets and creating tradeable instruments.

I wrote a concept paper for BHP in October 2014, but it took another two years of discussions with them and the market before we were ready to proceed to issue the bond.

Issue forth

The final version of the bond stated that each year bond holders could opt to receive a carbon credit instead of a cash coupon.

The credits would be allocated proportionally to their initial investment, and if the bond holder didn't specifically request the carbon alternative, then they would automatically receive the agreed cash payment.

In the case that the bond holders didn't take up the carbon credit option, then any remaining credits would flow to BHP who were acting as the backstop. IFC and BHP had agreed a fixed price for the credits under an ERPA.

Once we had locked down this structure, we worked with three banks in different parts of the world who went out and shook the tree to find potential buyers.

We ended up with enough interested parties to finally issue a bond for \$152 million in late October 2016. The buyers were all large institutions, including some pension funds.

The issuance passed off successfully and the innovative nature of a forestry bond with the optionality of receiving cash or carbon credits made quite a splash. The bond was listed with fanfare on the London Stock Exchange.

The Forests Bond won *Environmental Finance*'s Best Sustainable Forestry deal of the year and also won an innovation prize internally at the World Bank Group, which was very gratifying.

More importantly though, the bond succeeded in its objective of funding a really excellent project. The finance from the bond supported the development of the Kasigau Corridor project in Kenya.

The Kasigau Corridor is located between two national parks, Tsavo West and Tsavo East, and created a new reserve protecting wildlife and over 2,000 square kilometres of forest. The project offsets one million tonnes of carbon dioxide per year and around five million carbon credits were delivered to IFC during the life of the bond.

The bond linked a project in a remote part of Kenya to the global financial markets. I thought that was both very beautiful in a way and innovative: investors in the world's financial centres engaged in something that was very meaningful and different to their day-to-day experience.

The bond gave the developers of the Kasigau Corridor project the certainty that they were going to get paid for their carbon upon delivery. The money would come from either the bond holder or BHP, with IFC responsible for the exchange of money and credits between the recipient and the project developer.

New learnings

The bond worked well: throughout its five-year duration, there were no missed payments, and the carbon credits were created as intended.

What was a surprise to us was that none of the bond holders ever requested the carbon credits; they always took the cash payment.

Most of them didn't really need the carbon credits because they didn't have large carbon footprints to offset.

The bond holders were there primarily to learn and to support the development of a new type of instrument, so the credits generated from the Kasigau Corridor ended up going to BHP.

We also learned that, although using a bond structure brought in new potential financial investors, it also ruled out some of the more typical investors in carbon projects.

The typical carbon trading desk that was active in the spot and forward carbon markets didn't necessarily have the internal approvals in place to buy a bond.

Carbon traders weren't authorized to buy bonds, only their treasury departments. That meant the instrument didn't find a natural home in the carbon market because the people who buy bonds are a completely different cast of characters.

The other takeaway for us at IFC was that there was a limit to how creative you could be when you issued a carbon bond.

Our initial thought had been to design the bond to always pay out in carbon credits unless the bond holder specifically requested a cash payment.

But it turned out that issuing a carbon coupon bond was not easy to get approved by the U.S. regulators.

The regulators required issuers of bonds to spell out what are the financial risks from this instrument. Well, it would require a crystal ball to have any idea about how the carbon market was going to perform going forward.

We tried with a few well-respected banks to come up with some models about how the price of carbon might evolve and what might be the variability in value. But it was ultimately too tricky, so we reversed the structure and made cash payments the default option for bond holders.

The forestry bond worked well overall and was a good proof of concept. I'm not saying that bonds are the perfect solution or the only instrument that we should focus on in carbon finance. But bonds should certainly be part of the toolbox we have at our disposal.

Keep on moving on

One of the fundamental roles of a development bank, like the World Bank or the IFC, is to crack open a new market. Then, when the market is working well and you start to see different players emerge, the question that should come up internally is, 'what are we still doing there? are we crowding out the private sector?'

When you get to the point in market development where the big banks – JPMorgan, Goldman Sachs etc. – are participating actively, and are throwing their big origination teams at the problem, then there's no need for a development bank any more.

Once the market is functioning properly, the development bank needs to get out of the way and go and work on a new area that hasn't been cracked yet.

The motto of a good development bank should always be, 'let's try something different'.

I guess that's why I have always found my various jobs so interesting. There's always something new to learn and to work on.

My roles have put me through plenty of mental hoops. You have to be a realist if you want to attract private sector investment, but at the same time you also have to be a keen believer in the environmental markets and in carbon pricing.

You also have to be very pragmatic. Nowadays, when my colleagues present something that is very ambitious or clever to me, I ask them, 'do you really need all of those bells and whistles? why don't you just go ahead and get the first project launched?'

My view is that when it comes to the environment, our priority should always be to get something done as quickly and efficiently as possible.

Just as with the Forests Bond, once you have an initial success, you can always go on and make the next project bigger or better.

Part VIII

Trading water markets

Water markets have developed in various forms across the globe, with the most established and liquid – pardon the pun – markets found in Australia and the United States.

The Australian water market began in the late 1980s and has evolved organically, relying on a clear legal regime for water rights that are registered, transferable and can be traded independently of land ownership.

Most market participants are farmers, and trading allows for flexible water use, supporting agricultural production through periods of drought and abundance. The introduction of water markets has notably improved resource allocation, enabling more careful water usage and maximized productivity even as climate conditions become more variable.

Some limited water markets also exist in the United States, while there are also water-related environmental mitigation markets that are particularly important for wetlands and streams.

These markets have become an important vehicle for enforcing 'no net loss' policies, obliging developers who impact aquatic resources to purchase environmental credits that fund restoration elsewhere.

Beyond Australia and the United States, formal water markets remain less developed in most regions, though interest in market solutions is rising as water scarcity intensifies.

DOI: 10.4324/9781003359739-42

Chapter 34

Trading water forwards

After graduating from the University of Melbourne in 2008 with a master's degree in water resource management, Lex Batters went to work as a project manager for specialist environmental consultancy Psi Delta. Lex joined water brokerage firm Ruralco Water in 2012, and in 2014 he moved to water marketplace H2OX as business development manager. Lex currently serves as chief executive of H2OX, after being promoted to the position in 2015.

The Australian water market is probably the most advanced water market in the world, but it's still relatively young by commodity market standards.

I would guess the first water trade might have happened in the mid- to late 1980s, and it would likely have been a deal done over the fence between two neighbouring farmers.

The farmers would have fixed a dollar amount and then one would have probably stuck his pump in the other guy's water channel and taken delivery that way.

Since then, the water market has evolved, but developments have come very slowly and very organically. In part, that's because there has been very little guidance from the government, which is highly unusual for an environmental market.

For some reason, officials in Australia have taken the view that they shouldn't interfere in any way, shape or form with the water market.

We don't have any specific regulations that cover the water market, we just follow the general regulatory guidelines that apply to the whole financial sector.

In general, this hands-off approach has worked well. Of course, water rights are listed on government-owned registers, so a buyer can have confidence that the seller is actually holding the water rights that they are selling.

DOI: 10.4324/9781003359739-43

The vast majority of participants in this market are farmers, and most deals are for water that is immediately available. The typical trade might be a water utility or a small farmer with some water left over who will sell 50 or 100 megalitres to someone like a dairy farmer who might need a little extra water.

Forward liquidity

The Australian water market is pretty straightforward: we don't offer lots of sophisticated products. The most exotic product you can trade at the moment is a 'forward' deal, where the water is not for immediate delivery but for delivery at a future date.

The most innovative water trade that I've seen was the five-year forward trade that we arranged in 2016 between a large almond grower and an investment fund. That was the first water trade to have such a long duration and I haven't seen anything similar since.

Multi-year forwards are a challenging product to price, and it is very challenging to hedge the exposure, which deters a lot of participants. It's a shame because a forward product is so useful for certain farmers who tend to sell their crop ahead of production.

Cotton is the classic commodity that needs water certainty. Farmers come to us and say I've forward sold my cotton for the next three or four years, so now I need to make sure I have enough water to grow it.

The risk with a multi-year forward is that one side is likely to end up either hugely in or hugely out of the money.

Potential buyers know they can get the water they need for free from the sky sometimes, so it takes a lot of foresight for someone to pay a premium for certainty.

It's quite brave for any potential water user to say, 'I want to lock in a price, so I don't mind paying well over the market today and even well over where the market has traded for the last five years'.

In the case of our five-year forward, the market price of water was trading at around A$50–60 per megalitre when we struck the deal at A$180.

I remember sitting with the almond grower and her asking why on earth it was a good idea for her to pay A$120 more than the current market price, and then to lock that elevated price in for five years.

My argument was that water is very, very volatile.

To put it in perspective, the water price was A$1,000 per megalitre in 2020, but by June 2023, you could buy the same volume for just A$2 because of the floods, while by October 2023 the market had traded back up to A$200.

There's no commodity quite as volatile as water: with droughts and floods ever more common, the price jumps all over the place.

That was what I needed to explain to the almond grower, who had only really been active in wetter periods when market conditions favoured the farmer.

My argument was that a farmer would only need to be in the money for one of those five years for this multi-year forward to potentially pay for itself.

Cash flow

That's the way it ended up working out.

During the first year, the almond grower was behind in terms of having overpaid relative to the spot price. In the second year, they were well ahead. But in the third year, the water price shot up to over $400 when the grower had paid A$180, so they were more than 100% ahead.

Then 2022 was a blowout year. There was a regional drought that sent water prices soaring. The spot price at delivery that year ended up being over A$900, costing the poor investor on the other side around A$750 on a trade that they had struck at A$180.

I remember having lunch with the trader from the investment fund during that fourth year. We were sitting in a restaurant by the Brisbane River, and by that point the fund was probably a couple of million dollars out of the money on the five-year forward.

I remember this very nice boat sailing down the river past where we were sitting. I turned to the trader and said, 'hey, you could have bought that boat if you hadn't done the water trade'.

I hope he took it in good spirits.

The fund's paper loss was obviously enormous but it likely wasn't that bad in reality because the trader would have offloaded some of the risk. The fund would have traded an offsetting forward or leased some physical water to partially hedge their exposure.

Nonetheless, it is bound to feel sore to deliver water at A$180 that you could have sold at A$900. Fortunately, the investment fund had their eyes wide open, and they are still active in the market to this day.

The almond growers were clearly very happy. You don't hear 'thank you' a lot in the trading business and sadly I didn't get a lifetime supply of almonds, almond milk or anything like that.

But when you put someone onto a trade that works out so well, at least it means they will take your phone call next time and give whatever you are proposing some extra attention.

Drought-buster

The introduction of a water market has worked really well for the agricultural sector. The volatility of water availability here is such that most farmers wouldn't have survived the millennium drought if we hadn't had water trading in place.

The drought severely affected southern Australia between 1996 and 2010, with 2006 declared the driest year since the arrival of European settlers to the country.

During the millennium drought, if you owned a megalitre of water rights in Victoria, you might have received at best 20 or 30% of your rights, and in some instances less than that. Meanwhile, rights owners in New South Wales went for years without being allocated any water.

Without enough water to grow crops, trading their water rights was the only way that some farmer could make an income.

The market performed really well during the millennial drought.

In a dry year, a rice farmer might not be allocated enough water to grow anything meaningful, but instead he or she had the opportunity to sell the water rights to someone like an almond grower.

For the almond grower on the other side of the trade, their most important concern is to maintain water availability, almost at any cost, because their trees need water to survive. If an almond tree dies and the producer needs to replant, they will be years without any production.

Thanks to the market, the rice grower can always decide to skip a year of output and wait for better times. Trading the water rights to a grower who needs it more urgently allows that rice grower to stay in business for the next 12 months.

The market essentially gives people in agriculture the flexibility to scale up their production when water is plentiful and then scale it back down when there are droughts. Trading water rights allows farmers to ride out the cycle.

The market also makes it easier for new entrants to get into agriculture. Farmland in Australia, like everywhere else, is ferociously expensive. If you had to buy water rights at the same time as the land, the upfront costs might be prohibitive.

But because we have a market, the new entrant can go and buy a property and start farming, secure in the knowledge that they can buy water in the spot market to meet their requirements.

Waterproof rights

The reason why the Australian water market has developed so well is that we have a good regime in place: we have underlying water rights, caps on extraction and fungible rights. That combination of factors makes it very easy to trade water rights.

We can do trades here that are finalized the same day, whereas in the U.S. there are trades that have been going on for years.

The way water rights were issued in the U.S. is more about who went West first and claimed the river. As a result, there are cases in the U.S. where there's been a deal done for delivery in a particular year, but three years later the parties are still working through the contract.

What might look like a straightforward deal in the U.S. can end up with the counterparties stuck in a courthouse in some remote town trying to decipher a deed from 1870.

Perhaps because Australia is a very young country, the government sat down and thought about water rights a bit more deeply and that has paid off.

Australia is quite unique in that you can own water separately from land. From a market point of view, this is a very good thing. From a political point of view, it has its issues: some farmers were initially very nervous about a market developing because there was a fear that all the water was going to be bought up by investors.

That hasn't played out. Investors are certainly a significant portion of the market, but their market share is no more than high single figures.

Investors appreciate the non-correlated nature of water as an asset. It gives them a different type of exposure, or else it fits with a broader agricultural investment programme.

The first group to invest in water in a big way was the Harvard Endowment Fund, which has more money than God, and which decided to park some money in water with a very long-term investment horizon. Harvard came to the market in 2007–8 and invested $30–40 million into the first stand-alone water fund.

There's certainly a lot of offshore money that comes into Australian agriculture, but that's always been the case: the whole development of agriculture here has been underpinned by foreign capital.

It was initially British money, then from the 1950s and 1960s it was mostly American money, then Japanese money, after that came the Chinese and now it's mostly the Canadians. The nature of the investors changes depending on geopolitics and investor interest.

At this point, Canadian pension funds are probably the biggest single owners of water in the country. There's always some concern about foreigners owning water, but water is a unique commodity in the sense that buyers have to make use of their water rights here in Australia.

After all, water isn't typically a commodity that is suitable for export. If someone figures out an economic way to put water onto a tanker at the bottom of the Murray River and ship it offshore, then good luck to them.

Drying up

To be fair, the environmental benefits of the water market are a somewhat double-edged.

If the water market went away overnight, there would probably be a whole lot of water that wouldn't get used because it would be valueless. People with excess water would just leave it in the river, which would ultimately benefit the environment.

Introducing the market, and giving water a value has definitely increased the usage of water within the capped amount. Most water now gets used, but I would argue that it gets used far more efficiently. The market enables us to grow much more with the same amount of water.

The productivity gains that have been achieved in the water space in Australia in the last 15–20 years since the market emerged are simply amazing.

That matters because the Australian climate is getting drier, while at the same time demand is increasing.

Water availability is a growing issue in Australia, and no one can say what water availability is going to look like three years from now. Predicting availability next year is already difficult enough because of the variability of the weather and the limited nature of storage.

But the market ensures that people use water much more carefully, whatever the climate scenario, because they appreciate its value. People treasure water now as opposed to wasting it.

Chapter 35

Trading from the wetlands

After graduating with a master's degree in environmental law, George Kelly began his career in Baltimore, Maryland, in 1987 with law firm Ober Kaler, where he became a partner. In 1998, he founded environmental mitigation firm Environmental Banc & Exchange, LLC, which was acquired by Resource Environmental Solutions (RES) in 2014. George stayed on at RES as chief markets officer and later as a strategic advisor to the board. He was appointed managing director of environmental investor Quantified Ventures in 2021, but left the following year to found Earth Recovery Partners (ERP), where he currently serves as chief executive. ERP is based in Denver, Colorado, and provides advisory and capital support for companies and projects in the environmental markets.

When you talk about the environment, there is often this cultural dynamic whereby the non-governmental organizations (NGOs) have had an aversion to private for-profit enterprises operating in the environmental sphere.

To some of those folk, the idea that someone might make a profit from restoring the environment is a terrible thing. When we started out in business, we experienced all kinds of opposition from folks in the resource agencies, the NGO community and plenty of others. Everyone was trying to undermine the private sector's involvement in the environmental space.

The first area I looked at when I started my own firm was wetland restoration in North Carolina. There was a robust approach and strict enforcement of mitigation rules that were set up nationwide. North Carolina embraced a market approach that required developers that impacted on wetlands or waterways to mitigate or pay an *in-lieu* fee to the authorities, which would then use that finance to offset the negative environmental impact of the development by developing positive environmental projects elsewhere.

Well, when we looked at that scheme, the first thing we found was that the state authorities had taken in something like $60 million in fees, but were only actively restoring around 10 acres of wetland. They were using that money for other purposes.

DOI: 10.4324/9781003359739-44

The other thing we found was that they were charging developers that needed to offset their impact only about $40 per linear foot of stream. That was a very cheap rate that was lower than the true cost of stream restoration, so they were kind of subsidizing the developers from day one.

Bringing accountability

There were similar in-lieu fee programmes all around the country run by states and operated by NGOs, and no one was holding any of them accountable. There was no real market, so no one knew the true cost of restoring wetlands or streams.

Meanwhile, the private sector – the for-profit black hatters – were being held to the highest standards possible. Of course, that made our credits way more expensive. They cost more because they had more integrity.

We had to fight a cultural fight. The *in-lieu* fees and the cultural disdain for the private sector were killing any chance of a real market developing.

It became a policy fight for us. We started asking why these programmes were charging such low fees; why were states only developing water projects six, eight or even ten years after they had taken in the funds from developers and why weren't the programmes held to higher standards.

But we were getting nowhere at state level, despite our lobbying efforts, and we realized we needed a federal law that would promote a level playing field for the private sector and would bring some transparency into the mitigation business.

A couple of us worked with a congressman from North Carolina to introduce a bill. We tried four times and every time the NGOs fought us, even though we were pushing for higher environmental standards. Our theme was: it's not who delivers environmental projects, it's the standard of delivery that matters.

Iraqi legacy

We finally got there via the Iraqi Appropriations Bill of 2003. We managed to sneak a provision relating to improving wetland and stream restoration standards into that bill because it related to the military and the Army Corps is the regulatory body for wetlands and streams in the U.S.

The only senator that paid that clause any attention was Hillary Clinton and once she realized it was raising environmental standards, she was OK with it. Remember that it was private industry that was pushing to drive up standards; it wasn't the NGOs or the resource agencies.

The Iraqi Appropriations Bill was transformative for wetlands and stream projects. I remember some French visitors asking about the development of the market and we told them, 'We basically have to thank Saddam Hussein for the U.S. mitigation markets'.

After the Iraq bill passed, it still took five years to create the federal mitigation rule of 2008, which finally levelled the playing field. At that point, private equity firms started showing up at mitigation conferences, and the finance guys started taking us seriously. I even named my first firm Environmental Banc & Exchange because it was oriented to appeal to Wall Street.

The mitigation rule also covered streams for the first time, as well as just dealing with wetlands. There was a lot of back and forth on that, but ultimately streams were included. Now the market for stream credits today is larger than the wetland market so that was another major achievement of the rule.

Growing revenue streams

In the years between the bill passing and the final rulemaking, I started to think hard about the imbalance between the multiple stringent permit requirements under both federal and state law that required multiple forms of mitigation but did not allow restoration projects to encompass all of those type of credits in one project.

Essentially, if you were working on a project in the riparian zone in North Carolina, you might have to deal with four separate mitigation obligations, relating to streams, buffers, nutrients and wetlands for one acre of impact of floodplain.

These four types of environmental attributes were recognized at the permit stage as requiring separate mitigation obligations and yet the mitigation site could not integrate these attributes into one site to obtain regulatory approval. In other words, there was no permit symmetry between the rules relating to assessing impacts and assessing mitigation solutions.

The concept was that, as an eco-asset restoration project, we should be able to aggregate the different types of credits into one restoration project, and then sell those credits separately.

We called it 'stacking': we wanted to be able to stack multiple credits on the same acre. We argued that if states were requiring multiple actions on the debit side, then they should be allowing multiple actions on the credit side.

We took this concept of 'permit symmetry' all the way up to the attorney general's office in North Carolina, where it was finally approved, and everything was hunky dory.

That approval meant we could get multiple credits issued on the same acreage. We had already sold the wetlands and stream credits for that acreage, but now we were getting additional nutrient and buffer credits as well.

Things were going great, and our stacking meant that we were providing inexpensive credits to the market because we had already covered our cost basis with the wetlands and stream credits that we had already sold.

The big dipper

The idea of stacking promotes projects that have the most ecological attributes on any individual site.

Conversely, since there are multiple forms of credits at one site, we were minimizing the cost of each type of credit since those costs were spread out. We were maximizing our market position by selling credits for less, which is just good for the buyers, but our competitors hated it. They got the NGO community to complain, and we ended up on the front page of the North Carolina paper.

There was a big brouhaha, as you can imagine. They all said, 'you're stacking and there's no additionality', which was the big buzzword at the time.

I became known in the market as 'Double-Dipping George' because I had stacked all these different credits on the same acreage. The reality was that this stacking approach allowed us to sell our credits at a cheaper rate and our competitors were just mad at us.

The noise was too much though, and ultimately the 2008 rulemaking established that if you are selling permits for wetlands or streams, you can't sell credits for any other purpose. It still makes no sense to me, none at all.

You see the same debate nowadays in the voluntary carbon markets, where a developer wants additional payment for a project's biodiversity improvements or for its gender equality achievements, above and beyond any payment for carbon dioxide mitigation. The multiple benefit dynamic that I called 'stacking' is still a hot topic in the environmental markets.

Anyway, after that rule came out, some of the folks in North Carolina wanted us to relinquish our additional credits from stacking. We fought it at the state level, and ultimately, we said, 'if competitors want to sue, they're going to have to sue the state, because that's who issued the credits'. Of course, the sabre rattling never resulted in a suit against the state. In the end, we sold the remainder of our additional credits, but going forward there were limits on stacking.

I guess my stacking trade became pretty famous.

I used to go to the mitigation conferences, and people would be sitting at the bar with some chips and a dip, and they'd start calling out to me, 'Hey, George, come over here and show me how to double dip. Do I dip once and then dip again?'

So that was me, Double-Dipping George.

Waiting for the army

Wetland and stream restoration has become a $3 billion per year industry, and a big part of that is due to the federal mitigation rule, but there are still a lot of inefficiencies holding the market back.

The ultimate regulatory body is the Army Corps, and, especially in the early days, the only real strategy to get a project's paperwork approved was simply pleading with the Corps because no one was really holding them accountable.

There were times when we would wait months for changes to be approved. We might add ten commas to a document, nothing really substantive, and it would still take four months to get a response.

I think on average it takes around three years to get a mitigation instrument approved, even five years in some places.

I would take my documentation everywhere just in case the Corps called me. If I was in the field, I would have those papers with me. I remember being in the women's bathroom at a Wendy's burger joint – the men's was closed – when, guess what, the Corps calls me to go over the documentation.

Well, I carried those documents everywhere, so I spent an hour reviewing them by phone with the agent from the ladies' room of a Wendy's, while the women outside were lining up to go to the restroom.

I recall a lot of knocking on the door.

We finally got through the instrument and got it so that it was approvable, and when I came out there were probably 20 ladies out there giving me the hairy eyeball.

But it was worth it because in the environmental markets, until you have official approval, you have nothing. Once you've got that title, you've created an asset. In the mitigation market, official approval is like the moment in alchemy when lead turns to gold.

Power of profit

In order to get those approvals to issue a credit, you have to show that your improvement to the environment is permanent. That means either buying the land outright, or more commonly, establishing an easement in perpetuity over the land.

My costs include paying a landowner for the easement and the restoration, enhancement or creation work that we carry out on the stream or wetland. My revenue comes from the value of the credit that I sell in order for permits to be issued to a land developer to offset the impact of his project.

The concept of 'no net loss' means if a developer has a negative impact on a wetland, then they have to show an equivalent ecological uplift that is protected in perpetuity.

Getting the private sector to fund permanent easements on land is a huge value to the community. You can quibble with the technical restoration standards here and there, but you can't quibble with the fact that we have permanently protected valuable environmental resources and we're using markets and private-sector dollars to do that.

The beautiful thing about the market is that it allows us to offer good money for an easement, which allows farmers to retain their land.

We had a scenario with a dairy farm where we put in 11 miles of new fencing for cattle, we added nine water tanks, we restored all of their creeks, and we paid the farmer $600,000. Even after all of that, we still made a profit on our credits. Try doing that without a compliance market.

We should be proud that we are making money from credits. Historically, the drive from the NGOs was always to make environmentalism cheap. They would always be asking: how can we get conservation for free; how can we save the planet through donations. They don't want to pay, or if they pay, they want to pay nickels.

My view is totally the opposite. We need to reward land owners. We are very adamant that if you don't pay the landowners for doing good things and being good stewards of their land, then the system will break down.

Many environmental organizations hate the concept of markets; they just hate it. They think that markets are terrible. We try to explain to them that markets actually bring more transparency, higher standards and higher integrity, but sometimes it's easier just to change the name of what we are doing.

In the context of water quality markets, instead of 'trading', we have started saying 'implementation of cost-effective and flexible ways to reduce nutrient loadings'. Anything to get people more comfortable with so-called market solutions.

When I was an environmental lawyer, I saw that the environment was just considered to be a cost centre and was always considered as a negative. I always wondered if we could make the environment into an asset instead, and I think we are moving in the right direction.

When I started EBX all those years ago, our aim was to put a value on environmental attributes that would be recognizable by society so that those attributes could be bought and sold.

When you are looking at land, you should be able to have the highest and best use including the value of the environmental services as part of the bundle of sticks that make up land.

Should we build another mall with parking lots on a headwater stream, or should we restore that headwater stream and ensure the integrity of that water source downstream?

We all know long term that the best use case is probably the latter. But without markets, without price discovery, and without transparent and effective market mechanisms, there would be no way of showing that relative value and so it would be harder for people to make the right choices.

Part IX

Trading as a project developer

Project developers generate the carbon offset credits that fuel the voluntary carbon markets by identifying, designing and implementing projects that deliver environmental benefits such as emissions reductions or ecosystem restoration.

This involves such varied roles as identifying suitable land or other opportunities, engaging stakeholders, navigating regulatory requirements, arranging project finance and overseeing delivery and monitoring.

Project developers are effectively the 'upstream' producers of the voluntary markets in the same way as oil drillers, farmers and miners are the primary sources of production for the traditional commodity markets.

Project developers are active market participants in that they live or die on the market prices that they can achieve for their projects, but few are genuine traders who speculate directly in the market.

Project development is, nonetheless, a highly risky activity.

Project developers need to ensure compliance, transparency and community involvement to achieve an environmental impact, but without ever losing sight of the need to maintain profitability.

Pricing projects correctly, surviving political upheavals and regulatory changes, often while operating in difficult jurisdictions, represents a huge challenge for the sector.

We will see in the following chapters how experienced project developers seek to navigate all of these market uncertainties to achieve the best results for their projects, allowing them to continue to deliver positive environmental impacts.

DOI: 10.4324/9781003359739-45

Chapter 36

From trading to projects

Of mixed Argentinian and French descent, Alexis Leroy is the founder and chief executive of ALLCOT. After holding several senior roles in different sectors, Alexis established the business in 2009 as a group of companies specializing in end-to-end sustainability solutions for individuals and businesses of all sizes. ALLCOT, which is headquartered in Switzerland, develops emissions reduction projects as well as trading in all sectors related to emissions mitigation. The firm operates in both voluntary and compliance markets and handles both carbon credit origination and trading. ALLCOT was acquired in 2025 by climate solutions firm Karbon-X, where Alexis now serves as chief sustainability investment officer. Alexis has served in numerous international roles, including board member of the Climate Markets and Investment Association (CMIA), co-chair of IETA's Business Partnership for Market Implementation (BPMI), and founding director of Sport and Sustainability International. He is also a strong advocate for pricing equity in the voluntary carbon market and supports institutions such as the West African Alliance for Carbon Markets and Climate Finance, helping to elevate regional voices. Alexis and his family are resident in Bogotá, Colombia.

It seems that in life, there sometimes has to be big drama to generate big change. It feels like everything fantastic in my life has happened either as a result of something dramatically good or dramatically bad.

When we started ALLCOTT, it was a small boutique firm that specialized in trading carbon emissions, mainly European Union Allowances (EUAs) along with some certified emissions reductions (CER) and even a few emission reduction units (ERUs).

We thought we were clever traders but looking back the atmosphere in the carbon markets at that time was pure euphoria.

Then the drama came, and in this case, it was dramatically bad. It took some time for the contagion from the global financial crisis of 2008 to reach carbon, but, when it finally did, the market spiralled into a terrible situation.

DOI: 10.4324/9781003359739-46

We saw EUAs trade as low as €2.75–€2.80 per tonne, and at that point we even wondered whether the EU Emissions Trading System (ETS) would survive because at €2.75 it was basically dead and useless.

That pushed me to think differently because I realized there was no trading margin at those price levels. It was basically impossible to do anything relevant in a market that was in limbo.

I began to think to myself, 'well, if trading is dead, then let's go to the source of the carbon'.

Instead of dealing with allowances, I started to look at carbon credits and I decided to create them myself rather than just trade them.

I would still do some limited trading in the secondary markets, but my focus would be on building a position in the primary market.

Pivot to projects

I started by developing two projects in the Ukraine. The first one went well and we sold the credits, but the second one, which was in Donetsk, didn't work at all. That was dispiriting and made me wonder if the pivot to project development wasn't going to work.

Fortunately, soon afterwards in 2012, I was invited down to Colombia by a good family friend who was a shareholder in a sugar mill in Providencia.

The sugar mill was generating 24 megawatts of power, and it was transitioning to using waste products from the sugar manufacturing process, like bagasse, as fuel. That qualified the mill for carbon credits under the clean development mechanism (CDM).

Spending time at that sugar mill was like an epiphany for me.

The premises were fantastic, the employee gender balance was great, even the gender balance on the board of directors was good. The workers were proud of working at the mill; they had sports facilities and medical care.

I didn't discover just a sugar mill; it was global impact entity.

I was planning to stay for ten days and I stayed for three months. When I saw gender balance, worker dignity, clean energy and carbon revenue all in one place, I told myself, 'this is what carbon markets were made for'.

It really resonated with me, and I said to myself, 'instead of pushing trades, this is what I want to do'. I realized I wanted to develop projects that have an impact both on the environment and the social side, and which are genuinely transformative.

In my view, carbon credits are not a commodity; they are more of a financial instrument that can deploy micro-finance and enable climate justice.

I see carbon markets as the bridge. They translate macro-finance into tangible local transformation: schools, clinics, reforestation, female-led businesses. The idea is to make money for sure, but above all to generate impact.

Since that first experience in Colombia, ALLCOT has grown into a firm managing a pipeline of over 200 projects, including forest conservation, agroforestry, waste management, regenerative agriculture, clean cooking and methane avoidance.

Community spirit

For a project to work, the community needs to feel ownership; they need to be involved and they need to be empowered. Particularly with nature-based projects, it's absolutely obvious that if local people don't see any benefit from conservation, we will see deforestation.

Our flagship project in Sur del Meta, Colombia, is in a post-conflict zone and involves over 950 families as forest stewards and local decision-makers. Revenues are used by the communities as an investment engine for health, education and regenerative production systems.

The idea is that we're not imposing top-down solutions. The community decides. That's what makes it sustainable.

We have employed a similar approach in Senegal, where we have been active since 2017. With the government's support, we launched a low-investment, high-impact waste-to-compost programme that transforms urban organic waste into agricultural inputs.

The idea is to build a circular economy financed by carbon. The programme has now evolved into a multi-credit system, integrating plastic credits and creating local green jobs.

We convinced the Senegalese government to authorize international transfers under Article 6 of the Paris Agreement instead of retiring credits domestically. Today, those credits are seen as high value, with estimates ranging from $35 to $100 per tonne.

Financing the future

It's not all plain-sailing. Attracting and deploying climate finance remains extremely challenging. While traditional infrastructure like wind and solar enjoys concessional capital, high-impact carbon projects in rural or politically complex geographies do not.

If we want to build the next 1,000 climate projects, we will need a new finance architecture. That's why we push for forward sales, blended finance, and higher voluntary market prices.

My view is that it's time we priced fairness into the market. Because this isn't just about carbon. It's about power and inclusion.

That's why I helped to launch the Environmental Market Fairness Foundation to advocate for pricing justice, especially for Global South nations producing low-cost, high-integrity credits but receiving disproportionately low returns.

I am very passionate about transparency. I am willing to provide total transparency about the cost of developing a project, even showing the margin that ALLCOT is making.

That transparency will hopefully allow us to charge prices that are based on the realities rather than on market sentiment. That way we can make carbon more of a climate finance vehicle than a commodity.

The problem right now is that the market is quite ruthless for projects.

Market pricing might work when it comes to technical-based solutions where the cost of origination is very clear. If you are working on methane flaring or on landfill gas in Brazil or in Mexico, you might not care as much.

After all, if the market goes up, it's great because you make more money, but at the end of the day, it's not fatal if the price goes down significantly because a lot of the projects can still work at less than $1 per credit. The absence of upside limits co-benefits, but it works.

That is absolutely different for those of us working on nature-based solutions. We draw up a plan with the community, but then we might have to go back to them and say, 'our projections were based on $15 but we need to work on $5 now' because that is what the market is telling us the project is worth.

That's a pretty tough message. You need the community to conserve the planting you have done, and their decisions are financially driven because people live with a first-necessity focus.

We have planted 5,500 hectares of mangroves in Senegal and we want to get to 7,000 hectares. The mortality rate of those mangroves is just 10%, which is thanks to the community's involvement.

At some point, the plantation work becomes conservation, but that can only work if the community is rewarded and protected from the vagaries of market price volatility.

If you tell communities that their income is going to be reduced by two-thirds just because the market says so, the reaction in Colombia or Senegal might be 'thank you very much, I'm going to go back to what I was doing before'.

It's been a long journey for someone who came out of the traded markets, but I'm increasingly looking to move away from pure market pricing.

Trading DNA

Despite my shift to project development and my concerns about market volatility, I believe my background in trading remains a core strength. We understand markets, which helps us structure projects, evaluate risk and create value for both investors and communities.

ALLCOT continues to run a strategic trading book and supports local stakeholders in making informed sales decisions.

If we sell credits, our partners sell too. That's part of our transparency model: shared value, shared timing. Having a trading background does absolutely help on the project side.

I don't think we would see projects as a financial tool as much, if we hadn't started out as pure traders. I think that experience in the markets gives us a much less sentimental approach. We are more comfortable in putting a price tag on projects.

We still do some speculative trading, and we run our own trading book, but it's usually in the secondary market. The market is challenging at present. Unless you are really cash rich and you can sit and hold positions, then you need to take care.

If you are holding inventory, you might also get a nasty surprise. Recently, the market seems to have decided that any voluntary carbon credits older than five years are horrible. That makes zero sense, at least in nature-based projects.

I am a firm believer that older, high-integrity credits — particularly from nature-based projects — should gain value, not lose it. A ten-year-old forest credit with proven permanence is an asset, not a liability. It's time we updated our narrative.

Just transition

I'm increasingly speaking less about 'carbon projects' and more about climate impact platforms: locally owned, globally financed, and policy aligned. I emphasize building capacity — not just technical, but also social and governance — within communities and national systems.

As the VCM matures and Article 6 becomes a global framework, I believe the next chapter must be led by the South, for the world.

We're not here to replicate the old models. We're here to build a new one — one that speaks the language of dignity, equity and climate ambition. If we can achieve that, the carbon market can truly become a force for good.

What I mean by that is that in the projects we develop, carbon is more of a financial product than a commodity. The carbon markets are simply a very effective mechanism for channelling finance to local communities so that they can manage their environment appropriately.

My transition from trader to project developer began with the drama of the market crashing and looking for a way to survive.

The journey has been transformative for me as an individual. I am still looking to make money, but that aspect doesn't dominate everything in the same way as it did in my trading days. Now, I believe it's more important to generate impact.

I guess that's the difference between life as a trader and life as a project developer, you become aware of factors that generate value that are beyond just market prices.

The switch completely changed my life. I would have never been ready to get married when I was a trader because my drive was completely different; I was too focussed on making money and being the biggest guy in the room.

That side doesn't worry me at all now: what matters to me instead is that I can have an outsized impact.

Chapter 37

Pricing voluntary projects

Daria Dyncheva graduated with a master's degree in international economics from Donetsk National University in Ukraine. She worked as an analyst for Ukrainian mining and metals company Metinvest Holding from 2010 to 2014, before joining steel trader NLMK Trading in Switzerland in 2016. She stayed with NLMK Trading until 2024, holding a number of roles of increasing seniority from assistant trader and business analyst through to director of marketing and finally chief financial officer for the export division. In 2024, Daria joined clean cooking company Circle Gas as head of strategy and business development.

Perhaps some people might think that it's fairly straightforward to trade voluntary carbon credits as a project developer.

After all, in theory, first, you develop projects that either mitigate or remove carbon emissions. Then, once you have generated some offsets, you simply look to sell the certificates to a buyer.

Obviously, the key is to sell the offsets for more than the cost of developing and running the project.

On the surface, that process probably sounds very similar to how most standard commodity markets work. Across commodities, whether it's energy, agriculture or metals, sellers try to source or develop a product and then sell it for more than the initial cost of acquisition or production.

Sounds obvious, right?

But in reality, putting together a trade in the voluntary carbon market is challenging. I would argue that there's really no such thing as a 'classic' trade in voluntary carbon.

Every deal is distinct and the motivations of different buyers are so different. One of the only common factors between trading a standard commodity and voluntary carbon is that it generally pays to do your research.

DOI: 10.4324/9781003359739-47

Fuelling the poorest

Circle Gas supplies liquefied petroleum gas (LPG) to some of the poorest households in Kenya and Tanzania. We use a proprietary technology system and a vast network of local distributors to sell tiny volumes at a time, allowing buyers to pay for enough LPG to cook a single meal.

Our buyers previously could only afford cooking with biomass or charcoal, or occasionally kerosine, so their health benefits from using clean-burning LPG at home are huge. Switching from charcoal to LPG also means our communities have reduced their emissions from more polluting fuels, so we have registered the business with the Gold Standard carbon registry under one of its 'cookstove' methodologies.

Every kilogramme of LPG that our clients in Kenya and Tanzania use definitely saves potential emissions because we know for sure that our customers would previously have only been able to afford energy with a high pollution content.

We can see real positive changes already in our communities from introducing LPG to them. After all, the areas that we cover are decades away from getting access to electricity or to pipeline gas. Carbon credits are a very important part of our business model. Sustainability projects are inevitably focussed on nature or on poor people so they don't tend to be projects that have big profit margins. Selling credits allows us to reach the poorest families that cannot afford LPG even with the smallest price premium that would cover our additional expenses.

But when I joined the business, I was taken aback to discover that the way to obtain the carbon revenue is not straightforward.

I came from the steel market, which is rather a classic commodity market, where prices typically fluctuate according to the balance of supply and demand, underlying assets have standard specifications, and the role of each market participant has a defined role with a corresponding price.

But the voluntary carbon markets are quite different and more confusing.

Supply-demand balance

Once I joined Circle Gas, my priority was to make a transparent pricing strategy. I decided to build a supply-demand model for the voluntary carbon market along the lines of my previously built model for the steel market.

But something that would be standard procedure in virtually every commodity market proved to be virtually impossible in the voluntary carbon market.

Supply was the easier side to model. You can see how many credits have been issued by the registries; you can also see how many new projects are under development. Some estimates are possible, and different agencies also supply analysis.

We could more or less model supply, and, as soon as the supply goes up, I know that the competition to sell will be even harder.

But, in my view, you cannot estimate demand at all.

You can arrive at some kind of estimate by collecting together all of the various commitments that companies and other entities have made about their desire to have 'net-zero' emissions by certain dates. That implies a figure about how many offsets each entity will need each year.

That figure is just a ceiling, though. After all, that demand is entirely voluntary.

The more problems there are in the global economy, the less firms will prioritize their sustainability commitments.

I don't know what will happen by 2030 or 2040 but I suspect a lot of companies won't have the same mindset or financial position that they had when they made their original commitment to net-zero emissions.

I'm a believer

Modelling the voluntary carbon market accurately is somewhere between very difficult and impossible. That means that the supply-demand balance is clearly not the primary price driver that it is in commodity markets like steel.

What then drives prices in this market?

In my view, price is generally defined by the buyer's perception of value. Nothing else.

People buy projects that they believe in. If they don't believe that the project helps the environment in some way, they don't buy, and there's no reason why they absolutely have to buy.

That means that you need to become the chief storyteller and evangelist for your project. People get excited only when they touch and when they see. Ideally, you need to bring the buyer to your project to show it off.

Most buyers also don't tend to respond well to technical complexity in a project. They just want a clear and strong story. When I first came to Circle Gas, I was mailing with one of the European funds. I tried to answer some of their questions with technical details, only for them to write back to say they were dropping out because it was all getting too complicated.

I realized that you need to make it as easy as possible. We have a technically very sophisticated cooking solution, and databases to support our carbon savings calculations, but I have to explain the project differently if I want people to 'feel' it.

For this I need to show them a Kenyan woman, a mother of four who makes $2 per day and cannot afford to buy a full cylinder of LPG and therefore burns charcoal for cooking every single day.

That's an image that a buyer can understand. If I start getting into how our meters connect to multiple mobile networks for calculation and verification, then it will be 'thank you, next!'

School for scandal

What I have learned about this market is that the project's reputation is everything. Lack of unified methodologies lead to the risk of being accused of lack of transparency or even fraud.

The voluntary carbon market does not have a tangible underlying asset you can see, weigh or touch, and the issued carbon certificates lack clear and standardized specifications.

There are so many ways to calculate is how much carbon dioxide (CO2) the project has captured, reduced or saved. The project developer does their own market analysis, and it's up to the developer whether that is based on one, 100 or 1,000 surveys and analyses. After the initial analysis, you do calculations, apply certain coefficients, some of which are provided by the carbon registry that issues the offsets, others by research companies or institutes. But these coefficients change all the time as new methodologies emerge or better studies are carried out.

Ideally, you need to constantly update your documentation to reflect the latest and greatest research, and visit your project on-site to ensure that your solution is actually being used, not just sitting in storage.

Whether or not that any of that best practice is applied relies entirely on the project developer.

If a new standard comes out for steel production, then obviously any sensible steel producer will adopt it, even if it raises costs, to ensure that their material still attracts top dollar. Another problem with the carbon voluntary market is that even after you apply the most conservative assumptions and reduce the credits you issue several times; it does not guarantee that the demand and price will grow proportionately.

A developer can apply and update everything constantly but it is still entirely unclear whether that will influence the price or not.

Developers generally want to do the right thing or they wouldn't have gone into this space in the first place, but on the other hand they might be competing to sell offsets with other less scrupulous sellers who don't apply the same standards and don't care that much about the reputation.

In Circle Gas we take our reputation very seriously, keeping up with methodology updates and collecting all the evidence that our project is protected from over-issuance.

I start every day by reading all of the sustainability magazines. I check the news to see whether any new methodology or methodology update has dropped, but I also need to look out for any scandals that might affect my project.

In 2022–24, there were quite a few scandals in the voluntary carbon markets, particularly around 'over-permitting' where a developer claims more credits that are truly warranted.

Scandals hit both sides of the supply-demand equation.

As soon as any new scandal is revealed, I know that some carbon credits will be taken out of the system because credits that are deemed over-permitted can get cancelled.

But then on the demand side, a scandal will call buyers to pull back from certain categories. Prices tend to drop immediately because firms lose confidence.

The impact of a scandal can also last for some time because of the slower pace of the voluntary carbon markets.

In most commodity markets, sellers need to sell because they are holding production, while buyers need to buy to supply their processes, but players in the voluntary carbon market are quite relaxed.

After all, buyers can store carbon credits for years. They can wait till their reporting date before they commit, while many project developers also sell very infrequently.

That all means that nothing can happen for months. Any new scandal stops the market dead; there are no deals at all for some time, then some people digest, reconsider and slowly restart buying and selling.

Scandal insurance

Keeping accurate carbon calculations and selling the story is by far the best ways to sell a project because the only real alternative is simply to sell cheap.

Corporations will typically either pay a higher price for what they consider to be a reliable project that they can fully embrace, or else you will need to drop the price for them, which gives them something like insurance if anything goes wrong.

Some buyers acquire carbon credits, but they do not claim the reductions immediately by retiring the credits. Instead, the buyers keep the credits on the registry for some time, or at least for long enough to check that there are no problems with the projects.

The information about who owns which projects only becomes public when the buyer retires the credit and claims the offset reduction or chooses to talk about the purchase.

In order to mitigate against the risk that a project attracts bad publicity before they retire its credits, some buyers prefer to buy multiple projects across different categories.

The majority of companies do not have big internal teams carrying out analysis into which projects are most reliable. For them, it's a legitimate strategy to try to pay minimum prices for a lot of different products that they can treat as an additional extra buffer.

All these market inefficiencies lead to an exponentially increasing number of market players and rules to follow.

Rating agencies analyse projects on behalf of firms that don't want to develop in-house expertise. The number of registries issuing new standards and methodologies is growing; each claiming to be the most reliable. Sustainability associations, platforms and registries establish specialized bodies to provide opinions and quality labels.

Naturally, buyers who do not follow the market closely risk becoming frustrated.

Passing responsibility

Given the quirks of the voluntary carbon market, the only way to really guarantee solid demand for carbon credits and support the projects is to give transparency to the buyers. One of the ways is to switch from voluntary to compliance.

We have high hopes for fresh demand coming into the market from the airlines covered by the mandatory CORSIA scheme. To get this label we in Circle Gas are working on obtaining a certificate of 'corresponding adjustment' from the Kenyan authorities.

This certificate guarantees that the credits we generate will not be counted towards Kenya's own climate targets and can therefore be transferred without any risk of 'double-counting'.

That is one controllable way of increasing the price for our product without relying on the vagaries of the market.

All of this makes me wonder if there is a future for the purely voluntary market. It feels like the market wants some form of regulation, whether from governments or from official programmes. Everyone is looking for someone to take responsibility for approving credits.

Companies don't want to take responsibility for something that they cannot understand and they don't want to pay for something that they do not understand. After all, some firms that bought credits voluntarily have since been criticized because they did not choose the right credits.

I would love for this market to develop and become a standard commodity market with all of the typical tools: a genuine supply-demand balance, a forward curve, indexation and even risk management.

At present, that is still a way off.

On the positive side, though, carbon people are so much more friendly and they even seem happier than folks from the other commodity markets.

Carbon people love to talk about their projects and their impact, and they don't generally like to talk about money. That's great but there are times when we need to face up to reality, raise some money and pay salaries.

Hopefully, this market will work more like a regular commodity market, letting impactful projects grow and multiply.

Chapter 38

Dealing with political risk

Torleif Haugland studied statistics and economics at the University of Oslo in Norway, before pursuing a career in energy and the environment, first with Statistics Norway and then with the International Energy Agency. From 1990, Torleif has worked as a consultant and entrepreneur in the environmental sector in more than 25 countries and served as director of the department for energy and environmental Studies at the ECON Centre for Economic Analysis in Oslo. He co-founded specialist emissions firm Carbon Limits in 2005 and co-founded CL-Invest in 2021. CL-Invest identifies and develops commercial projects to reduce emissions, particularly from methane. Torleif is the author of several research reports and books, including 1998's European Energy Structures and Environmental Futures.

Carbon credits is a commodity market where the commodity is greenhouse gas (GHG) emission reductions, but it is striking that demand is more affected by political factors than is the case with any other commodity.

The trade in carbon credits has similarities with, but is also distinct from, the EU Emissions Trading System (EU ETS) where companies trade emission allowances in a closed cap-and-trade scheme.

Carbon credits come from outside the boundaries of the cap-and-trade scheme but can under certain conditions be used as compliance tools, instead of purchasing cap-and-trade allowances. This is what, 20 years ago, propelled the carbon credit programme of the Kyoto Protocol (the Clean Development Mechanism, CDM) into a principal vehicle for cost-efficiency in climate change mitigation.

CDM carbon credits were allowed to be 'imported' into the EU ETS. Substantial cost savings were created since emission reductions under the CDM could be created at a much lower cost than inside the EU ETS boundaries.

The concept had a very strong economic rationale, and initially also political appeal. But unlike traditional commodity markets it didn't cover a fundamental need. Hence, it was exposed to shifts in public policies and politics, and this is what brought it down.

DOI: 10.4324/9781003359739-48

The decline of the CDM started with the Global Financial Crisis of 2008–9, which cooled economic activity and, therefore, demand for credits. Four years on, the EU decided, for various political reasons, to discontinue the scheme whereby CDM credits were a compliance tool under the EU ETS.

This wasn't so difficult because the price of internal ETS allowances was low at the time, unlike today.

The result was a collapse in volume and prices of international carbon credit trades. The international market for carbon credits degenerated into trade in so-called voluntary markets where the carbon credit is often not vetted for environmental integrity in the same way as under the CDM.

CDM enthusiast

My interest in carbon credit trading dates back to the mid-1990s. When the CDM market came along, soon after the turn of the century, I saw an opportunity to do something practical.

For me, the CDM market represented a realistic approach to a problem that we had talked about for a long time; how to channel investment funds to mitigation measures confronted with financial barriers and through this ensure greater cost-efficiency in global emission reduction efforts.

I think you can get a bit tired of writing studies and reports on these matters at a certain point so I co-founded Carbon Limits in 2005. The firm's focus was on developing decarbonization projects for the oil and gas industry.

I had already spent a long time looking at the implications of climate policies on the petroleum sector because Norway was one of the pioneers in this area.

One of my co-founders Arve Johnsen had previously been chief executive of Norwegian oil and gas giant Statoil, now Equinor. Arve had a great reputation in the industry and a strong network, which was important to attract potential partners in the oil and gas space.

We focussed on working with national oil companies in developing countries in Africa and the Middle East and in economies in transition, such as the former Soviet Union.

Carbon Limits generates revenue from two sources. First, we work with local oil and gas producers to capture natural gas that would otherwise have been flared – burned off during oil processing – and then we bring that gas to market.

Second, we generate environmental credits, which reflect that reduction in flaring and which we can sell to third parties in the open carbon markets.

Methane release

The CDM was a powerful concept to reduce flare reductions and subsequently became even more powerful for elimination of direct methane emissions from oil and gas sector installations.

Man-made methane emissions account for around one-third of all global warming to date because methane is such a powerful greenhouse gas. Of those emissions, around 20% are generated by the oil and gas sector, with agriculture and waste management the other major factors.

By far the lowest hanging fruit, the area where you actually can achieve significant emission reductions quite quickly is the oil and gas sector. Of all the climate mitigation options we have today, reducing methane emissions is one of the most cost-efficient activities.

The cost of reduction is not large relatively speaking, so many environmentalists would say, ‘well, the oil and gas industry is wealthy and so it can afford to clean itself up’.

In a way they are correct, the industry should, and they have the means to fix it. However, in developing countries and transition economies they aren’t doing it. Moreover, these countries, by and large, don’t have regulatory institutions strong enough to impose solutions on the oil and gas industry.

Certainly, waiting for governments to step in or for voluntary action by energy producers hasn’t proved a winning strategy in the past.

That means that decarbonization, particularly reducing emissions from the upstream part of the oil and gas industry, is largely dependent on industry-led initiatives and this in many cases require some market incentives in order to get started on the oil and gas sector ‘decarbonization journey’.

We are currently seeing some interest in developing green bond-style financing for methane and flaring emissions reductions, but to date the generation and sale of emission offsets has been the most productive mechanism for delivering reductions.

Of course, it’s controversial to provide market incentives to this rich industry. We also have to ask ourselves if providing support for reductions is just extending the lifetime of the oil and gas industry, which could actually disincentivize broader decarbonization and the energy transition.

There is also the argument that the oil and gas industry shouldn’t get financial support for something they ought to do themselves. These are legitimate argument, but we at the same time have to be realistic: we can’t let the (unrealistic) perfect be the enemy of the good, after all.

Criteria and rules must be in place so that carbon credit revenues are not allocated to projects that doesn’t make a very clear positive difference.

Trading credits

The toughest challenge for any project developer is to find buyers for the credits that are generated. When we came to sell, we always felt very vulnerable because we were exposed to all the ups and downs of the market, whether that was pricing or political sentiment.

We managed the inherent price risk successfully for a while but eventually the collapse of the CDM took us down. My CDM experience is classic, in that it reflects the experience of so many project developers who ultimately couldn't control the direction of the carbon market.

Everything essentially went away for us in 2012–13 and we could no longer operate projects on a pure risk basis anymore. The market just disappeared.

I still have the scars from this period, and I like to use the example of 2012–13 as a warning example whenever I speak to young people. My message is that you cannot rely on a single framework or scheme that is entirely dependent on political will.

We found that out the hard way.

Bounce back

The collapse of the CDM in 2012–13 was a shock and deterred us from carbon credit development, but actually for a somewhat shorter period than we had expected.

Most people think that it hasn't been possible to make use of carbon offset certificates in European compliance schemes ever since 2012. But in 2018, the German government allowed fuel suppliers to buy upstream emission reduction (UER) credits from flare and methane reduction projects outside the EU ETS to offset up to 1.2% of their official emissions limit.

It was a new and innovative transposition to German law of the EU Fuel Quality Directive which had allowed for use of offset to meet the targets of the Directive, under certain conditions, as an alternative to blending in ethanol and biodiesel to achieve the Directives requirement of reduced carbon footprint of transport fuels.

The UERs could be sourced anywhere in the world, and were usually generated by reducing flaring, which made them a perfect fit for the work that Carbon Limits was doing to reduce emissions from the oil and gas sector.

The scheme worked very well for a while and generated significant emission reductions (more than two million tonnes CO2e per annum and prices good enough to incentivize a scale-up of flare and methane emission reductions outside the EU.

However, as with the CDM–EU ETS ten years earlier, the scheme led to political controversies and allegation of fraud and the German authorities decided in mid-2024 to close the scheme down by mid-2025.

Lessons learned

Our experience of selling UERs into Germany was basically a repeat of our earlier experience with the CDM. Everything seemed to be going well, until everything came crashing down.

Fortunately, unlike the CDR collapse, it wasn't fatal because we have investment behind us and we believe in what we are doing.

An important lesson learned is that to be durable and successful any carbon credit scheme and market must have greater scale and be predictable in terms of the framework conditions.

The smaller the market, and the more limited its appeal is to a single jurisdiction, the more exposed it is.

I don't think we are going to get a stable carbon market unless there is actually significant demand for credits from different countries and different jurisdictions so that the impact of any single political decision is reduced.

I think we are now in the formative years with carbon credit schemes and carbon markets being developed that will be more robust because there is good communication and collaboration between the United Nations Framework Convention on Climate Change (UNFCCC) process and those independent schemes led by a number of non-governmental bodies which provide carbon credit to the voluntary market.

This market and the independent schemes for vetting and approving credits, which have been plagued with lack of transparency and great variation in quality and prices, are now being improved and we will hopefully soon have a consistent set of rules, procedures and institutional structures so that quality of credits and predictability of market conditions are established, and stable market growth can be achieved.

For us this is essential given the risk exposure we have. Currently we have important projects under development in countries like Nigeria, Algeria, Iraq and Uzbekistan.

The projects offer large and near-term emission reductions but there are typically significant capital expenditures involved, and these will not be disbursed unless it is likely that carbon credit subsequently will be earned to make the projects financially viable.

Voluntary to compliance

It's obviously great if countries want to bring offsets into a compliance instrument as a way to hit their emission reduction targets. That's a good thing. But our experience shows that you can't count on these schemes to last.

There can be shocks in any commodity market but these kinds of political shocks are unnecessary. Some people in the voluntary carbon market want to see more governments getting involved, but these examples show that government intervention is not always beneficial.

The re-emergence of compliance demand is essential to achieve stable demand, even if this demand is exposed to sudden political shifts. Hopefully, a re-established EU demand can be expected; it is now being debated as part of future commitments (2035 and beyond) under the Paris Agreement. There is an increasing recognition that the EU's climate policy is far too expensive, and hurts consumers, both households and industry.

The carbon price under the EU ETS is around €70 and it traded above €100 in February 2023. Moreover, other policies imposed by the EU and its Member States have abatement costs many times this level. Those costs are passed on to consumers through power prices and in other forms such as the cost of transport fuel.

Reducing flaring from the oil and gas sector can deliver major emission reductions at a cost of €10–20, so there are major cost savings to be had for EU climate policy if carbon credits could be imported into the EU ETS.

Given the challenges we are facing with public budgets due to the growing pension burden and increased military expenses, it is unlikely that politicians will draw on public funds in the same way as in the past to finance climate policy.

There are economic and even moral arguments for not doing so since you clearly can achieve the same results in climate mitigation with use of fewer economic resources.

We need to approach environmental problems in a cost-efficient way. In Europe, we have been taking measures on the steep part of the climate abatement curve rather than choosing cheaper options and the low hanging fruit.

There needs to be a shift in climate policy to reflect the new realities. We have seen over and over again that environmental markets can work fantastically well when properly managed.

Politicians need to allow global markets to deliver the greatest number of emission reductions at the lowest possible price.

Chapter 39

Writing the trading rules

Jeff Cohen has been instrumental in some of the most significant environmental success stories of our time, including work on the International Panel on Climate Change, restoration of the earth's stratospheric ozone layer, watershed protection, and the sharp reductions in lead exposure and particulate and sulphur dioxide emissions. From the time he was in high school, he set his career path in what was then simply called 'ecology'. After graduating with a master's degree in public health and environmental management, Jeff began his career with the U.S. Environmental Protection Agency (EPA) where in 1998, he was appointed to lead the team responsible for domestic implementation of the Montreal Protocol – a position at the intersection of critical industry sectors and international policy on stratospheric ozone and climate. His expertise led to his role as a senior policy adviser to the California Air Resources Board, where he helped develop early action regulations under the state's landmark climate change law. He returned to graduate school to earn an MBA in sustainable management and in 2009 co-founded the San Francisco-based carbon project developer, EOS Climate, and later Xpansiv, the largest environmental market exchange. He continues to innovate to mobilize capital to scale decarbonization across the transition economy.

Sometimes in the environmental markets, you can come up with a concept, but the concept is so novel that you have to kickstart a market to turn your idea into a reality. That's what my co-founders and I encountered when we launched EOS Climate in 2009. We literally had to write our own rules to make our concept work.

At the time we met, I was managing the group at the U.S. EPA that was implementing the Montreal Protocol and guiding the transition to alternative, next-generation chemicals and technologies.

DOI: 10.4324/9781003359739-49

On weekends, I was a graduate student working on an MBA at the Presidio School of Management in San Francisco, focussed on sustainability and impact, which was then a groundbreaking programme and is still thriving today.

A gigaton-scale policy gap

The Montreal Protocol is recognized as one of the most successful and one of the most important demonstrations of international cooperation. It prevented a catastrophic loss of the Earth's shield that protects all living things from dangerously excessive ultraviolet radiation.

By phasing out production of nearly 99% of chlorofluorocarbons (CFCs) and other 'ozone-depleting substances' (ODS), the global ozone layer is on track to recover by roughly 2050.

It turns out that the Montreal Protocol has been an incredibly successful climate treaty as well. CFCs not only destroy stratospheric ozone but have a pound-for-pound global warming potential up to 11,000 times greater than carbon dioxide (CO2).

By phasing out new production of CFCs, the Montreal Protocol eliminated a significant contributor to climate change, avoiding an additional increase in average global temperature of 0.5–1 degree Fahrenheit.

Despite this success, there was a ticking time bomb in the form of millions of pounds of CFCs and other ODS produced before the phaseouts that remained in legal use in older equipment, buildings and stockpiles around the world.

Under business as usual, these powerful gases were being released to the atmosphere from old legacy systems. In 2006, this 'installed bank' represented potential emissions equivalent to between 16 and 18 billion tonnes of CO2.

An MBA start-up

I was inspired by the pioneering work at the Chicago Climate Exchange at the time and asked myself what could we do to incentivize the collection, aggregation and destruction of CFCs and other ozone-depleting greenhouse gases from legacy systems and equipment?

Two of my MBA classmates – Todd English and Joe Madden – already had experience in greenhouse gas accounting and market-based systems. When I shared my idea, they agreed to develop a business plan around the concept.

Then, being excellent MBA students, they went out and raised a million dollars from a venture firm in the Bay Area to jumpstart the business.

EOS Climate was born.

Overcoming market challenges

Our business – and any hope of developing projects to generate credits to market and trade - faced significant challenges at the outset.

First, there was no centralized CFC 'bank' – refrigerants and other ozone-depleting chemicals were dispersed in millions of pieces of equipment around the world.

Second, financial incentives for CFC recovery and destruction were needed to compete with an established and profitable aftermarket, which was stoked by high demand for reclaimed CFCs to service older (and leaky) refrigeration and air conditioning systems.

Third, CFCs were considered under the control of the Montreal Protocol and therefore not considered eligible for greenhouse gas 'crediting' programmes such as the Clean Development Mechanism.

Given these challenges, we needed several things to scale a business and create the market catalyst for this new project type.

The first was a standardized protocol. Years before, with support from DuPont (now Chemours), I had submitted a rudimentary methodology to the Chicago Climate Exchange for crediting destruction of ODS. It presented an ideal project type with clear additionality, clear permanence, clear and verifiable metrics.

Some folks did use that early methodology for early projects and to start their own businesses. However, I felt we needed a bigger platform with greater reach.

We approached VCS (now Verra) and the Climate Action Reserve (CAR) with a proper ISO-compliant protocol. After a full stakeholder review process, CAR published it.

While developing the new ODS protocol, I was also advocating for ODS destruction inclusion in the federal Waxman-Markey cap-and-trade legislation then pending on Capitol Hill. I spent months meeting with congressional and White House staff, industry associations and environmental groups and ultimately ODS destruction was listed as an eligible offset in the bill.

Once we were able to explain key issues: that the Montreal Protocol did not regulate end-of-life disposition of CFCs, destruction of CFCs recovered from old equipment was completely unrelated to 'R-22' clean development mechanism (CDM) projects in China and Mexico, and that the threat of illegal imports was managed, there was universal understanding that this offset type provided a high degree of certainty of real, permanent and measurable greenhouse gas emission reductions.

Even though the federal legislation did not pass, winning the seal of approval in Waxman-Markey opened the door for the California Air Resources Board (CARB) to consider, and eventually list, ODS destruction as one of only five eligible compliance offset types under its cap-and-trade programme.

This was a breakthrough.

A combination of sound science and forward-looking policy created a new market for end-of-life management of powerful greenhouse gases that would otherwise be emitted to the atmosphere. It was up to us to execute.

Demonstrating impact

From a three-person start-up business we grew to a team of 20+ and created a partnership ecosystem with leaders in appliance recycling, refrigerant reclamation and hazardous waste management to re-orient the secondary refrigerant market across the country with an alternative and financially viable 'reverse supply chain' in which carbon credits were more profitable than keeping CFCs in circulation to maintain older cooling systems.

On the strength of California's approval, and our partnerships and operational system, EOS became the leading source of compliance offsets for the state's cap-and-trade programme and held that position for about six years until forestry credits became dominant.

The ODS protocol used for projects by EOS Climate, as well as by other project developers who followed our lead, has generated CO2e reductions involving hundreds of trades with a market value in the hundreds of millions of dollars.

I am especially gratified to see that the first three protocols approved in June 2024 by the Integrity Council for Voluntary Carbon Markets (ICVCM) as meeting the Core Carbon Principles were the ODS protocols that I originated and that were published in different forms by the Climate Action Reserve and the American Carbon Registry (now ACR).

Keeping our cool

At EOS, we continued to build on our success with other greenhouse gas protocols also focussed on fluorochemical refrigerants that I originated and were published by the ACR.

One credited installation of climate-friendly technologies in supermarkets – a market-based solution picking up on the U.S. EPA GreenChill programme. The other created credits for reclaiming hydrofluorocarbon (HFC) refrigerants, which like CFCs are also powerful greenhouse gases.

Collectively, these methodologies have created market-mechanisms tackling one of the most important climate challenges remaining today.

Project Drawdown estimates that by replacing fluorochemical refrigerants with more climate-friendly alternatives we can prevent greenhouse gas emissions equivalent to between 43 and 49 Gigatons of CO2 through 2050, roughly equivalent to ten years of total U.S. annual emissions.

From carbon to other markets

The lessons learned, partnerships and friendships gained at EOS Climate were a stepping stone to building Xpansiv.

We gradually realized that our work could be extended to transform larger global markets – leveraging advanced data systems to differentiate energy fuels, metals, agricultural commodities and other raw materials at the base of global supply chains based on their environmental attributes.

Through its merger with CBL Markets and subsequent acquisitions, Xpansiv is today the world's largest environmental commodity market exchange, with partners including CME Group, S&P Global, and Blackstone.

In retrospect, coming to carbon markets with the mindset of a regulator and scientist contributed to our success in driving gigaton reductions and will continue to be key as we as an industry go forward – science-based protocols, rigorous monitoring and data systems, predictable delivery of high integrity credits, creating 'win-win' industry partnerships and finding the right balance amidst the 'carrots and sticks' that policymakers in different jurisdictions provide.

And while it may be cliché, it is still true: having great people by your side who can imagine and actually deliver bold outcomes is just as important as having a good business model.

Our original MBA team with Todd and Joe has since multiplied several times over, continuing to innovate to efficiently connect capital to decarbonization solutions at scale.

Chapter 40

Bringing the JI to Russia

Tatiana Fayzullina holds law and chemical engineering degrees from Kazan State University and Kazan University of Technology in Russia as well as at Oxford University in the U.K., before completing a master's degree in environmental technology at Imperial College London. In 2005, she was hired as a senior project manager by pioneering carbon project developer and consultancy company EcoSecurities Group. In 2008, Tatiana joined Gazprom Marketing & Trading, now SEFE Marketing & Trading, where she built a carbon project portfolio under the mechanisms of the Kyoto Protocol and managed a satellite office in Moscow, before setting up a small-scale LNG team to continue her career in decarbonization. Since 2017, Tatiana has consulted with energy trading and utility companies like Axpo Solutions, Origin Energy and E.ON Hydrogen, among others. She also assists energy and sustainability entrepreneurs with commercialization and go-to-market strategies.

The worst enemy of sustainability and environmental markets is perfectionism.

There is a lot of criticism and negativity in the media towards carbon projects and, although there may be a certain merit to some of it, much of the criticism misses the mark.

Given the complexity of the cosmos, ecosystems and microsystems that guide life on Earth, we may never achieve perfectly defined operating rules. The carbon markets are part of a process and an evolution.

Surely, we should do what we can rather than just waiting for a magic wand to sort it all out?

Carbon emissions cause climate change that affects everyone, but at the same time countries, companies and people all point at each other in terms of who is responsible. And unconstructive and idealistic views often provoke a 'limbo' effect that justifies delaying necessary action.

I also find it very hypercritical when there is so much negative attention on companies. Businesses are solely driven by value and this value is created by each of us individually and jointly buying goods and services. In other words, each of us has 'wallet power'.

DOI: 10.4324/9781003359739-50

Next time you order something on Amazon, don't pick a one-day delivery option, unless you really need it, because your action is highly likely to result in a higher transportation emission profile than could otherwise be achieved with better planning.

Carbon is a commodity that is not really easy to price and not really easy to deal with. Carbon emissions affect everyone but at the same time no one really wants to accept accountability.

We as consumers and investors should recognize and bear our fair share of responsibility for climate change.

Joint implementation

In my view, the perfect environmental market does not exist. The best we can hope for is a system that works and where there is some chance of improvement. It has to be better to do something than to do absolutely nothing.

The Joint Implementation (JI) mechanism is one area that has come in for a lot of criticism over the years, but I worked on many JI projects, and I can assure you that many projects did make a difference.

JI and Clean Development Mechanism (CDM) projects under the Kyoto Protocol were the very first project standards that allowed for the quantification, circulation and pricing of carbon emissions on a global scale.

The major difference between the two is that 37 industrialized countries and countries in transition accepted binding emission targets (JI host countries), while CDM countries had none.

The JI countries also had to submit national inventories and report on their progress. This mechanism was taken as a base for the Paris Agreement Crediting Mechanism (Article 6.4).

The JI allowed industrialized countries to invest in carbon abatement projects in other industrialized countries by buying the Emissions Reduction Unit (ERU) credits generated by JI projects.

When I started working for EcoSecurities in 2005, many governments and companies were struggling to understand the commodity nature of carbon emissions.

I spent good three or four years working with governments and companies explaining that the emerging carbon market was a new reality and not some kind of global conspiracy movement.

Despite all of the efforts by many colleagues across the industry, Russia was one of the very last JI countries to step into this market.

Russia only entered in 2010, which was just before the carbon market price collapsed in 2011. In my view, it was a missed opportunity, as with a different regulatory approach Russia could have become a major beneficiary of carbon financing.

JI projects in Russia

The delayed response and a lack of clarity from the Russian government on the approval of JI projects caused hesitation with companies interested in benefitting from carbon finance.

Although quite a few Russian state and private companies such as Gazprom, Rosneft, Surgutneftegaz, Lukoil, Novatek and others were in discussions with carbon buyers, they were all waiting for a 'green light' from the government. It is hard to attribute this delay to anything besides interministerial power fights.

In the end, Russia finally started issuing letters of approvals for JI projects from 2010 onwards.

The oil and gas industry had its fair share of JI projects. The majority related to the avoidance of associated gas flaring.

It is disappointing to admit that, even almost 15 years later, the fight to eliminate these emissions globally is still ongoing. The Oil and Gas Decarbonization Charter was signed at COP-28 in December 2023, which proves that there is still more that ought to be done.

Critics of the JI point to the early days when the regulations were kind of loose and there were some projects that probably were not truly additional, in the sense that their supposed carbon reductions would have taken place anyway.

But in Russia and in many other countries of Eastern Europe, the additional carbon finance that the JI attracted was the main reason why many, although not all, carbon projects happened.

My most vivid memory from that time is a visit to one of the landfills in Moscow region. We were wrapping up a dialogue with the director of a landfill about the utilization of biogas when somebody came over and placed a huge wooden box on the desk with some dark metal bats.

The director asked what was inside. The guy said that they had found some objects that morning in the landfill and they seemed to be grenades.

The director started shouting, 'are you f***ing crazy? Why did you bring them here? What if they are live?'

We found out later that they were just 'dummy grenades'. And I learnt the lesson – you never know what you might find in a Moscow landfill.

Managing deal flow

To develop JI projects, we had to persuade often sceptical stakeholders that it was possible to make real money out of the carbon markets.

Our classic trade looked something like: plan, sell, hedge and develop.

The first step was to come up with an idea for a JI project. We would then do a lot of work to understand the commercial aspects, after which we would go out and look for potential buyers, even before work had begun on the project.

We were not going to be the ultimate end-user of the ERU credits we were generating, so we knew we would need to trade our ERUs in the open market. And we had to sell them at a premium, given the commercial risks we were taking.

These were not risk-free trades. We were investing funds in developing projects, and we were also tying up capital in margin calls for the hedging that we were doing in the futures market.

Using the futures market to hedge against price moves was critical to our success.

After all, we were trying to sell our credits as early as possible in the process when the credits hadn't yet been created.

There were no exchanges offering trading of ERUs because their liquidity was too low compared to Certified Emission Reductions (CERs). Our ERUs were all proxy hedged on exchanges using the CER market and were then rolled forward as required.

The liquidity wasn't there to hedge the multiple years that it takes to develop a project, so we would end up hedging one year ahead and then rolling our position forward and so on.

We sold ERUs and hedged with CERs, all the while hoping that our projects would actually come through.

Chinese benefit

Despite our push to develop projects, Russia missed out on much of the benefits of the JI.

In contrast, China was certainly the major beneficiary of CER trading. It had hosted near to 4,000 CDM projects equal to approximately 2.9 billion CER credits. Using an assumed price of €8 per CER, China received over €23 billion in carbon finance.

These days China is a recognized leader in many technologies that are advancing decarbonization. China also operates a CDM Fund worth $1.5 billion, which was created from the profit-sharing mechanism established by the Chinese government for the issuance of CERs, and which provides grants for energy efficiency and other decarbonization projects.

Given that majority of buyers of CERs were European companies, one could argue that the technological transformation of China was paid for by European consumers.

Environmental stirrings

I was born in Kazan, the capital of Tatarstan, which is located 800 km east of Moscow. I was working in the Tatar Parliament when an external affair advisor suggested applying to a programme called 'Leadership for Environment and Development' (LEAD) funded by the Rockefeller Foundation.

The programme was a global initiative to support talented young professionals to learn and collaborate on all aspects of sustainable development. I was lucky as I was selected for the programme to represent Russia.

What followed was a rigorous international and regional training programme on sustainability. Its uniqueness was in a multidisciplinary approach and a global outreach. It was a union of truly passionate, professional people who were very generously sharing their knowledge and experience gained from environmental and social challenges in their home countries. I caught a bug and couldn't imagine doing anything else other than having an international career dedicated to sustainability. After the programme, I was fortunate again to get a scholarship to Imperial College London, which led to my first professional role.

I was very fortunate to get so many fantastic opportunities, but I like to think I made the most of them, and I am looking forward to contributing further, using my experience, passion and drive to lead the transition of energy and environmental markets.

Further reading and bibliography

There is a substantial amount of academic literature available that discusses various theoretical approaches to the environment, particularly as regards policymaking.

There are also plenty of practical engineering studies that cover biofuel production or carbon management.

Works that deal with the markets themselves, or the professional lives of environmental traders are less common. Unfortunately, even the more market-oriented works can quickly get outdated, given how quickly government mandates and market practices change.

The following represent some personal recommendations for further reading.

Some works by contributors

If you enjoyed the stories told by our leading figures, then the next logical step would be to also enjoy some of their published works.

Haugland, Torleif, Bergesen, Helge Ole, & Roland, Kjell (1998) *Energy Structures and Environmental Futures in Europe*, Clarendon Press. Examines the history and prospects of the European energy sector, with a focus on the risks related to climate change.

James, Tom (2012) *Energy Markets: Price Risk Management and Trading*, Wiley Finance. A comprehensive overview of the energy markets and of risk management techniques.

James, Tom & Fusaro, Peter (2011) *Energy & Emissions Markets: Collision or Convergence?* Wiley. Discusses traditional energy-trading markets, the impact of emissions trading schemes and the early days of renewable energy trading.

James, Tom & Zerenghi, Francesca (2010) *The Global Biofuels Market: Trading and Operations*, Wiley Finance. Focuses on the practical trading and distribution of biofuels.

Ringius, Lasse (2000) *Radioactive Waste Disposal at Sea: Public Ideas, Transnational Policy Entrepreneurs, and Environmental Regimes*, The MIT Press.

Sandor, Richard (2012) *Good Derivatives: A Story of Financial and Environmental Innovation*, Wiley. Shows how financial innovation has been a positive force in the last four decades, and tells the story of the creation of the Chicago Climate Exchange and its affiliates: the European Climate Exchange, the Chicago Climate Futures Exchange, and the Tianjin Climate Exchange.

Sandor, Richard (2017) *How I Saw It: Analysis and Commentary on Environmental Finance*, World Scientific Publishing Company. A collection of articles providing historical analysis and commentary in the field of environmental finance. An insightful overview of carbon markets around the world that also offers personal stories and a compelling look at how the markets developed and what might be next.

Sandor, Richard, Clark, Nathan, Kanakasabai, Murali & Marques, Rafael (2014) *Sustainable Investing and Environmental Markets: Opportunities in a New Asset Class*, World Scientific Publishing Company. Looks at how environmental asset classes are incorporated into commodities, fixed income, and equity instruments.

Sandor, Richard & Diperna, Paula (2025) *Carbon Hunters: Reflections and Forecasts of Climate Markets in the 21st Century*, World Scientific Publishing Co Pte Ltd.

Taylor, Mike (2022) *Reduce Carbon Compliance Costs: Strategies for Facilities in a Carbon Cap and Trade Program*, Aegis Hedging Solutions. A practical guide for firms looking to optimize their approach to compliance with a mandatory carbon regime.

Further reading on emissions

Bossley, Liz & Kerr, Andy (2009) *Climate Change & Emissions Trading: What Every Business Needs To Know*, 3rd Ed., Consilience Energy Advisory Group. One of the original guides to the carbon markets; a great snapshot of the markets' early incarnations.

Bryant, Gareth (2019) *Carbon Markets in a Climate-Changing Capitalism*, Cambridge University Press. Explores the relationship of capitalism and climate change and offers a socio-political critique of existing carbon markets.

Eyre, Nick, Brohe, Arnauld, & Howarth, Nicholas (2015) *Carbon Markets: An International Business Guide*, Routledge. Comprehensive guide to both the regulated and voluntary carbon markets.

Rathi, Akshat (2024) *Climate Capitalism: Winning the Global Race to Zero Emissions*, John Murray. Profiles ten individuals creating the key breakthroughs for a green economy.

Rudolph, Sven & Aydos, Elena (2021) *Carbon Markets Around the Globe: Sustainability and Political Feasibility*, Edward Elgar Publishing Ltd. Offers a thorough comparative study of emissions trading schemes around the world.

Further reading on bioenergy

Kumar, Sunil & Kumar, Rena (2023) *Biofuels: Technologies, Policies, and Opportunities*, CRC Press. Comprehensive guide to biofuels.

Manuel, Jeffrey & Rogers, Thomas (2025) *Ethanol: A Hemispheric History for the Future of Biofuels*, University of Oklahoma Press. Provides a history of ethanol development in the U.S. and Brazil.

Pahl, Greg (2008) *Biodiesel: Growing a New Energy Economy*, 2nd Ed., Chelsea Green Publishing Co. Survey of biodiesel in 80 countries and a helpful review of all the current debates.

Rauch, Marc (2019) *The Ethanol Papers*, Dialog Press. Punchy analysis of gasoline versus ethanol.

Further reading on water markets

Burnett, Kimberly, Howitt, Richard, Roumasset, James & Wada, Christopher (2014) *Routledge Handbook of Water Economics and Institutions*, Routledge. Essays on water resource problems including market development.

Maestu, Josefina (2017) *Water Trading and Global Water Scarcity: International Experiences*, Routledge. Explores various types of water trading arrangements in different parts of the world.

Raffensperger, John & Milke, Mark (2017) *Smart Markets for Water Resources: A Manual for Implementation*, Springer. Explains why traditional water markets often fail and proposes solutions using optimization and auction-based mechanisms.

Wheeler, Sarah Ann (2021) *Water Markets: A Global Assessment*, Edward Elgar Publishing. A comprehensive overview of water markets worldwide.

Index